RACING POST
ANNUAL 2016

Racing Post One Canada Square, London E14 5AP. 020 7293 2001
Irish Racing Post The Capel Building, Mary's Abbey, Dublin 7. 01 828 7450

Editor Nick Pulford
Art editor David Dew
Cover design Jay Vincent
Chief photographers Edward Whitaker, Patrick McCann
Other photography Alain Barr, Clive Bennett, Mark Cranham, Steve Davies, Getty, John Grossick, Caroline Norris, Louise Pollard, Matthew Webb, Liam Woulfe
Picture editor David Cramphorn
Graphics Samanatha Creedon, Stefan Searle
Picture artworking Nigel Jones, Stefan Searle
Feature writers Scott Burton, David Carr, Steve Dennis, Nicholas Godfrey, David Jennings, Tom Kerr, Lee Mottershead, Jonathan Mullin, Julian Muscat, Nick Pulford, Brough Scott, Peter Thomas
Contributors David Bellingham, Mark Bowers, Paul Curtis, Graham Dench, Steve Mason, Dave Orton, James Pyman, John Randall, Martin Smethurst, David Toft, Sam Walker

Advertisement Sales
Racing Post: One Canada Square, London E14 5AP.
0208 2630226 Cheryl Gunn, cheryl.gunn@racingpost.com

Archant Dialogue Prospect House, Rouen Road, Norwich NR1 1RE. 01603 772554
Kay Brown, kay.brown@archantdialogue.co.uk
Dean Brown, dean.brown@archantdialogue.co.uk

Distribution/availability
01933 304858
help@racingpost.com

Published by Racing Post Books
27 Kingfisher Court, Hambridge Road, Newbury, Berkshire RG14 5SJ

Copyright © Racing Post 2015

All rights reserved. No part of this publication may be reproduced, stored in a retrieval system, or transmitted in any form or by any means, electronic, mechanical, photocopying, recording, or otherwise, without the prior written permission of the publishers. A catalogue record for this book is available from the British Library.

ISBN 978-1-910498-04-0 [UK]
ISBN 978-1-910498-05-7 [Ireland]

Printed in Great Britain by Buxton Press. Every effort has been made to fulfil requirements with regard to copyright material. The author and publisher will be glad to rectify any omissions at the earliest opportunity.

www.racingpost.com/shop

Welcome to the Racing Pos

Time to celebrate v

Greatness is a rare commodity and yet, even at the risk of falling into the trap of affixing that label too easily, it is indisputable that racing was blessed in 2015 by momentous achievements and extraordinary people. Greatness walked among us.

Tony McCoy, the ultimate champion, walked that walk for two decades and the final steps were as remarkable as all his long years of rewriting the record books, perhaps for all time. The story of those last few weeks, from the bombshell of his retirement announcement to the tearful farewell, is retold in this year's Annual and it has everything: dreams, brilliance, glory, joy, determination, tears, humour, reverence. An astonishing career in microcosm.

Willie Mullins is another record-breaker in jump racing whose claims to greatness are becoming ever more obvious after his haul of eight winners at the Cheltenham Festival, marked by a Champion Hurdle 1-2-3 and breathtaking performances from Faugheen, Un De Sceaux, Vautour and Douvan. He looks back on the festival in a revealing interview, while we turn the spotlight on his hopes for a first Cheltenham Gold Cup.

In what might be termed the Year of the Jockey, McCoy was not the only one to leave an indelible mark. Ryan Moore set a modern-day record at Royal Ascot, three-time Flat champion Richard Hughes hung up his saddle to start a training career, Silvestre de Sousa took his first title and Frankie Dettori crowned a glorious comeback with Derby and Arc success, while Richard Johnson and Barry Geraghty set about filling McCoy's boots.

The stories of all those jockeys are here, along with others recounting the awe-inspiring fortitude of Robbie McNamara and Brian Toomey in bouncing back from catastrophic falls. Greatness of a different kind lies there.

For all the human endeavours, horses are the heartbeat of the racing world and there was plenty to set pulses racing in 2015. Golden Horn, Muhaarar, Jack Hobbs, Treve, Gleneagles, Air Force Blue, Coneygree, Faugheen, Un De Sceaux, Don Cossack, Many Clouds, American Pharoah, Solow and Hurricane Fly provided many high points, but there were others from Arabian Queen's giantkilling act to breakthrough successes for the trainers and jockeys of Cole Harden and Mecca's Angel.

As well as reflecting on a great year, there is already so much to look forward to. The Cheltenham Gold Cup is shaping up as one of the most competitive and exciting in recent memory, while the next generation of Flat horses is rich with promise. In the Annual 20, our regular look at the year to come, we highlight the horses and people expected to go on to better things.

Some will stand tall, others will fall, but one thing's for sure: 2015 will be a hard act to follow.

Nick Pulford
Editor

CONTENTS

66

26

BIG STORIES

42

FINAL FURLONG

HORN OF PLENTY

Time and again Golden Horn proved himself the top performer of the European Flat season with dazzling displays at Epsom, Sandown and Longchamp

By Steve Dennis

GOLDEN years. Every now and then there is an efflorescence of brilliance from within the root and branch, a great collective blossoming, a sustained splash of colour so bright it remains on the retina even after the moment has passed.

At the beginning of the 1970s Nijinsky, Mill Reef, Brigadier Gerard and Dahlia came crowding in upon each other's heels, and 40 years later the pattern repeated itself with Sea The Stars, Frankel, Treve and now Golden Horn, whose magnificent campaign entitles him to be mentioned in the same contented exhalation as the aforementioned stars. His dominance of the season's highlights was the keynote of 2015, a golden year indeed.

Victory in the Prix de l'Arc de Triomphe, a strong iteration of the race with a ready-made story seemingly in place, that of Treve's bid for a unique hat-trick, set the seal on Golden Horn's status in terms as black and white as owner Anthony Oppenheimer's silks. The dashingly dark son of Cape Cross did not have to transcend humble beginnings, or defy convention with a rise from a lowly source, but his ascent was compelling nevertheless.

His trainer John Gosden is one of the most articulate members of

» *Continues page 6*

his profession, seemingly forever bending from his lofty height to offer words of wisdom and illumination into a waiting microphone, and there were few gaps on the CV in what has been a gloriously glittering career – but the Arc was one. An autumn crisp and dry – Golden Horn's triumphal progression during the height of the summer was first delayed and then derailed by sticky ground – offered the opportunity to set the record straight.

Gosden had chuckled about a 'rosbif draw' when Golden Horn was drawn near the peripherique in stall 14 of 17, but any fears would quickly have been allayed by jockey Frankie Dettori, whose deeds need no introduction. Dettori, whose reinvigoration – largely to do with Golden Horn – was the other main theme of the year, produced a masterclass of inspiration and experience to defy the draw and the destiny of supermare Treve.

When the stalls opened at Longchamp, Dettori charted a wide course for the first couple of furlongs, keeping Golden Horn to his draw and avoiding the usual scrimmaging towards the rail as the field packed down. At first sight it was a blunder, a 'what the hell?' moment, but it enabled the free-going Golden Horn to settle away from the madding crowd, and by the time Dettori angled his mount in behind Treve's pacemaker, into the perfect spot in a relatively modestly run race, most of the work had been done.

The rest was relatively simple: when the pacemaker dropped away like a bird with a broken wing at the entrance to the straight, Dettori soon had Golden Horn in full flight and, with his stamina and class proven beyond doubt, his lead always looked unshrinkable. The mighty Treve flattered on the outside but then flattened out, and all the while Golden Horn galloped gloriously into legend. His winning margin over the Poulidor-esque Flintshire was two lengths. Treve was only fourth. And if there had been a scintilla of doubt about Golden Horn before the race, there was no longer any room for manoeuvre. With the Arc added to the Derby, the Eclipse and the Irish Champion, Golden Horn was an undisputed champion.

"Today you saw the real Golden Horn," said Dettori, whose fourth Arc win equalled the record for a jockey. "He put to bed a great Arc field like a real champion. Over the last furlong and a half it would have been impossible for any horse to get near me. I pressed the button and he flew. Think of the horses he has beaten, and beaten well. I spent the last furlong enjoying myself. He has given me some tremendous pleasure and is probably the best I've ridden.

"I told John this morning, 'Listen, I'm not going to spend all the race trying to get in and have him pulling. Leave it to me, I know what I'm doing'. He was a bit keen but I've got strong arms and really the race worked out exactly as I thought it would. My tactics were good but his performance was unbelievable."

Truth be told,

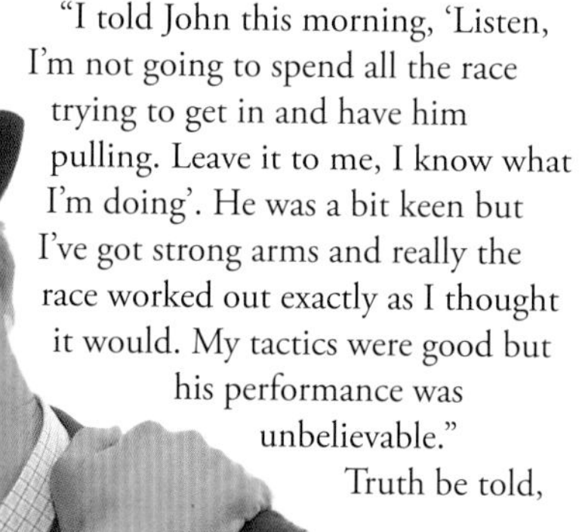

▸▸ Head and shoulders above the rest: (from left) Frankie Dettori stands tall to celebrate Arc victory after his brilliant ride; the jockey salutes the crowd at Longchamp; Dettori after winning the Irish Champion and (below) with John Gosden after that race

ARC ACES

Frankie Dettori's quartet of winners

Lammtarra *1995* Made good use of a pacemaker before beating off stern opposition up the straight to score by three-quarters of a length

Sakhee *2001* Always handy and galloped home six lengths clear in one of the most impressive Arc wins of modern times

Marienbard *2002* Always in touch and, in a wide-open finish, had the greater staying power to score by three-quarters of a length

Golden Horn *2015* A masterclass from start to finish and proved uncatchable in the straight with a winning margin of two lengths

OTHER FOUR-TIME WINNERS

Jacques Doyasbere
Djebel (1942), Ardan (1944), Tantieme (1950, 1951)

Freddy Head
Bon Mot (1966), San San (1972), Ivanjica (1976), Three Troikas (1979)

Yves Saint-Martin
Sassafras (1970), Allez France (1974), Akiyda (1982), Sagace (1984)

Pat Eddery
Detroit (1980), Rainbow Quest (1985), Dancing Brave (1986), Trempolino (1987)

Olivier Peslier
Helissio (1996), Peintre Celebre (1997), Sagamix (1998), Solemia (2012)

Thierry Jarnet
Subotica (1992), Carnegie (1994), Treve (2013, 2014)

Golden Horn's performance was thoroughly believable given what had gone before. But even those at the top of the bill have to start somewhere, small-time, small-town, playing to a handful of indifferent observers who'll one day be able to say "I was there when . . . " The homebred Golden Horn had run just once as a two-year-old, winning a Nottingham maiden from Storm The Stars, who would go on to finish third in the Derby and second in the Irish Derby. The Racing Post analysis said: "He looks a very nice prospect for next season."

Indeed he was. Golden Horn began his long season at Newmarket in mid-April, winning the Listed Feilden Stakes, which entitled him to take his chance in a more relevant Derby trial. In the Dante Stakes at York he showed the elan that became his trademark when scything down stablemate Jack Hobbs for a decisive success. Now for the Derby. Or maybe not?

In the aftermath of Golden Horn's Dante victory, there was uncertainty over his Derby participation because Oppenheimer was unconvinced of his prospects of staying a mile and a half and thus reluctant to commit to the £75,000 payment for a supplementary entry. The Prix du Jockey-Club was initially mooted as a more likely

> 'I pressed the button and he flew. I spent the last furlong enjoying myself. He has given me tremendous pleasure and is probably the best I've ridden'

target, but a day or two later Oppenheimer – cognisant of his horse's ability and his position at the head of the Derby market – reached into his deep diamond-magnate's pockets and gave the go-ahead for Epsom.

In the premier Classic, Dettori again showed his mastery of the situation when – after regaining the ride on Golden Horn owing to William Buick's retainer with Godolphin – he strove to settle the impetuous colt in the early stages. The race might have been lost in the first two furlongs, but instead it was won there and Golden Horn was consequently ruthless in his dismissal of his would-be peers, streaking exhilaratingly clear inside the final furlong to beat Jack Hobbs by three and a half lengths.

Happiness was unconfined, in the

▸▸ *Continues page 8*

shape of the manically celebrating Dettori and of the less mobile Oppenheimer, whose Hascombe and Valiant Stud is a minor character in a bloodstock world dominated by Coolmore and Darley.

"I've won a Guineas with On The House [1982] and one or two other big races, but this is the biggest race in the world," Oppenheimer said. "It really is something I've been aspiring to, and my father was aspiring to. It's not easy, it's very difficult. Anything can go wrong and often does, so I'm immensely happy."

It was the performance of an above-average Derby winner. The Derby is a beginning, not an end, a springboard rather than a soft pile of laurels, and in Golden Horn we had a horse who looked to have unplumbed depths of talent. Given his innate speed, and the fact that stablemate Jack Hobbs was the very model of an Irish Derby horse, the Eclipse Stakes against his elders was his next target.

There have been better Eclipses – many better – but at Sandown Golden Horn ran arguably his most admirable race, setting the pace to confirm his tactical versatility and then going head-to-head with the tenacious The Grey Gatsby up Esher's climactic climb before dropping him and driving on for another three-and-a-half-length victory.

Derby winners do not always shine here – Erhaab, Benny The Dip, Motivator, Authorized were all beaten – but Golden Horn positively gleamed. His Eclipse victory was the standout performance of the European Flat season with a Racing Post Rating of 132, 5lb better than the mark he recorded in the Derby and Arc. No other European horse, of any age or over any distance, could even surpass his Derby and Arc standard, let alone reach the high point of the Eclipse.

"In none of the races I've ridden him in has he ever felt tired," Dettori said at Sandown. "He just keeps on galloping. He's a remarkable horse. His constitution is unbelievable. I've never got to the bottom of him."

He would. Golden Horn was a late withdrawal from the King George VI & Queen Elizabeth Stakes (which suffered notably for his absence) on account of the unseasonably soft ground, and his sights were then trained upon the Juddmonte International at York, a race notorious as the 'graveyard of champions'. Surely not Golden Horn, though.

And yet. The ground was Knavesmire tacky, his pacemaker went off like a ton-up merchant up the Great West Road and was ignored, and Golden Horn proved intractable in the early stages, fighting Dettori while the unconsidered Arabian Queen set her own fractions behind the impotent pacemaker. Golden Horn's brilliance carried him into the firing line, carried him to level pegging with Arabian Queen, but the final flourish was absent and his unbeaten record expired in a stunned silence. The filly beat him by a thoroughly meritworthy neck.

▸▸ Dominant force: Golden Horn leads a John Gosden one-two in the Derby from Jack Hobbs; (below) Frankie Dettori celebrates his second Derby victory

"Golden Horn was always doing too much, you can see him throwing his head around," said the habitually level-headed Gosden. "He didn't run in the King George and was a very fresh horse and he's rather gassed himself out in the ground. He's gone in front of the filly and then just tired in what is dead ground. There's no doubt he's a much better horse on fast ground, as we know. But take nothing away from the filly – she's outstayed them all well and if you look back to The Grey Gatsby you see the form of the Eclipse still there."

It was disappointing, but even though Golden Horn had lost his perfect formline he had hardly been disgraced. There were substantive reasons for his defeat and neither his stallion value nor his public profile were affected by it. Three weeks later he bounced back – and bounced off Free Eagle – in the Irish Champion Stakes.

In one respect Golden Horn reasserted his old invulnerability, yet in another he was lucky to escape the wrath of the stewards for sideswiping Free Eagle as that horse came to his quarters a furlong out. It

▸▸ *Continues page 10*

DREAM DOUBLE

DERBY-ARC WINNERS

Year	*Horse*
1965	Sea-Bird
1971	Mill Reef
1995	Lammtarra
2000	Sinndar
2009	Sea The Stars
2010	Workforce
2015	Golden Horn

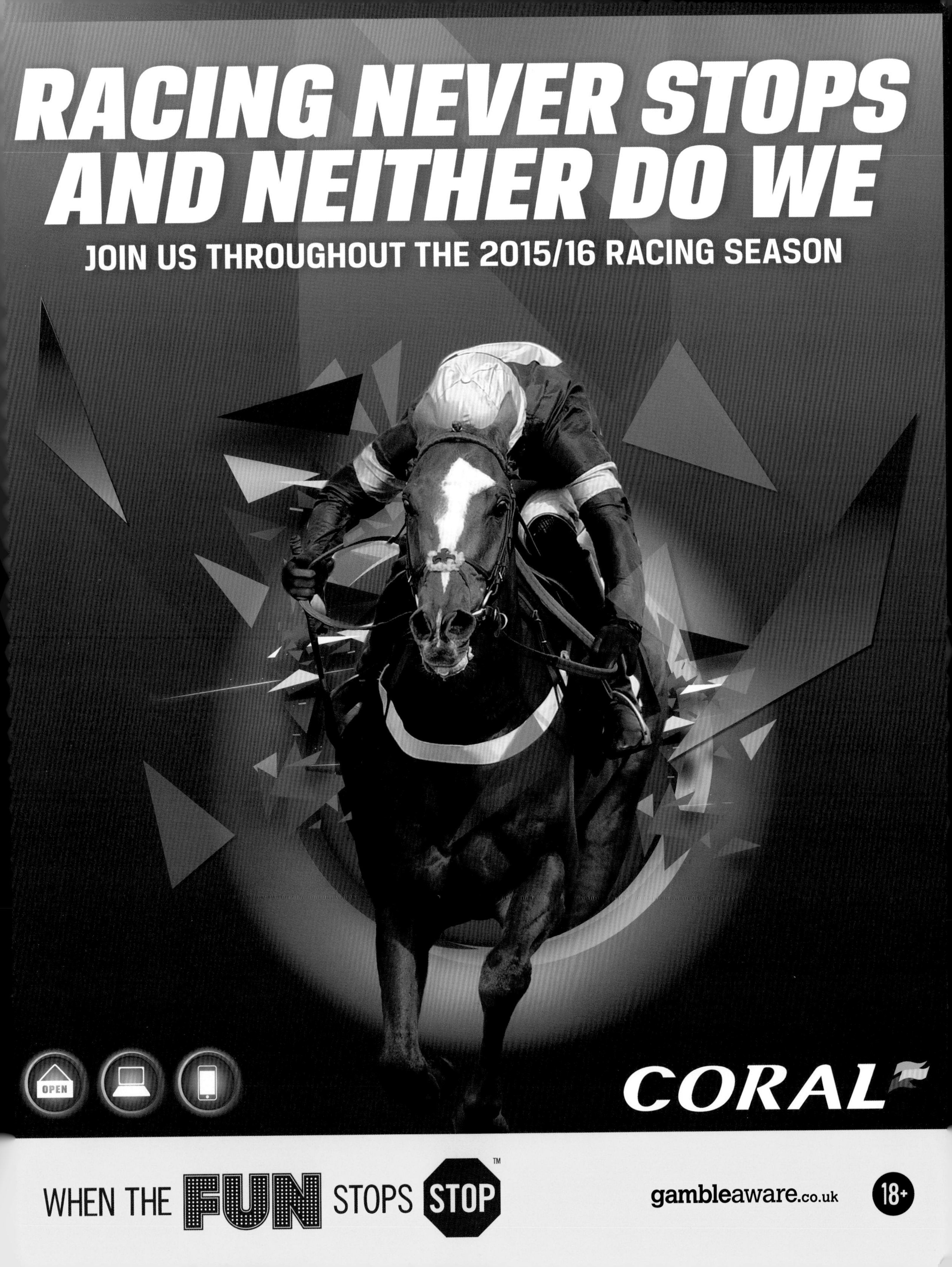

RACING NEVER STOPS AND NEITHER DO WE

JOIN US THROUGHOUT THE 2015/16 RACING SEASON

OPEN

CORAL

gambleaware.co.uk

18+

cost Free Eagle a fair crack at the race, and it was only because the filly Found ran on into second, relegating Free Eagle to third, that Golden Horn was not demoted in disgrace. Those with long memories would nod wisely at Gosden's excuse for his star's errant ways.

"I think it was the shadow of the grandstand and just as the ground gets dark he seems to have run across that line," he said, adopting the Dayjur defence. Dermot Weld, Free Eagle's trainer, voiced the thoughts of many when saying "Pat [Smullen] said the interference completely knocked the wind out of Free Eagle and cost him the race" but the rules are the rules and Golden Horn had already proved himself a hard horse to pass. It was not a satisfactory outcome, but those looking for a neat resolution to the Golden Horn story had only to wait until Longchamp and that triumphal Prix de l'Arc de Triomphe.

The thorny aspect of where Golden Horn fits in to the hierarchy will never be resolved, only barely illuminated by put-upon pundits and earnest offerings to the letters page in the Racing Post. Lester Piggott said he was "nearly in the same class as Nijinsky, Mill Reef, Sea The Stars, that sort of horse, but not quite as good as them" – a view backed up by Golden Horn's 132 RPR in the Eclipse, which was the second-highest mark reached by a Derby winner in the past decade but 6lb short of Sea The Stars' peak figure in 2009. To not reach that stratospheric altitude is no shame. What is not in question is Golden Horn's brilliance, his valour, his all-round excellence and consistency that lit up the season like a firework. Next February he will embark on a second career at Dalham Hall Stud, Oppenheimer's understandable desire to breed future champions from his present champion overriding the possibilities of a four-year-old career.

It was a year of headlines such as 'Golden Wonder', 'Golden Boy', 'Golden Moment', although the scientists among us would have loved some periodic table-literate headline writer to have used 'Au-some!', or 'Au-inspiring!'. Never mind; the memories will forever be golden.

'Lucky' Curran dealt good hand

EVERYWHERE Golden Horn went, so did Michael Curran; his devoted lad rode him every day at John Gosden's yard, apart from when Frankie Dettori or Robert Havlin were on hand for more serious work purposes, *writes Nicholas Godfrey.*

"You get to know every little trait really but he's a very laid-back horse with a lovely manner," said Curran (below, with Golden Horn and Dettori). "Sometimes people would look at him when you were leading him round because he'd have a bit of a holler but he always did that. If he didn't do it you might be worried. That's just his character."

For the two seasons before the Derby and Arc winner was put under his care, Curran had been looking after star miler Kingman. "You put your name forward for them and the boss decides in the end. There could be more than one person – if you know there's a good one, we'd almost literally be fighting over them. I've been lucky as I had Kingman all the way through as well. It could be a long time before another one comes around but you live in hope."

Curran, 49, from Galashiels in the Scottish Borders, realises he is privileged to work for one of the top trainers in Europe. "It's a great yard and we're very lucky. We've got top owners, top horses and he's a great bloke to work for – very straightforward, asks your opinion, likes hearing feedback – and you can have a bit of banter. He's firm but fair."

If the rest of the racing world was a bit slow on the uptake regarding Golden Horn's prowess, Curran suggests he was always held in some regard. "He won nicely as a two-year-old and the boss must always have thought a little bit of him because he allocates which box they go into and he put him in Kingman's box."

As well as their stable, Golden Horn and Kingman shared certain attributes, according to Curran. "This horse I rode out all the time but Robert Havlin rode Kingman and did a great job. Golden Horn has a bit of an air about him – he knows he's good and hasn't got a bad trait at all – and the exact same could be said of Kingman. Because he never won by far, Kingman probably never got the recognition he should have done. But when he galloped he showed how good he was. Golden Horn was similar."

Curran will never forget Derby day, when the nervous tension of looking after the favourite found joyous release in the closing stages. "I admit when our second horse [Jack Hobbs] went clear I did worry we were a little bit too far back. But once he got into top gear he was just eating up ground. There were a lot of people in the little stable lads' stand and I said sorry for bouncing around so much, but they said 'don't worry, just enjoy it!'"

THIS IS WHAT WE DO

AND WE WOULD LIKE TO DO IT WITH YOU

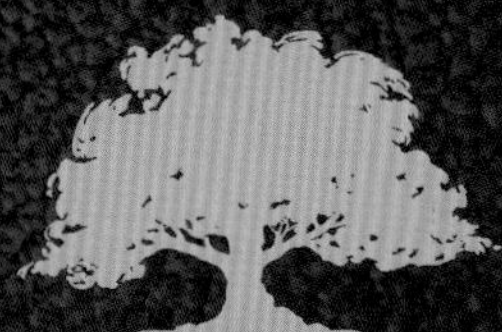

COULONCES CONSIGNMENT

HARAS DU GRAND CHENE

ANNA DRION: +33 6 76 74 94 74

ETIENNE DRION: +33 6 37 06 01 31 | HGCHENE@GMAIL.COM

A STAR IS REBORN

In true Hollywood style Frankie Dettori made an epic comeback with a spectacular year capped by his triumphs on Golden Horn

By Steve Dennis

THE old Hollywood moguls would have recognised the plot. Take a good-looking hero, take away his success, leave him on the edge of the action running a hand wearily through his six-day stubble, enviously watching a bunch of youngsters do the job he once excelled at, angrily shambling around his filthy apartment leaning on a bottle, all washed up and nowhere to go.

Then give him a chance, just a little one, a chance to pick himself off the floor, clean himself up. Shuffle the cards of life and deal him a decent hand for once. See what happens.

Watch him renew his faith in himself, watch him drag himself back up the ladder, watch him slowly progress towards the sort of heartsweet redemption that makes the audience stand up in the cinema aisles and shout, their eyes a little damp at the corners. Watch him rediscover his old magic in the last act and win the game, the fight, the race.

One old Hollywood mogul turns to another, shifts his fat cigar from one corner of his mouth to the other, and says: "You know who'd be perfect for this? That Italian guy."

The reinvigoration of Frankie Dettori was one of the Flat season's central themes, a breath of fresh air that filled the lungs of a sport that lacks natural celebrities and therefore relies over-heavily on everyone's favourite Sardinian to keep the temperature high.

Dettori's career had stagnated, his previous two campaigns having produced the lowest returns since his very first season as a wet-behind-the-ears 7lb claimer trading on the rawest of talents and his father's good name. His job as first jockey in Britain to Al Shaqab Racing was no doubt financially rewarding but it didn't keep him that busy, and the sight of Dettori making the leaky-roof tour of the likes of Leicester and Bath for one unsuccessful ride a day was a dispiriting one for onlooker and jockey alike.

There were even rumours that Dettori was considering quitting the sport, which is where our narrative arc reaches its nadir and we see our Italian hero sitting alone in his apartment in yesterday's clothes, in front of a television broadcasting big-race action, with some mouthy pundit

»» *Continues page 14*

declaring that Dettori is that guy he found in the 'where are they now?' file.

Our man slumps into a stupor, only to be woken by the jangle of the telephone. The second old Hollywood mogul nudges the first old Hollywood mogul. "We need a song here. Something poignant, get the blood moving. What about that old Joe Cocker number, the one about getting by with a little help from your friends?"

On the other end of the line, the patrician tones of John Gosden, Dettori's old ally, his old comrade-in-arms on so many big days. In an interview with Alastair Down in the Racing Post, Dettori recalled the conversation.

"We were having a family day out at a horse show – the missus driving the lorry and the kids in the back. When we were there I was having a salad and a glass of wine when I got a text saying 'William Buick has got the Godolphin job'. Purely as a joke I said to Catherine 'maybe I should text John and get my old job back', and we all laughed.

"But no more than five seconds later my phone rang and it was John saying 'hello matey, now listen, this is what I want to do – I want to use you a lot but keep it under your hat for now'. I didn't run round the lorry whooping but I did finish the bottle of wine!"

Racing's tight-knit community resembles a dense mat of electrical connections. When the lights go out in one place, they often come on again somewhere else. Dettori, of course, was once synonymous with the Godolphin operation, at home as securely in those royal blue silks as he was in his own skin, but a falling-out at the end of 2012 – allied to a six-month riding ban following a positive drug test – meant the end of that job and presaged his steady fall from grace and prominence. First the blue silks, then the blues.

Yet Buick's promotion to Dettori's old job meant a vacancy in Dettori's previous old job. He had enjoyed many great days in partnership with Gosden before those comfortable blue shackles slipped over his wrists, and perhaps here was a chance to rekindle those old glories. Dettori began riding out for Gosden in March. The first horse he sat on was called Golden Horn. See where this is going?

Yet there was still a twist in the tale, one almost too preposterous for a Hollywood scriptwriter to consider. When Golden Horn flashed to victory in the Dante Stakes at York, propelling himself to the head of the betting markets for the Derby, he was ridden by Buick, whose connection with Gosden still sustained. Runner-up was stablemate Jack Hobbs, ridden by Dettori, owned by Gosden's wife Rachel Hood.

Then Sheikh Mohammed purchased Jack Hobbs for his Godolphin empire, meaning that his retained jockey Buick would be required for the ride. After a degree of debate, Golden Horn was confirmed as a Derby runner, as Derby favourite, and guess who Gosden turned to as his new jockey. You guessed it.

Continues page 16

Animal kingdom: Frankie Dettori at home near Newmarket in June with an emu from the family menagerie, which also includes a gecko, an albino hedgehog and donkeys as well as horses

LUCKY CHARM

Superstition played a part in Frankie Dettori's second Derby victory, as RaceTech engineer Pete Binfield explained afterwards.

Binfield, 57, who has worked on course as a sound engineer since 1983, said: "We're always based in the weighing room and share the same tearoom as the jockeys. Back in 1989 a valet called Dave Currie came in asking me for some tape, as Willie Carson's saddle had a tear in it. I gave him a roll of white tape and he put a ring of it round the tear and Willie went out and won the Derby on Nashwan.

"Frankie was desperate to win the Derby on Authorized in 2007 and I said 'you need some of my lucky white tape'. He asked what it was all about and decided to put a wrap of it around his right stirrup. We were only 20 minutes from the race."

With Authorized having stormed home to give Dettori his first Derby triumph, it was little surprise that the Italian, who is known to be superstitious, came calling again when confirmed for the ride on Golden Horn.

"Frankie asked if I still had the white tape and asked me to bring it on Derby day," said Binfield (below, with Dettori). "Straight after the first we put a ring of tape round the stirrup and off he went."

After the tape worked its magic for a third time, and after Dettori had fulfilled his post-race commitments to the press, the rider took Binfield for a glass of champagne. Between them, they had it taped.

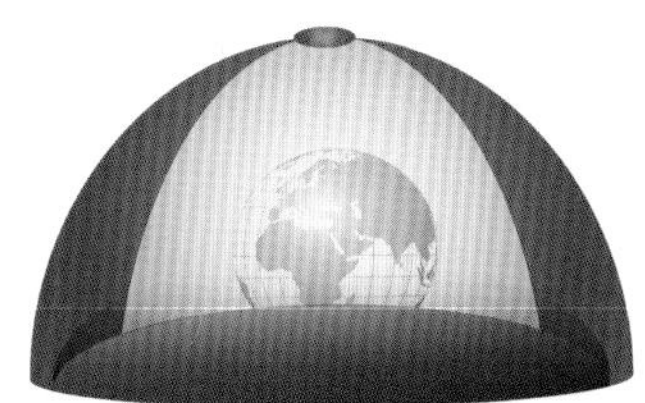

عالم
مهرجان سُمُو الشيخ منصور بن زايد آل نهيان
HH Sheikh Mansoor Bin Zayed Al Nahyan Festival
WORLD

Abu Dhabi The Capital

سمو الشيخة فاطمة بنت مبارك
HH Sheikha Fatima Bint Mubarak
Darley Awards
HOLLYWOOD 2016

April 1- 3 - 2016
DOLBY THEATRE
at hollywood & highland center

Sustained By

Coordinated By
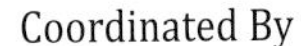

in Cooperation with

Official Partner
NATIONAL ARCHIVES
Ministry of Presidential Affairs

Official Carrier

Sponsored By

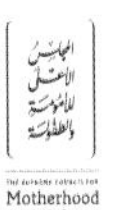

www.sheikhmansoorfestival.com

On Derby day, Golden Horn was brilliant in victory, the perfect vehicle to put Dettori back where he belonged at centre stage, the wheel of fortune come full circle, the narrative arc complete, the saga so sweetly resolved. Jack Hobbs was runner-up again, Dettori denying his former boss the Derby success he has long yearned for. If it hadn't happened, you'd never dare to make it up.

As he returned to the winner's enclosure, Dettori exploded into a display of sheer happiness. There was the flying dismount, kisses for everyone within range, shouts, screams, an irrepressible, irresistible performance that embraced not only those at the racecourse but all those watching on television, and all those reading their newspapers the following day. There is no better way of publicising racing than to have Dettori ride the Derby winner. He reaches out beyond our narrow confines and grabs the otherwise indifferent population by the lapels, shakes them, shows them what a great sport this is. To the man in the street, he is racing.

"I can't believe it," he said in the breathless aftermath, voicing the thoughts of millions. "I was about to say this is better than sex, but my wife wouldn't like that. But it's just as good! I told my dad after the race that this was the most thrilling moment of my career. It was even better than the Magnificent Seven at Ascot.

"John was my father figure 20 years ago. He gave me lots of advice. Now he's more of a friend. I've won the Derby without him and he's won the Derby without me. Finally after 20 years we're back together and we've won it together. That's really special."

A few weeks later Gosden, in a Racing Post interview, examined the Frankie phenomenon and the way in which he helped to rekindle it.

"Frankie is a bit like an Italian diva in that when he gets too high you have to gently bring him down but, just as important, you have to know how to lift him up. Nobody should underestimate his brains or his sensitivity. A lot of the bravado is a front, a way of getting through. Everyone does that in one way or another.

"When he came back here he was hugely enthusiastic even in the sleet and rain of March. The most important thing was that he felt at home again – it's part of that Italian family thing."

****

IT'S clear that, back in the bosom of Clarehaven, Dettori felt wanted again. The days when he was "struggling and frustrated at how short people's memories were because nobody would put me up" were behind him, and with Gosden's faith supporting him and Derby glory giving him an untold boost, the scene was set for a riotous summer of success.

A week after the Derby he rode the Gosden-trained Star Of Seville to victory in the Prix de Diane and a couple of days later came Royal Ascot, at which Dettori has long been a fixture but which also played a part in the story. In 2014, he rode Treve in the Prince of Wales's Stakes on what turned out to be her least magnificent performance, and consequently lost the ride on the great filly. In the receding tide of Dettori's fortunes, it may have been the lowest ebb.

And if this year's Arc was a new high-water mark, Dettori wouldn't be human if, in Golden Horn's defeat of supermare Treve on her hat-trick bid, a little frisson of 'revenge is sweet' hadn't shivered down his spine. He later said he was thinking only of Golden Horn, but the significance of the result and that particular beaten horse would not have been lost on him or anyone else despite his alliance with Treve's owner.

"For a couple of years I thought the

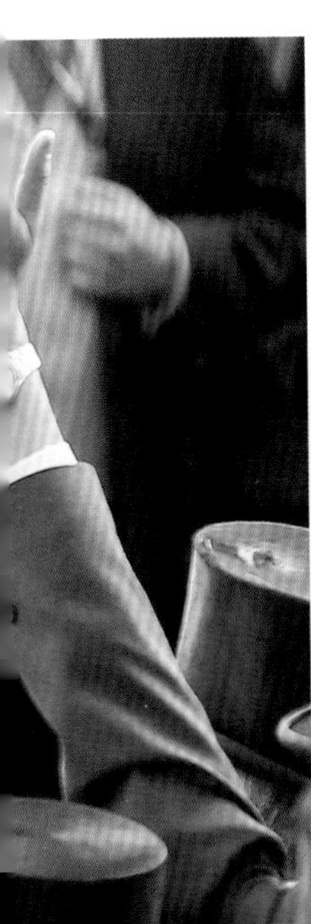

good times had gone and I came within an inch of retiring. I remember sitting at Royal Ascot with just a handful of rides and thinking 'I'll keep going until the end of the season and that's it'," he told Down. But the end of the 2014 season brought that call from Gosden, and 2015 was very different.

Dettori rode three winners at the royal meeting, the first of them – Osaila in the Sandringham Handicap – his milestone 50th at the five-day festival. Other victories on Time Test (Tercentenary Stakes) and Undrafted (Diamond Jubilee Stakes) set the seal on a remarkable week, and the big winners simply kept coming from all points of the compass. Sprinters, milers, middle-distance horses, stayers, two-year-olds – every house in racing's mansion opened its doors to Dettori.

There was the Eclipse Stakes, Irish Champion Stakes and Prix de l'Arc de Triomphe on the brilliant Golden Horn, the Stewards' Cup on Magical Memory, the Lonsdale Cup on Max Dynamite and, most encouragingly for the future, the Prix Morny and the Middle Park on the fleet-footed Shalaa.

Every big meeting was endowed with a sprinkling of the Dettori stardust, and although he'll never be champion again the feeling persists that it doesn't matter, that he's happy to cherry-pick from the biggest races and spend a little more time at home with the family while still bestriding the racing world like the colossus we have come to love.

"When I left Godolphin I knew I'd get another shot at things but I didn't think it would take three years. It was a big step that has only now paid off," he told Down. "I'm very content this time has come not only for my family, who are old enough to appreciate it, but for me too. I'm very humble and happy.

"As you get older you understand racing more and it means more. I've rediscovered my enjoyment and got something back that had been missing for seven or eight years."

And what he gets, he gives. Racing lost one superstar this year on the retirement of AP McCoy, but on the other side of the ledger it renewed its covenant with Dettori, that invaluable ambassador for the sport. He turns 45 just before Christmas 2015 and now, God willing, he will be with us for the next five or six years as he continues to chase big-race success around Europe and beyond.

Somewhere far out west, the first old Hollywood mogul grins at the second old Hollywood mogul, drains the day's third dry martini and sighs. "It'd be a great story, and I love that little Italian guy. But come on, who'd ever believe it could happen?"

▸▸ Frankie's golden summer: (from far left) Time Test wins the Tercentenary Stakes at Royal Ascot; a flying dismount from Shalaa after the Richmond Stakes at Glorious Goodwood; celebrations with John Gosden after Golden Horn's Derby; Undrafted (top, black) lands the Diamond Jubilee Stakes; Max Dynamite takes the Lonsdale Cup at York's Ebor meeting; Charlie Hills embraces the jockey after Stewards' Cup success with Magical Memory; (opposite page, bottom) Dettori celebrates after Osaila became his 50th Royal Ascot winner

CREST FALLEN

Frankie Dettori bade a sad farewell in March to Fujiyama Crest, famous for completing the jockey's Magnificent Seven at Ascot in 1996. The 'life-changing' horse died at the jockey's home in Newmarket at the age of 23.

Reporting his death, Dettori said: "He died peacefully in his paddock. He's been at my home since I bought him when he was up for sale 15 years ago and I'll never forget him. He changed my life. There would have been no Magnificent Seven without him.

"He's been a real family pet out in the paddock at home and all my children have sat on him."

Fujiyama Crest became part of racing folklore when he landed the Gordon Carter Handicap at Ascot after Dettori had ridden the first six winners on the card. He held on by a neck to complete Dettori's 25,091-1 seven-timer.

"Fujiyama Crest was the horse who made me famous, not the Group winners on that day," Dettori said. "I was doing well before that, but that day was the one that put me on the world map."

After a hurdling career Fujiyama Crest was due to go to the Malvern sales in the autumn of 2000 but Dettori stepped in to buy him for £12,000, having been alerted he was up for sale by the groom who had looked after Fujiyama Crest at Sir Michael Stoute's yard.

CLASS ACT

Treve failed in her bid for a historic third Arc but trainer Criquette Head-Maarek's magnanimity and the great racemare's feats left abiding memories

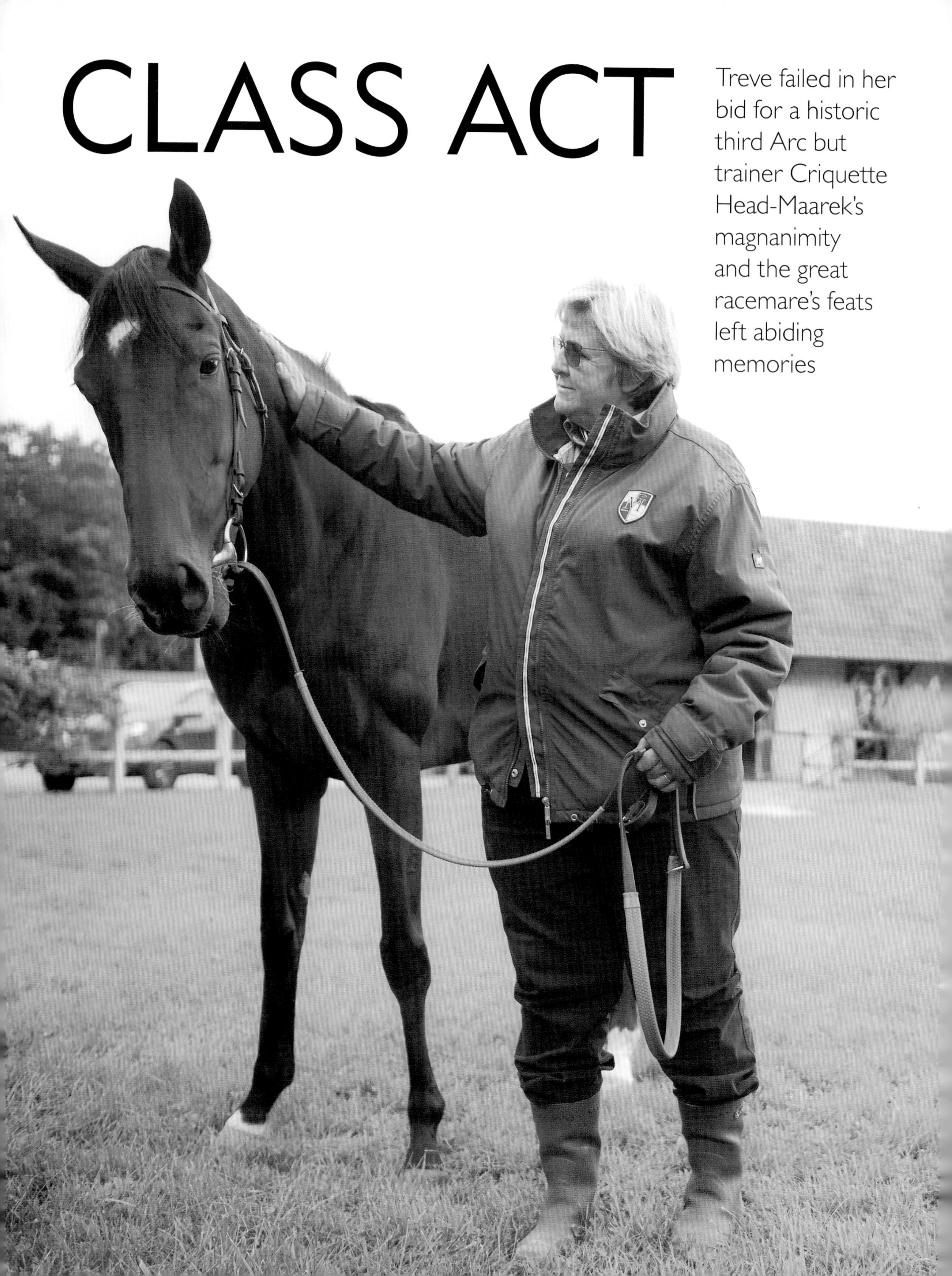

By Scott Burton

UNLIKE the major team sports, racing rarely demands formal inquisition of the vanquished after its key events. Win or lose, Premier League football managers are contractually obliged to face searching, prolonged questioning in a press conference. But the trainer of a beaten favourite can hope to slip away for quiet contemplation with the owner after offering the scantest of observations in the unsaddling enclosure.

Criquette Head-Maarek spent much of 2015 – much of Treve's brilliant career, in fact – tearing up those norms and was never likely to choose the easy way out after the dream of a third Arc slipped away in the 20-odd seconds it took the field to storm up Longchamp's home straight.

And so, having conducted a walking debrief in the Longchamp paddock for more than ten minutes in the immediate aftermath of Treve's fourth place behind Golden Horn, she was to be found standing patiently to one side in the lobby given over to media conferences, as Robert Cowell and Martin Harley relived Goldream's win in the Prix de l'Abbaye.

Head-Maarek was relaxed, chatting to a couple who may have been lifelong friends but could just as easily have happened upon her for the first time that day. She was about to go on the record again and wore not a hint of regret, in either her expression or her words. Treve had been beaten, and was now to be retired, but this was only the ending, not the full story.

When she was called to the top table and the microphone, Head-Maarek was applauded by a media pack that had scarcely been able to believe her open discourse with them over the 28 months since Treve dismantled the record time for the Prix de Diane by more than two seconds. Once more, she continued in the same vein, adding layers of understanding to her earlier analysis.

"I have watched the race back closely and I must say Dettori rode a remarkable race," said Head-Maarek, heaping praise on the man she very publicly had replaced as Treve's jockey before the Prix Vermeille 13 months earlier.

She was magnanimous at every turn, repeating there were "no excuses", and did not even jump at the chance to offer one when told of John Gosden's belief that on a softer surface the fortunes of Treve and Golden Horn would have been reversed. "I don't share his analysis. She was maybe slightly below her best, but that's all. We were beaten by a good horse and there is no disgrace to be beaten by Golden Horn."

Her admiration for Golden Horn had been second only to her feelings for Treve in dominating a dozen or more conversations with Head-Maarek since midsummer. Twenty-four hours after Treve had swept past Flintshire to claim the Grand Prix de Saint-Cloud in June, Head-Maarek paused during her rounds of evening stables to reflect that Golden Horn would be the one to beat on the first Sunday in October.

"I think the horse that won the Derby is very good," she said. "The second [Jack Hobbs] went to Ireland and won very easily. I don't know how well those behind stayed in the Irish Derby but that Epsom form is very good. If they come over you have to fear them."

It was a subject she would return to again and again, with French Derby winner New Bay also growing in her estimation following easy successes at Deauville and on trials day at Longchamp. Even in the wake of Golden Horn's unfathomable defeat at York, Head-Maarek repeated: "That doesn't mean he isn't a champion, he's a fantastic horse. He's the one I fear."

Treve's performances on the track in 2015 made her the one to fear most going into the Arc, for which she started even-money favourite with Golden Horn 9-2

▸▸ High point: (above) Treve gives her best performance of her final season as she streaks clear in the Prix Vermeille, passes the post six lengths in front and is welcomed back to the winner's enclosure; (opposite page) Criquette Head-Maarek with her 'exceptional' mare

and New Bay 5-1. She had earned her position, not only of favouritism but standing on the brink of history as the first three-time Arc winner, with three lead-up victories, each better than the last.

After dispatching the previous season's Prix de l'Opera heroine We Are over a barely adequate ten and a half furlongs on her seasonal reappearance in the Prix Corrida, Treve's victory in the Grand Prix de Saint-Cloud gave a taste of the public and media interest that would surround her in the autumn. Treve was applauded to the start, cheered as she passed the

▸▸ *Continues page 20*

post a length and a quarter in front of Flintshire and paraded around Saint-Cloud's tiny rectangular enclosure until every racegoer had a photographic souvenir.

The field for the Prix Vermeille on trials day may not have contained many fillies with genuine Arc ambitions but the way Treve took the race by the scruff of the neck in the false straight was out of the 2013 playbook. "I wanted to wait until the straight before letting her accelerate and so I was dabbing the brakes all the way round," jockey Thierry Jarnet said. "She's a bit stronger than at three. She took me by surprise in the false straight and I had to really get hold of her."

Head-Maarek was also reminded of that astonishing first Arc victory when Treve left Orfevre and Intello battling for scraps. "She is extraordinary and today I see her as being as good as when she was three. She has the same energy and the same will to win and this is really her backyard."

That victory moved the Group 1 counter up to six wins but it was to be the Queen of Longchamp's final success on a track where she had written much of her own legend. Treve's adoring public, though, could hardly envisage defeat in the run-up to the Arc. The buzz around the mare was remarkable, yet Head-Maarek was more than accommodating to every enquiry – from media and public alike – and exuded confidence and calmness as the pressure mounted.

The foundations of the serenity shown by Head-Maarek and Jarnet in the moments after Treve's defeat on Arc day were there for all to see in the press conference the previous Tuesday. "If Golden Horn is better than her he will beat her, let's find out on Sunday," the trainer said philosophically. "That's the great thing about a race, there is always something new which is revealed. If you have Golden Horn and New Bay then you have the best three-year-olds and it will be a good race."

After half an hour of cross-examination by both the racing and general media on every subject from what Treve eats to the size of her heart, Head-Maarek offered her own prescription for surviving the pressurised build-up. "I am quite relaxed. It's not snobbery on my part but I take the races as they come. We win, we lose but, once the horses pass the post, you just have to live with it. They are animals, not machines, and anything can happen, even during a race. You have to keep your feet on the ground whatever happens. You have to be a realist and recognise that anything can happen. What I need is that the people around me remain calm – that's what keeps me from being stressed, and the horses as well because they are very receptive."

For all the post-race questions of tactics – did Jarnet hang back too far or plot too wide a course? – the figures suggest Treve was below her brilliant best on Arc day. Still very, very good, but not exceptional. *Un jour sans*, in French racing jargon.

Back in the media conference, in the administrative building adjoining Longchamp's soon-to-be-demolished weighing room, Head-Maarek received even more rapturous press approval in taking her leave than when she had arrived. The day afterwards she would tell those gathered for the final time behind her yard that Treve had been "fantastique" across three brilliant seasons. "For me she was exceptional. It is difficult to find the words to describe what she has done and what she means to everyone. For me she is an exceptional horse, even though she got beaten."

MIGHTY MARE

TREVE IN NUMBERS

£6,002,918 Career earnings

131 Best RPR, achieved in her first Arc

29 Aggregate lengths by which she gained her wins

13 Races over four seasons

9 Wins

6 Group 1 victories

▸▸ French heroine: (clockwise from top left) Banners supporting Treve in the stands at Longchamp on Arc weekend; Treve and Thierry Jarnet go to post for the Arc; the great mare with her groom Stephanie Desjardins at Criquette Head-Maarek's stables in Chantilly

> 'It is difficult to find the words to describe what she has done and what she means to everyone. For me she is an exceptional horse, even though she got beaten'

Nobody held defeat against her, for all the disappointment as the expectant Longchamp crowd saw hopes of a third triumph unravel in the home straight. Twenty minutes after the race, with the television cameras absent for almost the first time on that tumultuous Arc day, Treve's two closest companions, Bertrand 'Capitaine' Clermont and Stephanie Desjardins, led their heroine back to her habitual box in the racecourse stables.

Clermont let go of Treve's bridle to embrace her, offering the consoling words: "It's okay, it's not so serious." No, Capitaine, it wasn't. Not after everything that had gone before. It was one hell of a ride.

MUHAARAR

MUKHADRAM

NAYEF

SHADWELL STALLIONS

Standing at Nunnery Stud UK

NEW FOR 2016

MUHAARAR

Oasis Dream - Tahrir

Quadruple Gr.1 winner.
European Champion Sprinter.

Applications close 2nd December

MUKHADRAM

Shamardal - Magic Tree

Beat: 2 Classic winners & 24 Gr.1 winners during his career.

80% of first season mares were winners/producers of winners.

Only Gr.1 winning son of SHAMARDAL to stand in the UK.

FIRST FOALS IN 2016

NAYEF

Gulch - Height Of Fashion

Sire of 4 Stakes winners 2015.

Sire of 7 stakes winners 2014.

31% Stakes winners/runners (Europe 2015).

49% winners/runners strike rate in 2015.

33% strike rate with 2YOS of 2015.

Discover more about the Shadwell Stallions at www.shadwellstud.co.uk
Or call Richard Lancaster, Johnnie Peter-Hoblyn or Rachael Gowland on

01842 755913

Email us at: nominations@shadwellstud.co.uk

JACK THE LAD

John Gosden is confident Jack Hobbs will become a man next year after a season spent in the shadow of stablemate Golden Horn despite his own Classic success

By David Carr

HE was the other horse. A Classic winner and one of the top-rated in Europe but just not quite as good as the stablemate who beat him twice and made most of the headlines from Epsom to Longchamp. When he was asked to play the leading role, Jack Hobbs delivered a signature performance in the Irish Derby and earned a rave review despite being upstaged on British Champions Day. The best news of all is that there is always next year, and Golden Horn won't be around then.

Being second best in a stable as powerful as John Gosden's does not mean second-rate and Jack Hobbs is a rattling good horse. Gosden is confident 2016 will be his year, and possibly 2017 too. Not only will Europe's middle-distance champion of this year be busy at stud by then but his less precocious, slower-maturing contemporary promises to be even better at four – which is saying something, considering what he achieved as a three-year-old.

For a while nobody was sure which of Gosden's pair was better. Jack Hobbs went off 2-1 favourite when they clashed for the first time in the Betfred Dante Stakes at York in May and still headed the betting for the Investec Derby at the time, having bolted up by 12 lengths in a handicap at Sandown the previous month. Significantly, that particular three-year-old handicap had been the intended starting point for Gosden's subsequent Oaks and King George winner Taghrooda in 2014.

Those who had backed Jack Hobbs for Epsom still had reason to hope despite his defeat against Golden Horn by two and three-quarter lengths at York. He had taken a bump around a furlong from home and had a pedigree more obviously conducive to staying a mile and a half than Golden Horn, who was not even entered for the Derby.

Sheikh Mohammed clearly still fancied him as Godolphin got out their chequebook and bought into the partnership, which included Rachel Hood, Gosden's wife. That meant William Buick, on a Godolphin retainer, would swap from Golden Horn to Jack Hobbs, freeing Frankie Dettori – the former Godolphin jockey – to make the opposite switch.

Once he was supplemented for the Derby, Golden Horn assumed favouritism ahead of his stablemate and this time the betting was right on the money. Jack Hobbs saw out every yard of the trip at Epsom, keeping on resolutely to pull four and a half lengths clear of third-placed Storm The Stars with the rest well beaten off. The only problem was that Golden Horn had passed the post three and a half lengths in front of him, leaving little doubt as to their relative abilities.

In some sports, being marginally inferior to an obvious star on your own side can be enormously frustrating. Think of England goalkeeper Ray Clemence, who was overshadowed by the legendary Peter Shilton, or wicketkeeper Bob Taylor, who was denied the Test match gloves for years by the peerless Alan Knott. It can be the same in racing if there is only one obvious prize to go for – as Aidan O'Brien's Theatreworld showed when banging his head against the Istabraq brick wall in the Champion Hurdle.

But there are an awful lot of good races for middle-distance three-year-old colts nowadays and there was no languishing on the bench for Jack Hobbs after Epsom. With Golden Horn dropped back in trip for the Eclipse, he was called up for the Dubai Duty Free Irish Derby over the stiff Curragh mile and a half – a perfect opportunity for a strong galloper with copper-bottomed stamina. Having been so far clear of the rest at Epsom, it was no surprise when he confirmed superiority over Storm The Stars. He extended the distance between them slightly to five lengths, with Derby fourth Giovanni Canaletto another five and a half lengths back in third.

Strikingly, the 150th running of Ireland's biggest mile-and-a-half race was the first to fall to a British stable since Balanchine had made it eight overseas triumphs in nine years in 1994 – so long ago that the filly was based with Godolphin's original trainer, the oft-forgotten Hilal Ibrahim. That

▸▸ First class: (opposite page) Jack Hobbs with Rachel Hood, one of the ownership partners, after his Irish Derby success; (above left) powering to his five-length Classic victory at the Curragh; (above right) winning the September Stakes

was the high point for Balanchine, who was beaten in all three subsequent appearances and has not bred anything remotely in her own league at stud, whereas Jack Hobbs continued to suggest there was more to come.

Not so much on the all-weather in the September Stakes at Kempton – he was a 1-5 shot and faced nothing of his own calibre as he comfortably defied a Group 1 penalty – but more so in the Qipco Champion Stakes at Ascot, after he was rerouted there when drying ground at Longchamp enabled Golden Horn to take his chance in the Prix de l'Arc de Triomphe.

Although Jack Hobbs could manage only third place, beaten a little under two lengths behind Fascinating Rock having started evens favourite, those bare facts do not tell the whole story. He was

▸▸ *Continues page 24*

drawn wide in stall 12 of 13 and Buick had no choice but to get him out quickly to chase his pacemaker Maverick Wave for fear of being caught in behind with nowhere to go in a mile-and-a-quarter race that was at the bottom end of his mount's stamina range.

That enforced early manoeuvre was bound to take its toll on the still immature colt, who had not made his debut in an all-weather maiden at Wolverhampton until two days after Christmas in 2014. Defeat certainly did not faze Gosden, who had seen exactly what was coming on the drive down from Newmarket.

"I said to Rachel coming down what would happen," he said. "We're drawn wide and we're going to have to use him with the pacemaker, and he's still such an immature horse it will catch him out in the final furlong. You're forced to commit from that draw and we had to use him quite a lot early, which would not be the normal plan. You'll pay the price at the other end and that's what happened."

Looking at Jack Hobbs's big frame and his pedigree, Gosden could see only good times ahead. It was in his later years that his sire Halling came into his own, landing the Eclipse and International Stakes twice each. The trainer likens his potential 2016 stable star to "a fifteen-year-old kid" who has still to grow into a man.

"It's all about next year," the trainer stressed in the aftermath of defeat at Ascot. "He's a big, overgrown kid and I couldn't be more thrilled with him. This horse will be bigger and stronger next year and I'm not in the slightest bit disappointed in him. He's a next-year horse, his dad got good at four and five. If you had told me this horse would do what he has done already I would have been blown away."

In his riding days, Jack Hobbs's breeder Willie Carson won a string of good races for Gosden on Muhtarram at four, five and six, notably the Irish Champion Stakes and the Prince of Wales's Stakes twice. The old team look to have something even better to go to war with next season when Jack the lad comes of age.

Weld's plans built on solid Rock

THERE was the one that got away but Dermot Weld still managed to land two of the biggest Group 1 middle-distance prizes, both at Ascot.

Free Eagle was first to strike, scoring a thrilling success in the Prince of Wales's Stakes at Royal Ascot by a short head from The Grey Gatsby. That was some performance on his first outing since finishing third in the Champion Stakes eight months earlier – and only the fifth of his entire career – and Weld admitted the four-year-old's preparation had been a calculated risk after a planned comeback at the Curragh was derailed by a head cold.

"This horse has had a lot of problems," he said. "He had a stress fracture, which is why he missed the Classics. We didn't put a lot of hard work into him, we just crept back into today. But I have huge confidence in him. I've always thought the Irish Champion and the Arc would be his long-term objectives."

When it came to those races, the getting there was not the issue; it was what happened on the track, especially at Leopardstown, that would cause all the problems.

Meanwhile, Weld had already set an objective for another of his four-year-olds. In the spring he decided to aim Fascinating Rock, then only a Group 3 winner, at the Group 1 Qipco Champion Stakes in October. It was an ambitious plan and by the time the colt arrived at Ascot he was still only a Group 3 winner – albeit a status he had achieved again with a runaway victory on his latest start – but Weld is a master at delivering on the big day.

The rain-softened ground was in Fascinating Rock's favour and the tactics were also spot on, with Pat Smullen – who enjoyed a vintage year himself – coming from off the fast pace to score from the three-year-olds Found and Jack Hobbs. They were both proven Group 1 performers and now Fascinating Rock is too, with plans to keep him in training at five.

"Pat gave him a brilliant ride and he had the ground he likes," Weld later told At The Races. "It was a really good Group 1, they went a cracking gallop all the way and the best horses fought it out. I've been lucky enough to have had a number of five-year-olds who got better with age and I see no reason why he won't. He's the classic stayer with speed."

In between those triumphs came disappointment. Many thought Weld was destined for another major success when Free Eagle launched a strong run in the Qipco Irish Champion Stakes but the colt was one of the year's unluckiest losers after he was knocked sideways by Golden Horn 150 yards from the line and pushed back to third.

"Pat said the interference completely knocked the wind out of Free Eagle and cost him the race," was Weld's frank assessment. There was no such hard-luck story in the Arc, where Free Eagle was sixth behind Golden Horn, and the baton then passed to Fascinating Rock.

In picking up the baton and running with it, probably all the way into next year, Fascinating Rock promises to keep Weld's eye on the big prizes.

▸▸ Plan into action: Fascinating Rock (centre) lands the Champion Stakes at Ascot from Found (left) and Jack Hobbs

5X G1 WINNER

POINT OF ENTRY

DYNAFORMER – MATLACHA PASS, by SEEKING THE GOLD

The Next Global Sire

PEDIGREE & PERFORMANCE

- **Dynaformer's Most Accomplished Son at Stud**
  Five-time G1 winner, twice Eclipse finalist
- **First Four Dams are G1 Winners and/or G1 Producers**
  Family of Eclipse Champions Sky Beauty and Gold Beauty

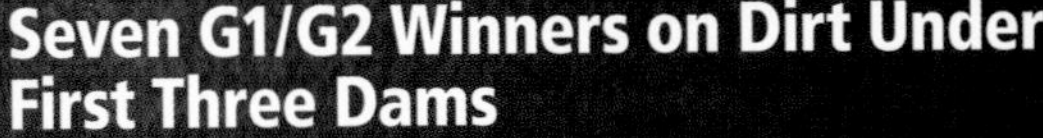

- **Seven G1/G2 Winners on Dirt Under First Three Dams**
  Half-Brother to G1 Winner on Dirt, out of a Sister to Breeders' Cup Distaff-G1 Winner
- **Exceptional First Foals**
  Selling this Fall

CLASSIC BLOODLINES

ADENA SPRINGS KENTUCKY

CLASSIC PERFORMANCE

AWESOME AGAIN ▸ GHOSTZAPPER ▸ MACHO UNO ▸ MUCHO MACHO MAN ▸ POINT OF ENTRY

Jack Brothers (859) 509-0879 ▸ Cormac Breathnach (859) 552-4345

www.AdenaStallions.com

By Scott Burton

ON Champions Day 2014 Freddy Head stood in the red, white and blue bedecked winner's enclosure at Ascot after Charm Spirit had landed Britain's miling championship, the Queen Elizabeth II Stakes. This was a victory to savour but Charm Spirit was about to be retired to stud and Head already knew what the project for 2015 entailed.

Two weeks earlier, a striking grey four-year-old called Solow – a failed stayer and one-time suspect traveller – had landed the Group 2 Prix Daniel Wildenstein over a mile under a hands-and-heels ride from Olivier Peslier, Head's long-time ally.

At Longchamp Head had mentioned the need to venture abroad in search of a Group opportunity for the gelded son of Singspiel, and by the time he arrived at Ascot a plan had been hatched along with owners Alain and Gerard Wertheimer and their racing manager, Pierre-Yves Bureau. Solow had already been put away for the year at the Wertheimers' Haras de Saint-Leonard and the objective was Meydan in March.

The newly rechristened Dubai Turf would prove to be the first in a wondrous five-card-trick of a Group 1 season, with Solow following up in the Prix d'Ispahan, Queen Anne Stakes, Sussex Stakes and finally at Ascot in the QEII. Such a collection of racing jewels required a level of consistency none of the other pretenders to the miling crown could even approach.

Twenty-four hours after Solow's final triumph of 2015, Head was at one of Chantilly's more low-key meetings and took time to reflect on a job well planned and well executed. "He's a very sound and healthy horse and I think his superiority helped because he wasn't taking as much out of himself," he said. "He had his races quite well spaced out and we gave him a rest after Goodwood. He's a crack and when they're as good as that they can do it."

All the more impressive is that Head hasn't had the luxury of picking and choosing Solow's targets. The list of races at the top level closed to geldings affords no room for error. "In one sense it's easier because you know exactly which races you're going to run in. Of course that means you have to be exactly right on the day but he's been in really good form and done all that we asked of him. He's easy to train."

Having blown away the cobwebs on the Chantilly Polytrack on March 3, Solow blitzed the field in Dubai, putting four and a quarter lengths between himself and French Derby winner The Grey Gatsby. Next, on what would be his only Group 1 start in France, Solow disposed of the talented and tough Gailo Chop in the Ispahan.

At that stage Head was finding excuses to doubt the veracity of the form book, even though Solow was rated just a pound off being the best thoroughbred on the planet by early June. Surely the marquee clash with Hong Kong's Able Friend at Royal Ascot would offer

FLYING SOLOW

Freddy Head's magnificent miler won in Dubai, France and three times in England to complete an unbeaten campaign

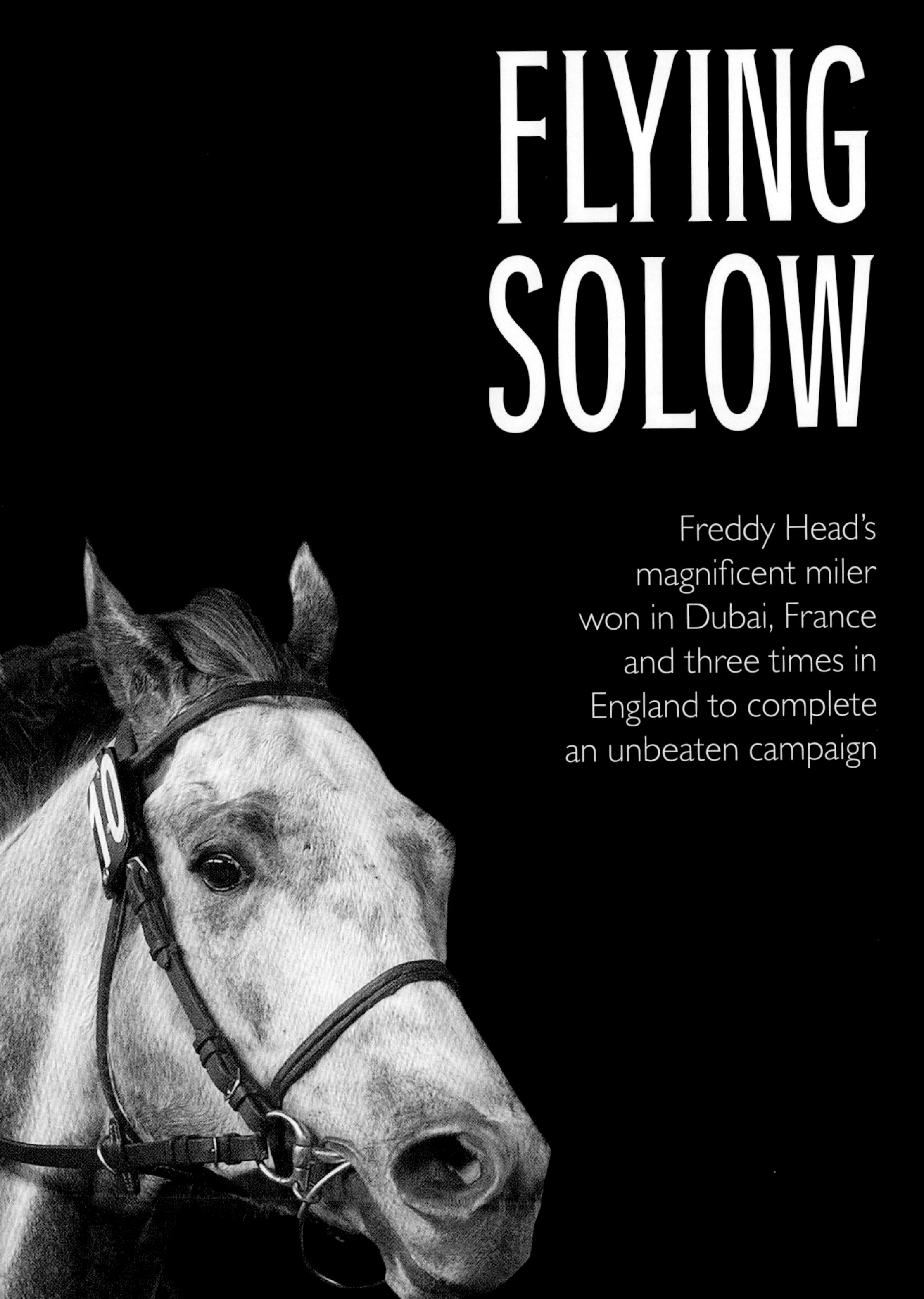

conclusive proof one way or the other.

Speaking to the Racing Post a fortnight before Royal Ascot, Head offered this insight: "You really have to get every step of the trip at Ascot. Goldikova was a champion and could do everything but I think Solow is really made for Ascot. He's a magnificent physical specimen and so easy to ride."

Head was right about Solow's suitability for Ascot. While a long season took its toll on Able Friend, the flying grey delivered a one-length success over compatriot Esoterique, who would carry that form on to victory in the Prix Jacques Le Marois and beyond.

Nobody doubted Solow now. Although a different challenge awaited the heavy-shouldered grey on the downland switchback of Goodwood in the Qatar Sussex Stakes, a large element of difficulty was removed with the no-show of Gleneagles and he was sent off at 2-5 in a field of eight. Guyon took all risk out of being locked on the rail by riding a positive race in second before motoring up the straight, always holding Arod to score by a deceptively comfortable half a length.

Guyon offered a measured assessment in the days before the QEII, his faith in Solow completely unshakeable. "I don't know that we should expect him to win his races now by the sort of margin he recorded in Dubai," he said. "He didn't win by far at Ascot either and I think he is learning to ration his effort. It certainly wasn't a lack of condition [at Goodwood] because the horse was really well in himself. He just lets up a little these days once he gets his head in front."

How prophetic that description turned out in the QEII as Guyon once again applied the pressure from some way out, with Solow's now familiar long crescendo of acceleration settling the matter. Gleneagles turned up this time but the good-to-soft ground was against him and in favour of Solow, as it had been all year. Head's grey again won by a relatively small margin, three-quarters of a length from Belardo, but always had the race in safe keeping.

James Doyle, who rode the runner-up, gave a clue as to why Solow has been able to live so comfortably in the rarefied atmosphere of the top mile races. "At halfway I wanted to be closer," he said, "but we didn't half quicken going down past the four-furlong marker."

Some would be tempted to chart a different course in 2016 but Head appears content for more of the same, something for which anyone who caught the Solow show this year can only be grateful.

In the twilight at Chantilly the trainer reflected: "One day perhaps we might go back up [to a mile and a quarter] but I'm in no hurry. You need to respect a horse like him. If he keeps having relatively easy races he could be running at the top level for two or three seasons."

For existing rivals and any new ones who might emerge next year, Solow has set the standard.

SUPER

A blockbuster opening day set the tone as Willie Mullins saddled a record eight winners at the Cheltenham Festival. Here he relives the preparation, pressure and pride involved in a job well done

The winning team: (left to right) Paul Townend, Wicklow Brave and Kevin McCabe; Luke Dempsey, Killultagh Vic and Qasim Raza; Willie Mullins, Faugheen and John Codd; Un De Sceaux and Anatoliy Yakovlyev; Douvan, Gail Carlisle and Ruby Walsh; Vautour and Dermot Keeling; Bryan Cooper, Don Poli and Linda Masterson; Glens Melody and Irfan Ali

EIGHT

By Jonathan Mullin

THERE is only one thing more disconcerting than a build-up wrecked with problems, and that's one where nothing goes wrong at all. As Cheltenham 2015 approached and Willie Mullins made the fog-breathed walk back to his warm kitchen from the gallops across the country lane from his home and yard, he found himself, in his own words, "in a sort of a daze".

It wasn't as if the pressure hadn't been mounting; there was enough to ensure the responsibility of an entire country's challenge seemed to rest on his shoulders. For months the Irish champion trainer's horses headed the ante-post betting for a host of festival contests, and these weren't reputations built on sand: throughout the winter and early spring, Mullins' horses dominated their rivals in the big Irish races and continually enhanced their standing.

"Two weeks out from Cheltenham and I was just there in a sort of a daze," he says, "because I realised I couldn't do any more and it was the first time for years I was looking forward to Cheltenham. So I'm saying to myself, this is the best prep I've ever had, and that means it's either going to be a fantastic Cheltenham for the yard or I've got it completely wrong and it'll be a total blowout. The training had gone right, the weather had been spot on, the horses were staying right, we had no major blows or injuries, no coughs or colds. Nothing."

It was only when the team arrived off the lorry at Cheltenham that the first issue arose. "The one thing we did different this time was to give our good horses bigger stalls, so they travelled business class. So what amazed me, and the big disappointment of the whole thing, was that Champagne Fever got into a fracas with his neighbour Un Atout. We had put the horses side by side that we thought would travel well together and we obviously got that match-up wrong. They live opposite each other in the barn at home, so there you go.

"It was only when we took them off the lorry that we could see they'd had a difference of opinion along the way

▸▸ *Continues page 30*

and it was unfortunate because it ruled Champagne Fever out of the Champion Chase. After spending so much time and effort planning the match-ups and the travel, it was disappointing for something like that to happen in the lorry.

"Some horses don't travel well and get grumpy but we never thought that with Un Atout. And maybe Champagne Fever might have been the one who started it, who knows? There are some horses that you give an extra stall to, or some you'll put on the back of the lorry with a stall in between. In going to Cheltenham we could put a lot more on the lorry and cut down on the expense, but we try to travel them business class and give them a bit more room. It costs more, but for a meeting like that you try to do everything right."

****

THE opening morning of the Cheltenham Festival is like no other. The foggy Cotswold hills throw a mystical blanket across the track as visiting horses stretch their legs and the sense of anticipation rises. That morning, as Mullins pulled the collar of his green anorak high around his neck and watched as the Channel 4 cameras beamed pictures of his team on to The Morning Line, he dared hope that today would be all it promised to be, yet with one niggly doubt eating at his ability to enjoy the final few hours before the tapes went up in the Sky Bet Supreme Novices' Hurdle. "It was that worry: if we had done anything wrong, the whole thing was wrong. It was all or nothing."

It will be some time before one trainer goes into the Tuesday of Cheltenham with such a strong hand. Along with a handy group of second strings – one of whom was to prove a timely parachute later in the day – he had four favourites with Douvan, at 2-1, the biggest price of the quartet in the Supreme. Later, there was Un De Sceaux in the Racing Post Arkle at 4-6, Faugheen in the Stan James Champion Hurdle at 4-5 and Annie Power, the 1-2 favourite for the OLBG Mares' Hurdle.

On his phone was a text from a friend wishing him "the worst day in bookmaking history". And while that wish didn't quite come true, Mullins' attempt scraped the top of the crossbar.

Douvan led home a 1-2 in the Supreme and for the travelling Irish it was the first sign that all they had seen at home all winter could now be believed. For Mullins it was a pressure-releasing moment of pure joy. "It was so good to get one on the board so early, and super to let the air out of the balloon and then I just . . . I seemed to be talking to you guys [the media] a lot of the time, which just shows what tremendous staff I have, they took over and ran the show. From weighing out jockeys, saddling them, making sure they're all right after the race. It was a huge effort on their part, everything went like clockwork. They knew what they were doing and it went fantastic."

Mullins is not in the habit of talking up his young horses in ebullient terms before their big assignments, but Douvan has become the exception. "Gail [Carlisle, head girl] rides him all the time at home and every day I left her on him. He was just so superior to the horses I was putting him with. Normally I'd put David [Casey] or Ruby [Walsh] or someone like that on, but this horse kept performing, with Gail looking around wondering where the rest were.

"I was surprised at how

▸▸ *Continues page 32*

▸▸ First class: Douvan jumps the final flight in the Supreme Novices' Hurdle to set the ball rolling for the Mullins team at the Cheltenham Festival; (below) Ruby Walsh after his victory on Douvan

Favourites Racing is one of the most successful racehorse syndicate ownerships in the country.

We have numerous exciting prospects in training both on the flat and National Hunt which are available for syndication.

Shares available to suit all budgets.

Festival successes include:

- ★ Godsmejudge, winning the Scottish Grand National at Ayr in 2013 and runner up in the same race again in 2014
- ★ The 2009 Cheltenham Festival Winner, Something Wells
- ★ Dutch Rose at York's Ebor Meeting
- ★ Livingstonebramble at Punchestown

To find out more about our horses please visit **www.favourites.co.uk** or to arrange a viewing of the horses available please call **01684 310565**, or email **info@favourites.co.uk**

Favourites Racing Syndication
Tyre Hill Racing Stables
Hanley Swan
Worcestershire WR8 0EQ

bullish I was about him when talking to the press before Cheltenham. Am I really saying this?" he recalls, scarcely believing his own words. "But this was what I was seeing every morning. When you look at some of the horses we had won with over there, you could get from me that I thought this fellow was better than any of them and I think I might have said that.

"What he was showing me . . . " he says, then hesitates. "Put it this way: it'll be a while before we'll see a horse do that again here at home as a novice. I'm hoping that what we saw last season was not all precociousness and he will develop more."

One leg down, three to go, and Un De Sceaux was a horse who jangled nerves for a different reason. He fell on his chase debut at Thurles and, while he was foot-perfect after that, his 'look, no brakes!' manner of front-running did not inspire confidence that, if he came to a fence on a disagreeable stride, a safe landing would be negotiated. Even after Douvan's sparkling win in the Supreme, Mullins couldn't relax just yet.

"That fall at Thurles affected the confidence of all of us," he admits. "You think back to that every time he runs. But there was no doubt at Cheltenham at any of the fences and he jumped like a handicapper in the Arkle. Whereas before all of the organisation had to be done by Ruby, at Cheltenham Un De Sceaux was setting himself up at his fences. It gives you the confidence to think he can go the whole way."

Two from two for Mullins and if anybody thought his powers – even by the law of averages – would soon dwindle, they were wrong. The day's big race, the Champion Hurdle, wasn't quite Michael Dickinsonesque, but it wasn't far off.

He saddled three of the eight runners – the odds-on favourite Faugheen, the old gunslinger Hurricane Fly and the improving Arctic Fire – and watched as all three filled the placings.

"To me Hurricane Fly is Hurricane Fly, there'll never be another one, and Faugheen has some amount of work to do to get near him. But Faugheen is a champion and there's no reason to think he won't reproduce those performances this season because he did it hard last season, he travelled to England twice. And he made all in the Champion Hurdle. Ruby said he wasn't going to take any prisoners; he asked a big question from Faugheen and he came up with the answer, which was fantastic.

"Faugheen certainly wouldn't be as good a jumper as Hurricane Fly but he gets the job done. He doesn't lose ground when he gallops out through them. Probably his point-to-pointing has taught him how to make a mistake and recover quickly.

"Just looking at him, he has come back in great form. The first year we went to Cheltenham there wasn't a pick on him. He was like a greyhound. That's what had me worried this time: could he improve? I worried whether he had the strength to improve if I really started to train him for Champion Hurdle-type races, Grade 1s in open company.

"That was always in my mind looking at him as we worked him this year. And he did, he retained his strength all season and it stood to him. Now I can ask myself, if I really go and train him, could

'Faugheen is a champion and there's no reason to think he won't reproduce those performances this season because he did it hard last season'

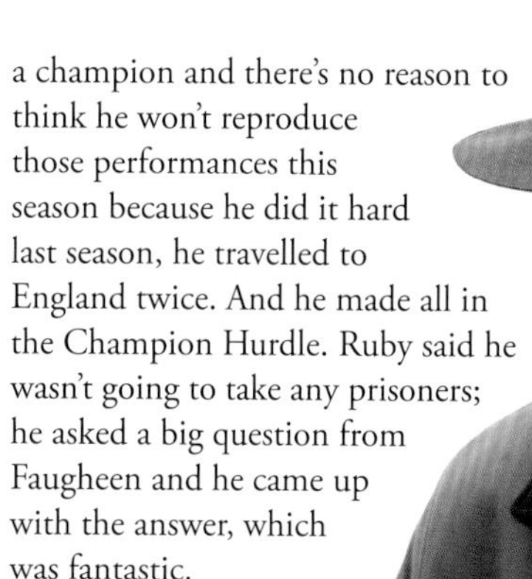

he be better?" A formidable thought for those looking to take him on in this season's big two-mile hurdle races.

The overall quality of the Mullins team was already evident from the placed horses, as well as the winners, and the trainer was sure glad he had Glens Melody as high-quality back-up to Annie Power in the Mares' Hurdle. The favourite's fall saved the bookmakers a massive payout, being the last of Mullins' four hotpots to run and the first not to win. As he came down from the stands, from the same spot he watches every race through his binoculars, Mullins feared the worst.

"I thought we were beat in the photo-finish and I looked back down the straight and saw the screens were up. Holy God, says I, we've lost one mare and the other has been done on the line. I came off the stand absolutely gutted until the result of the photo came out, and soon after the word came through that Annie Power was okay and was walking away. It was an extraordinary few minutes.

"Watching the replay, I think Annie Power probably stood way back. In fact Glens Melody did the same but she got the landing gear out. It was just one of those things.

"After Glens Melody had chased home Quevega in 2014, I thought Fiona McStay [owner of Glens Melody] would send her mare to be covered because breeders usually like to protect their stock and get them off to stud safely, so I was surprised when she decided to come back. I thought it was a very game thing for a breeder to do, most breeders I know wouldn't have done it. I admired her, I was surprised, but she showed great conviction to do it, and it took until the last 100 yards for it to pan out."

Success story: (clockwise from top left) Un De Sceaux and Ruby Walsh return in triumph after the Racing Post Arkle; Bryan Cooper punches the air as Don Poli lands the RSA Chase; Annie Power (Walsh) falls at the last in the Mares' Hurdle, leaving stablemate Glens Melody (Paul Townend) to win; Killultagh Vic (Luke Dempsey) takes the Martin Pipe Conditional Jockeys' Handicap Hurdle; Vautour powers up the hill under Walsh in the JLT Novices' Chase; Wicklow Brave (Townend) lands the County Hurdle; Faugheen (right) and Walsh pile the pressure on their rivals in the Champion Hurdle; (opposite page, bottom) Willie Mullins after Don Poli's success

It was a remarkable day's work and, while not quite the quartet everybody presumed, four winners was enough for Mullins to secure a stranglehold on the festival. He would end up with four more over the concluding three days, with Wicklow Brave (County) and Killultagh Vic (Martin Pipe Conditional Jockeys) landing handicap hurdles on the Friday and novice chasers Don Poli (RSA) and Vautour (JLT) stamping themselves as two ready-made Gold Cup contenders for this season, to join his 2015 runner-up Djakadam and the returning Sir Des Champs.

Eight winners was a record haul at the festival – eclipsing Nicky Henderson's seven in 2012 – and made Mullins leading trainer for the third year in a row. He moved past Paul Nicholls into second on the all-time list of festival trainers with a

Continues page 34

One of many: Willie Mullins with his trophy for winning the Racing Post Arkle with Un De Sceaux, the second of his eight winners at the Cheltenham Festival

total of 41 winners and, with 24 of those coming in the past five years, is fast closing the gap to Nicky Henderson, who leads with 53.

****

WHILE Mullins' patience means it will be deepest, darkest winter before most of his Cheltenham horses begin to beam their ambitions for this new season, don't expect him to be dining out on what happened last March. It's an exaggeration to say he 'moved on' straight away, but he certainly isn't the maudlin type.

"I don't think I've watched any of the winners on video, just on the day over there, but none since I came home. Oh," he says, a memory just sprouting, "maybe one."

That one was the JLT Novices' Chase, because you know earlier we said nothing had gone wrong save for some inter-barn rivalry on the journey over? Well, one horse had tested Mullins to his limits.

"For me, coming home from Cheltenham in 2014, he was the one. The media and plenty of others were all over Faugheen but for me what your man [Vautour] did was exceptional.

"But then he disappointed at Christmas, he wasn't right. I think he was sore, it must have been a muscle problem because he wasn't letting himself jump. We had to get him over that, and with that problem he probably wasn't doing everything right at home either. There was a rush to get him ready [for Cheltenham], he was behind and he definitely got extra homework. It was all or nothing."

With so much committed, and Vautour responding with a breathtaking performance, Mullins kept a tight grip on his binoculars as the crowd gasped at how Rich Ricci's horse took his fences. The reason why Vautour's JLT victory is the only one Mullins has watched back is simple: he couldn't enjoy it at the time.

"He was jumping so fantastically and so extravagantly but in one way – aside from the fact it's an honour to be training him – you'd love to be watching as a neutral. Because watching as a trainer my heart was in my mouth every time he jumped like that. Watching him as a punter every time you'd be thinking, 'wow, wow, wow'. When you see someone else's horse do that you think it's fantastic, but I never got to think that at Cheltenham because from my perspective I was thinking, he can't keep this 'wow' jumping up the whole time. But he did. Yeah, of all the winners we had, I might have looked back at that one all right, just to enjoy it."

After his crowning cluster of festival winners, Mullins was more than entitled to that.

RECORDS GALORE

Willie Mullins followed his record haul at Cheltenham with a new high at the Punchestown festival, sending out 16 winners over the five days.

Four of his Cheltenham winners – Faugheen, Un De Sceaux, Douvan and Killultagh Vic – followed up with Grade 1 victories, among an incredible ten successes at the top level for Mullins. One of the most treasured was Annie Power's win in the Mares Champion Hurdle, which provided compensation for her bad luck at Cheltenham, and the other Grade 1 scorers were Felix Yonger, Valseur Lido, Bellshill, Nichols Canyon and Petite Parisienne.

That brought down the curtain on another magisterial season for Mullins, who won his ninth Irish jump trainers' championship and the eighth in a row. He notched 187 domestic winners (203 with British winners included) and triumphed in an astonishing 30 Grade 1 races in Ireland and Britain – a record for a jumps trainer. His combined winnings in Ireland and Britain totalled more than £4.5m.

For Mullins' rivals there is the chilling impression that the best may be yet to come.

DON'T WAIT TO CELEBRATE

PRIORITY ACCESS

ONE CARD FOR **EVERYTHING**

The William Hill Priority Access Prepaid MasterCard®, puts you in total control. It lets you get to your William Hill online account winnings, the instant you win.

The Priority Access card gives you **INSTANT ACCESS** to your winnings as the **card is linked to your William Hill online account balance**, no more waiting, no more winnings being caught up in day to day banking. Simply carry on betting on all the top sporting action and choose how you want to use your winnings.... That's better, isn't it?

Contact us today on 0800 085 6296 or visit us at williamhill.com/priorityaccess to get started.

 **PLACE BETS**  **SHOP**  **EAT OUT**  **TRAVEL**  **BUY ONLINE**  **GET CASH**

ON MOBILE · ONLINE · IN SHOP

PRIORITY ACCESS
www.williamhill.com/priorityaccess

WHEN THE FUN STOPS STOP™

gambleaware.co.uk

William Hill rules apply. Over 18s only. FOR ADVICE & INFORMATION VISIT WWW.GAMBLEAWARE.CO.UK. NATIONAL GAMBLING HELPLINE 0808 8020 133.

GOING FOR GOLD

Willie Mullins, who has had five runners-up but never a winner in the Cheltenham Gold Cup, has his strongest team yet in his search for the holy grail

By David Jennings

HE COULD have won it ugly. Having watched On His Own, the handicapper he had supplemented at the 11th hour, carried towards the centre of the track by Lord Windermere in the 2014 Cheltenham Gold Cup, Willie Mullins had every right to try to win it ugly.

The stewards deliberated on the day for the best part of 15 minutes before confirming that Lord Windermere, who passed the post a short head in front, would keep the race. There was no guarantee that an appeal panel would agree with that ruling and it was surely worth a shot to find out. Many connections would have done that, bearing in mind the prize-money and the fact that opportunities to win a Gold Cup can be once in a lifetime, even for major owners like Andrea and Graham Wylie.

On His Own's team thought differently. "I had a good chat with Mr and Mrs Wylie and we just felt that as we didn't win it on the day

there was no point in trying to win it on a different day. It just wouldn't be the same," said Mullins less than 24 hours after another agonising reversal in the race that has eluded him so often.

Mullins wants to win the Gold Cup the right way. He doesn't want to get it in the stewards' room or in front of a panel at BHA headquarters in London. He wants to win the best race with the best horse, no questions asked. And so the search goes on.

Ireland's master jumps trainer came closest to the holy grail in that incident-packed 2014 edition but there are four other seconds on his CV too. Florida Pearl was runner-up in 2000, as was Hedgehunter in 2006, and Mullins has been second in each of the past three years – with Sir Des Champs in 2013, then On His Own and most recently when Djakadam chased home Coneygree. Seconditis is not a condition that usually afflicts Mullins and he looks set to try all possible remedies in an attempt to shake off the malady next March.

Mullins seems to have every angle covered this time. He has the sexy one in Vautour, the white-faced son of Robin Des Champs who cannot help but turn heads. Then there is Don Poli, the relentless one. The RSA Chase winner who loves the stamina test of Cheltenham's undulations. Djakadam is the precocious one. Few six-year-olds even run in the Gold Cup, never mind finish second. He has always looked more advanced than his years. And don't forget Sir Des Champs, the returning one. He suffered a tendon injury at the end of 2013 and has not been back to the Gold Cup since his second place, but he is ready again to fight for his place in the Closutton team.

Even Mullins, who is a dab hand at playing down expectations, is unable to hide away from the hype. "In terms of a team of Gold Cup horses, I've never had anything like it," he admits. "Don Poli is an out-and-out stayer, which you obviously need for the Gold Cup – a jumper and a stayer. Sir Des Champs is the same, and he came so close to winning. Djakadam was only six in March and by trying to win with a horse of his age and inexperience, we were trying to do something that hasn't been done since Mill House in 1963. I think Vautour will stay, we're definitely going down the Gold Cup route. They all look like they could win a Gold Cup – but it's never as simple as that."

For most of the Cheltenham Festival last March everything seemed simple to the Mullins team and there was no more dominant winner than Vautour, whose 15-length romp in the JLT Novices' Chase was about as good as it gets. Having been pestered for the lead by Irish Saint, he should have found his finishing effort compromised. Instead he powered up the hill and made a pair of previous Grade 1 winners, Apache Stronghold and Valseur Lido, look distinctly ordinary.

Nobody should have been surprised, especially not if they had seen Lydia Hislop's interview with Mullins on Racing UK after Faugheen had won the Neptune

⏩ *Continues page 38*

⏩ Fab Four: (from left) Vautour, Don Poli, Djakadam and Sir Des Champs are ready to battle for the No. 1 spot

Novices' Hurdle the previous year. In asking the trainer to compare him with the previous day's Supreme winner, Hislop was just chancing her arm. She certainly didn't expect the answer she got. Nobody did. "It's tough. Actually, it's not really. Vautour is at a different level, isn't he? I think he is anyway."

Vautour's performances in the build-up to the 2015 festival veered from fantastic to flawed and nobody quite knew what to expect at Cheltenham. What we got was like nothing we had seen before.

There will be a sense of the unknown again next March if Vautour lines up in the Gold Cup. Can we really expect a horse who never went beyond two and a half miles as a novice chaser or hurdler to stay the gruelling three miles, two and a half furlongs of the Gold Cup? It is not as if you can put him in cruise control out the back in an attempt to save petrol. But, just for a second, imagine if Vautour does get the Gold Cup trip. Daydreams do not get much more enjoyable than that.

If Vautour is Michael Johnson, Don Poli is Mo Farah. The further he goes, the better he looks. Apache Stronghold looked like he might have his measure halfway up the Leopardstown run-in in the Topaz Novice Chase last Christmas, yet he pulled away to win by three lengths.

A similar story unfolded at Cheltenham in the RSA Chase. Bryan Cooper was nudging away from a long way out and his mount looked a sitting duck as Southfield Theatre jumped the final fence upsides. Course commentator Mike Cattermole briefly began to get excited about the prospect of a tight finish but he soon realised who he was commentating on. "Don Poli, though, one thing he does is stay and he is pouring it on," Cattermole told racegoers. "He is turning on the afterburners coming up the hill. Don Poli is going to maintain his unbeaten record over fences."

Don Poli won by six lengths. Had there been another furlong (and there are an extra two furlongs in the Gold Cup, remember) he might have won by double that. Mullins wasn't holding back afterwards. He told us exactly what he was thinking. "Don Poli has

▸▸ *Continues page 40*

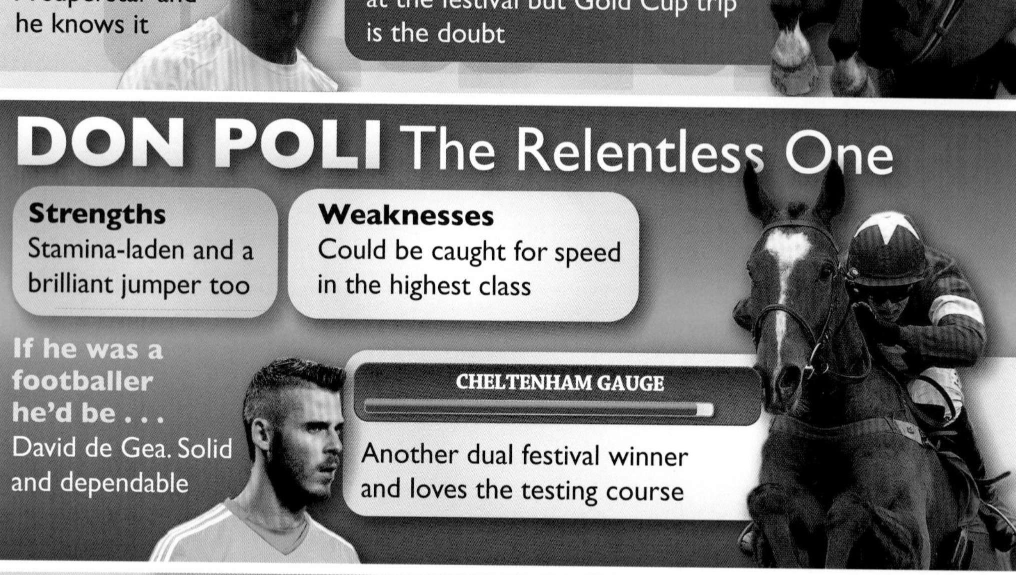

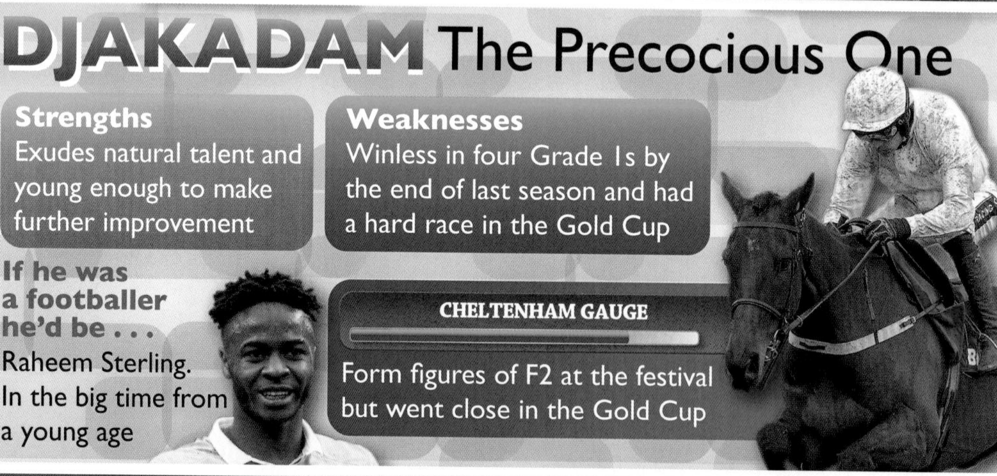

SECOND NATIONAL
THOROUGHBRED OWNER CONFERENCE
January | 2016

Don't miss this First-Class Entertaining and Educational Event that includes a chance to:

- Socialize and Network with Industry Leaders
- Meet Owners from the U.S. and Canada
- Hear Experts Discuss the Hottest Industry Topics for New and Longtime Owners
- Experience Exceptional Dining at Turnberry Isle and Host Venue, Gulfstream Park
- Make Plans to Stay After the Conference and Attend the 45th Annual Eclipse Awards

REGISTER NOW!

Visit ownerview.com for more details

KEYNOTE ADDRESS
Thoroughbred Owner and CBS Sports Personality
JIM ROME

Gulfstream Park — Hallandale Beach, Florida

PRESENTING SPONSORS: KEENELAND ASSOCIATION ○ THE STRONACH GROUP ○ WOODBINE ENTERTAINMENT

Hosted by OwnerView, a joint venture between The Jockey Club and Thoroughbred Owners and Breeders Association

Gold Cup written all over him. If he can do that to the best novices in England and Ireland at Cheltenham there is only one road on which to go. He's probably as good an RSA winner as we've had and he's won with a lot in hand."

High praise indeed when you consider that Florida Pearl, the first of Mullins' four RSA winners, went on to win seven more Grade 1s, including four Hennessy Gold Cups at Leopardstown. Don Poli is less flamboyant than Florida Pearl but he's a streetfighter and Mullins knows it will take one hell of a punch to knock him to the canvas.

Forget Don Poli's pitiful performance at Punchestown. His Cheltenham exertions were surely to blame for finishing last of five behind his less esteemed stablemate Valseur Lido in the Growise Champion Novice Chase. That just wasn't him.

Djakadam probably wasn't himself at Punchestown either. Having turned the Thyestes at Gowran Park into a procession on only his second start of last season, he traded blows with Coneygree and Road To Riches all the way up the home straight in an energy-sapping Gold Cup and, by the time the last week of April arrived, he might have been over the top.

Given that Djakadam does not turn seven until New Year's Day, there is every chance Mullins will be able to eke out a little more improvement. He was only a length and a half behind Coneygree – a novice but two years older than him – and doesn't have much to find.

Perhaps Mullins' greatest training feat would be to get Sir Des Champs back to the form of the 2012-2013 season, which saw him fend off Flemenstar in the Hennessy Gold Cup at Leopardstown and then beat all bar Bobs Worth in the Cheltenham Gold Cup.

In April owner Michael O'Leary said "it's probably over" when asked about the prospect of Sir Des Champs returning from his long layoff, but by the start of the winter season hope was rising again after Mullins managed to coax him back to fitness. Sir Des Champs would be another weapon in the owner's armoury, which also includes the Gordon Elliott-trained

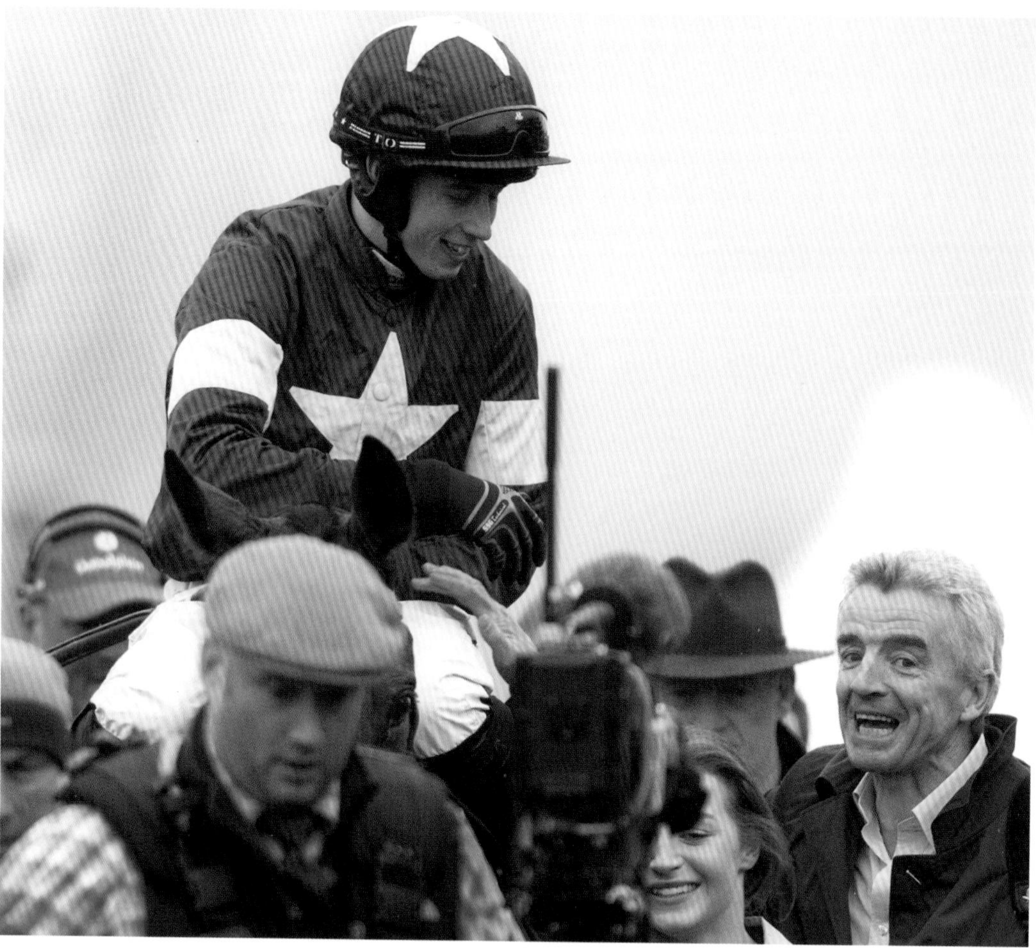

▸▸ Power sharing: Michael O'Leary (right) and Willie Mullins both have strong Gold Cup teams, including Don Poli (above) and Sir Des Champs as a partnership

MULLINS IN THE GOLD CUP

14 runners; **no** wins; **5** seconds; **1** third

THE FIVE RUNNERS-UP

Florida Pearl (below) *2000* Led two out, where Gloria Victis fell fatally, but was headed before the last by Looks Like Trouble, who stayed on stronger up the hill to win by five lengths

Hedgehunter *2006* Held up but was in contention as the field bypassed the third-last and chased War Of Attrition all the way from two out but fell short by two and a half lengths

Sir Des Champs *2013* Clear with Long Run coming down the hill but dropped to third after the second last as Bobs Worth launched his winning challenge and beaten two and a half lengths despite a brave rally

On His Own *2014* Bumped two out in a packed finish and only fifth jumping the last but finished strongly despite being carried right by Lord Windermere, who won by a short head

Djakadam *2015* Ridden in close third two out and minor mistake at the last before a valiant pursuit of all-the-way winner Coneygree, who scored by a length and a half

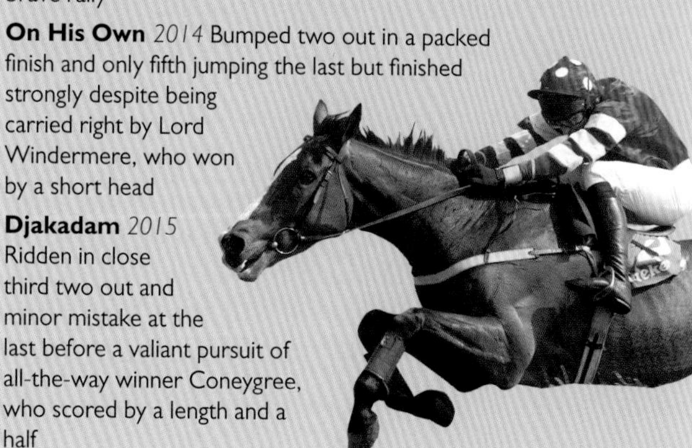

Don Cossack – last season's top-rated chaser in Britain and Ireland – as well as Don Poli and the Noel Meade-trained Road To Riches, third in last year's Gold Cup.

O'Leary, no less than Mullins, has a winter of Gold Cup dreams in prospect, but the difference is the Ryanair boss has won the race before; Mullins hasn't.

Yet when the foremost trainer of our time climbs the steps to his spot in the Cheltenham grandstand at about quarter past three on March 18, he is likely to look out across the course at the strongest team he has assembled for the Gold Cup. Somewhere among them, milling around at the start, could be the one who will end Mullins' Gold Cup hoodoo.

BREEDING LEGENDS, BUILDING LEGACIES

Since 1979, Lane's End stallions have been the source of some of the world's most coveted bloodlines, giving rise to Champions, Classic winners and Graded Stakes winners, primarily from the support of our outstanding group of breeders and shareholders.

850+ GRADED STAKES WINNERS

250+ G1 WINNERS

21 BREEDERS' CUP CHAMPIONS

3 KY DERBY WINNERS

4 KY OAKS WINNERS

6 PREAKNESS WINNERS

7 BELMONT WINNERS

Versailles, KY 40383 | p (859) 873.7300 | f (859) 873.3746 | lanesend.com

TOP OF THE TREE

WHEN the dust settles on Don Cossack's career, the victories won and the battles recalled, his connections may well conclude that the turning point came not in one of his outstanding successes but in a race that ended in disappointing defeat.

By the end of the 2014-15 season, Gordon Elliott's stable star had developed into one of the best Irish chasers of recent seasons and a Cheltenham Gold Cup prospect to rival any of Willie Mullins' powerful squad. Indeed, on Racing Post Ratings he was the top-ranked chaser of the season on 181, 3lb clear of Gold Cup winner Coneygree, 4lb better than King George VI Chase winner Silviniaco Conti and 5lb ahead of Djakadam, the highest-rated of the young breed in the Mullins camp.

For the most part it was a smooth climb to the top of the tree, but it took an unfortunate mistake at the wrong moment in Cheltenham's Ryanair Chase before he could take a firm hold on the division. He arrived at the festival with four straight wins under his belt in his second season of chasing and was 5-2 favourite for the Ryanair – the race sponsored by his owner Michael O'Leary – but his challenge was undone by a mistake at the second-last.

With the race lost, it was a case of damage limitation but Don Cossack did more than that. In fighting all the way up the punishing final climb to finish third behind Uxizandre and Ma Filleule, he revealed an hitherto unseen spine of steel that convinced connections he had the toughness to go with his talent.

Elliott had long been confident of Don Cossack's potential, describing the strapping son of Sholokhov as the apple of his eye, but here was proof that he had a chaser with that rare ability to stand up to adversity.

Reflecting later on what many saw as an unfortunate defeat, Elliott said: "I thought he ran a very good race. He made a mistake at the top of the hill and was stopped to a walk at the second last. You can't do that in a beginners' chase, never mind in a race like that. He had a lovely position before his mistake. He looked like he was going to be sixth going to the last and finished third. He could have thrown in the towel."

Even in defeat, Don Cossack's RPR of 170 in the Ryanair was a career-best and there was plenty more to come. Elliott had no hesitation in throwing him back into the fire at Aintree, where a red-hot Betfred Melling Chase would meld his steel with the iron will of AP McCoy. "Gordon told me he had a high cruising speed and not to be frightened to be positive, and saying that was like a red rag to a bull," McCoy said after Don Cossack had taken a wrecking ball to a talented bunch of rivals, including Champagne Fever and Cue Card, and demolished them by 26 lengths.

That was the best chasing performance of the season in Britain and Ireland – 11lb better than his Cheltenham effort – and Elliott considered pulling up stumps for the season, but there was still an important question to answer: could Don Cossack cut it at the top level over three miles-plus? Either it could be left hanging until the new season or Elliott could send him to Punchestown in an attempt to find out.

Elliott left the decision late but in the end Don Cossack's wellbeing made up his mind. If Aintree's two and a half miles was an exercise in speed and power, then Punchestown's Gold Cup, five furlongs longer, would test Don Cossack's stamina and strength, with the Cheltenham Gold Cup second and third, Djakadam and Road To Riches, lined up against him.

With a true gallop all the way from flagfall, there was no hiding place and Don Cossack sought none. He moved powerfully into contention for Paul Carberry off the searching pace and left his rivals toiling from the final fence. Djakadam and Road To Riches were second and third in this Gold Cup too, but at a greater distance than they had been behind Coneygree at Cheltenham.

Despite a reduced winning margin of seven lengths, compared with the Aintree romp, the Punchestown performance was the Oscar-winning one according to Elliott.

Although Racing Post Ratings put the two victories at the same level, the trainer said: "I thought that was even better than Aintree because they were flat to the boards all the way and he proved he stays."

O'Leary's racing involvement was sparked by the desire to win the Cheltenham Gold Cup and next March will mark the tenth anniversary of War Of Attrition's victory in the festival showpiece. The Gigginstown recruitment policy has changed emphasis over the years from a complete focus on that race to a more rounded approach of acquiring horses with the potential to win different types of Grade 1 races, but still the Gold Cup dream lives on for the Ryanair boss.

Don Cossack could make it reality again. At the age of eight, going on nine, the four-time Grade 1 winner with the mighty frame must surely be coming into his prime.

Don Cossack ended the 2014-15 season as the highest-rated chaser in Britain and Ireland after a pair of outstanding victories at Aintree and Punchestown

O'Leary certainly hopes so. "Gordon has managed to find more improvement from him. When you get the right trainer and the right horse, anything is possible. Don Cossack is huge. He was 17 hands over hurdles and as a novice but had probably not filled into his frame. Gordon says he's a totally different horse now."

A titanium constitution is one of Don Cossack's strong points. He ran seven times last season from October to the end of April and no other horse competed in a Grade 1 race at each of the spring's big festivals with the record of Don Cossack, who won twice and was placed once.

There was no better compliment for Elliott than Mullins' comment after Djakadam had been beaten at Punchestown: "It was a tremendous training performance by Gordon to keep Don Cossack fresh and improving all season."

Mullins has Gold Cup hopes of his own as he seeks his first victory in the race, but he is all too aware Don Cossack will be a tough nut to crack. As for Elliott, he says he has not looked ahead to the extra distance of the Cheltenham Gold Cup – "I'll worry about that next March" – but everyone else has, and most reckon the view is distinctly promising.

equimedia

GOLD RUSH

Coneygree's connections gained a famous victory after bypassing the traditional novice route to go straight for the Cheltenham Gold Cup – and now time is on their side as they look forward to a new challenge

By Brough Scott

IT WAS the Friday morning of Royal Ascot and the Gold Cup winner was lying flat out in a field. But this was not Trip To Paris recovering from his Flat-race exertions in the Ascot Gold Cup 18 hours earlier, this was Cheltenham hero Coneygree. In distance we were less than a hundred miles from the top hats and fashion statements; in racing terms we were on another planet.

Just six miles south of Cirencester this was Hill Farm, Oaksey, where Coneygree was born and raised and where his legendary breeder John Oaksey held court until his much-mourned death three years ago. The rooks were in the trees, the buttercups among the grasses and Coneygree, resplendent in lightweight fly-prevention pyjamas, was stretched out alongside his four years senior half-brother and best friend Carruthers. It was all a million miles from that unforgettable afternoon in March when the crowds (and no doubt Oaksey's ghost) looked down and Coneygree jumped off to stamp his name in history.

The greatness of the contrast only emphasises the enormity of the achievement. Nothing on this idyllic June morning could cloud the memory of the mounting disbelief and delight of watching Nico de Boinville and Coneygree put their Gold Cup rivals to the sword as the

▸▸ *Continues page 46*

fences came thick and fast at Cheltenham. Many 'experts' maintained that as a three-race novice he should not even be running in the Gold Cup. His jockey had cracked a collarbone in a neck-breaking fall on the Wednesday and earlier in the day a hoaxer had got into the Weatherbys database and declared an almost unknown conditional rider instead. It only made what happened better.

"We had 30 emails saying how stupid we were being, how he should run in the RSA because he was a novice," says John Oaksey's daughter Sarah Bradstock, who with her trainer husband Mark can now look back with a smile at how the know-alls huffed and puffed at the decision to tilt at the Gold Cup. "When it comes to horse safety I am the wuss," she adds, before setting out the reasons why they felt it was safe to run Coneygree. "Sure, he was a novice but he was an eight-year-old novice who had had some time out, had accumulated a bit of wisdom and had become one of the best jumpers we had ever seen. As for running in the RSA, it had Don Poli and the ground was going to be unsuitably fast for Coneygree, while the forecast was always for rain by the Friday."

'We had 30 emails saying how stupid we were being, how he should run in the RSA because he was a novice'

****

IN 24 years of training the Bradstocks may never have reached double figures for a season but Carruthers' Hennessy Gold Cup victory in 2011 had shown us both their expertise and the firmness of their opinions. They weren't going to come over all dithery just because it was the Gold Cup, although critical emails were as nothing to the event that pressurised them on the Wednesday of festival week. "Have I been jocked off?" was the plaintive call from De Boinville when Coneygree's regular rider spotted that some joker had got conditional Joe Cornwall down to partner the horse in the Gold Cup. A few hours later, the more legitimate question was "will De Boinville be fit to ride anything by Friday?"

Computer hackings can be put right in seconds, but the sort of crash that De Boinville took when Rolling Star fell at the last in the County Hurdle can put you out for much, much longer. Poor Rolling Star broke his neck on impact and, although De Boinville staggered dizzily from the carnage, you could see the pain coursing through the jockey. Officially he returned unhurt but in Royal Ascot week he confirmed how close had been the call.

"I wasn't in great shape," he admitted. "I had got a bit of a hit to the head and my left shoulder was very sore. I knew I had to get myself

CONEYGREE'S CRAZY RIDE

Nov 17, 2014 Coneygree is withdrawn on veterinary advice from a Plumpton novice chase that carried a £60,000 bonus if the winner also won at the Cheltenham Festival. The Bradstocks threaten legal action

Nov 28, 2014 Wins chase debut when digging deep from the front to beat Dell' Arca in the Grade 2 Berkshire Novices' Chase at Newbury

Dec 26, 2014 Stuns his rivals with a 40-length win in the Grade 1 Kauto Star Novices' Chase at Kempton, decimating the field with a strong pace from the front

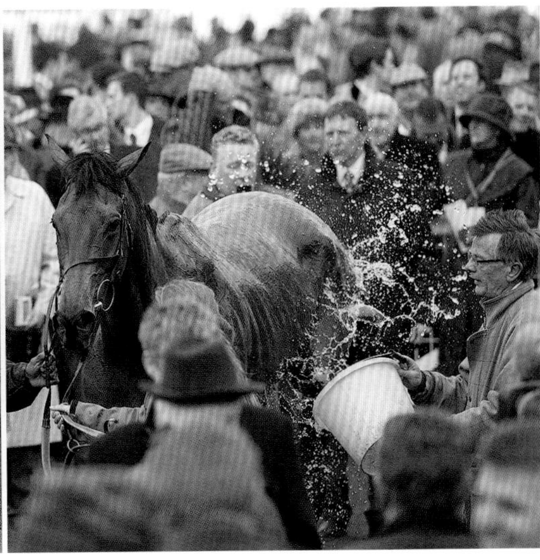

together because Gold Cup rides like this don't come every day for someone like me. So I couldn't afford to let the pain be a problem and got myself to Towcester on Thursday for two rides for Ben Pauling. They didn't do any good but the main thing was I got through them. The shoulder was still pretty tender on Gold Cup morning but I rode out at Nicky Henderson's and rode Caracci Apache for him in the Albert Bartlett, the race before the Gold Cup.

"It rained that morning and the ground had really turned against Caracci Apache. He couldn't handle it and as I pulled him up I remember thinking it would suit Coneygree. Dickie Johnson pulled up at the same hurdle and said, 'Nico, this is really testing, so make sure you conserve as much as you can in the Gold Cup.' Dickie had ridden Coneygree at Newbury and to say that was very kind of him."

To us outsiders Coneygree's jumping was going to be the big concern but jockey and trainer are adamant this was the one element that did not worry them. Their concerns, as ever, were more down-to-earth ones. Like the insurance of Mark Bradstock driving the little horsebox behind Sarah in the cattle truck containing Coneygree and his pony companion Heidi for fear of breakdown on the way to Cheltenham. "He doesn't travel well in the little box," says Sarah, "so he goes in the big truck with Heidi and no partitions. The crowd love it when they watch the pair of them unloading."

The practicality of this eccentricity was matched by the intensity of the jumping tuition Coneygree was given. Not only weekly sessions in the sand school with both De Boinville and the Bradstocks' professional show-jumping son Alfie, but steeplechase-fence experience that included jumping the obstacles downhill. "The first time was hysterical," remembers Sarah,

▸▸ Born leader: (from left) Coneygree flies to victory in the Cheltenham Gold Cup; Nico de Boinville drives for home up the hill; moments after passing the winning post; the triumphant walk back; a congratulatory pat from Sarah Bradstock; Mark Bradstock cools down the hero of the hour; (previous page) De Boinville's wild celebration in the winner's enclosure

"because Lily [Alfie's sister] led Nico, who then said 'let me lead' and the horse went and refused. It took Coneygree a long time to get the idea but think how stupid we would have felt if he had fallen at the downhill fence in the Gold Cup and we had not built a fence like that."

Two weeks before Cheltenham, De Boinville had given hostage to fortune by publicly stating Coneygree's jumping was "bombproof" and indeed as he walked out to the paddock it was not that but the fight for the lead that worried him.

Mark Bradstock remembers the moment. "Nico came out and said 'Patrick Mullins [On His Own's jockey] says he's going to take me on for the lead. It may be difficult.' I just said 'you're better than him. Just go out and enjoy.' We were completely confident in the horse's jumping because the more people try to take him on, the more focused he is. He just wants to keep on. He looks for

▸▸ *Continues page 48*

Feb 7, 2015 Emulates Kauto Star and Denman when winning Newbury's Grade 2 Denman Chase (formerly the Aon) by seven lengths, jumping superbly from the front again

Feb 11, 2015 Described as better than Denman at the same stage by BHA handicapper Phil Smith

Mar 11, 2015 Mystery surrounds apparent booking of journeyman jockey Joe Cornwall for Gold Cup ride on Coneygree as Bradstocks wonder whether their account with Weatherbys was hacked

Mar 13, 2015 Gallops the field into submission under Nico de Boinville and wins the Betfred Cheltenham Gold Cup at 7-1

the stride himself and he loves to outgallop them."

Buoyed by that pep talk, De Boinville gunned Coneygree towards the first two fences and up away from the stands with On His Own and Road To Riches straining to press errors from him. "He established such a rhythm early on that he made my life easy," says De Boinville with the firm self-confidence of a rider in whom all-round horsemanship was ingrained from childhood. "He never made a novice mistake. There was never a time when he came up unexpectedly out of my hands. I now know him well enough to know what he's going to do. He knows exactly where his feet are because of all the schooling the Bradstocks put him through and anyway he's a very smart horse."

The third fence, taken after the field swings downhill off the bend away from the stands, was a perfect example of what De Boinville means. It's a place where horses are still keen and many find themselves pitched towards the obstacle with more momentum than control. Yet Coneygree at full gallop adjusted his stride and crossed the fence in perfect rhythm.

"The best thing in that race," says De Boinville, warming to the memory, "was when we reached the far end of the course and turned to come home downhill the first time and he really took hold of the bridle. I remember thinking 'if he's like this when we come round again, we'll be all right.' He finds it so easy to travel within himself like that. He's deceptive and relentless. Going down the back he was the one putting the others under pressure. He just maintained that high cruising speed but it was not until we began to come down the hill the final time that I began to think about winning. He kept his jumping together but the one time I was a bit worried was going to the last where I could see a good way away that we were going to be very tight. But luckily he was so quick with it that we didn't lose much momentum."

By now there was bedlam up in the stands and baffled bystanders were wondering why the demented Bradstocks were shouting "come on Max" – Coneygree's stable name. Down on the racetrack it suddenly looked as if the fates would end the

Continues page 50

Shooting star: (clockwise from top) The Bradstocks (Mark, holding the Gold Cup, and Sarah, left) are interviewed by Alice Plunkett on Channel 4 Racing as family and neighbours welcome Coneygree back to Letcombe Bassett, Oxfordshire; Nico de Boinville with his Gold Cup-winning mount; the homecoming hero; Coneygree eats an apple piece from the Gold Cup

BUNCH OF FIVE

Captain Christy, the last novice before Coneygree to win the Gold Cup, was a truly great steeplechaser.

Trained by Arkle's rider Pat Taaffe, the brilliant but wayward champion triumphed in 1974 after the hot favourite Pendil was brought down. He survived a wholesale blunder at the final fence to score by five lengths from the previous year's winner The Dikler.

Captain Christy was the champion chaser for three seasons, although he never won the Gold Cup again. He was pulled up on bottomless ground in 1975.

The Dikler's trainer Fulke Walwyn had won the Gold Cup with a novice, Mont Tremblant, in 1952.

The first two novices to win the Gold Cup were both five-year-olds: Red Splash in its inaugural year, 1924, and Golden Miller when he scored the first of his record five victories in 1932.

When Dawn Run won the Gold Cup in 1986 she was inexperienced but had won over fences the previous season and was therefore not a novice.

NOVICE GOLD CUP WINNERS

Year	*Horse (SP)*	*Trainer*
1924	Red Splash (5-1)	Fred Withington
1932	Golden Miller (13-2)	Basil Briscoe
1952	Mont Tremblant (8-1)	Fulke Walwyn
1974	Captain Christy (7-1)	Pat Taaffe
2015	Coneygree (7-1)	Mark Bradstock

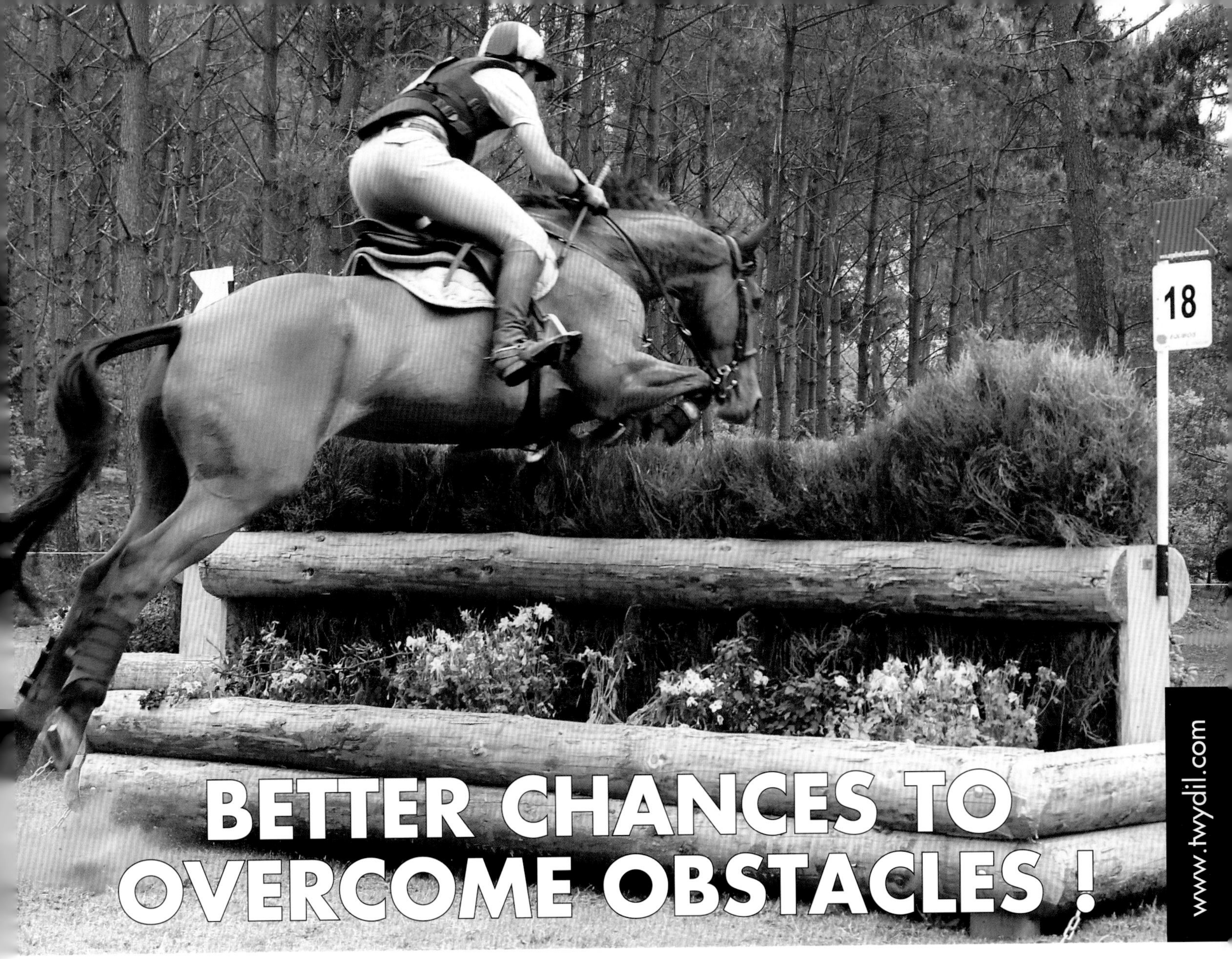

www.twydil.com

BETTER CHANCES TO OVERCOME OBSTACLES !

TWYDIL®

TWYDIL® is used by most of the successful professionals in the world.

TWYDIL® MUCOPROTECT

Complementary feed for horses containing notably vitamin C, prebiotics, Ginseng panax, Glycyrrhiza glabra and Berberine which helps support the natural defences of the body. Particularly indicated in the event of sudden cold, red mucosa, fatigue or lack of energy.

- *Withdrawal period: 48 hours*
- *Officially certified by the LCH (following controls on final product, urine and blood) can be used without risk if a withdrawal period of 48 hours is respected. According to the current «Clean Sport FEI list», can be used without risk with no withdrawal period in FEI competitions.*
- *Declared content guaranteed until expiry date.*

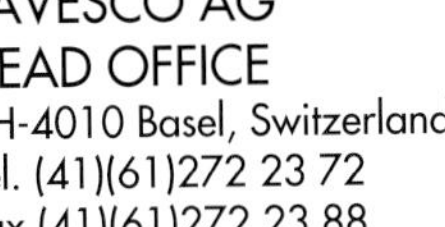

PAVESCO AG
HEAD OFFICE
CH-4010 Basel, Switzerland
Tel. (41)(61)272 23 72
Fax (41)(61)272 23 88

PAVESCO U.K. LTD.
116, High Road
Needham, Harleston, Norfolk IP20 9LG
Tel. (01379) 85 28 85
Fax (01379) 85 41 78

e-mail: info@twydil.com

GOLD TOP

THE RPR VIEW

The 2015 Cheltenham Festival was marked by a series of superb performances from novice chasers and the best was saved until last with Coneygree posting the week's top figure in winning the Gold Cup.

His mark of 178 is the highest achieved by a novice in the history of Racing Post Ratings, bettering the previous best of 176 recorded by Sprinter Sacre in the 2012 Arkle Chase.

Vautour was given a mark of 174 for his JLT Novices' Chase success and Arkle winner Un De Sceaux recorded 169 (having earlier reached 171 at Leopardstown).

Even allowing for the Foxhunter having had a standing start, the Gold Cup-winning time of Coneygree – more than 17 seconds quicker than that posted by impressive Foxhunter winner On The Fringe – is indicative of the brutal pace set by the front-runner, who is clearly a very good Gold Cup winner.

GOLD CUP WINNERS BY RPR

Year	Horse	Rating
2015	Coneygree	178
2014	Lord Windermere	168
2013	Bobs Worth	179
2012	Synchronised	171
2011	Long Run	181
2010	Imperial Commander	182
2009	Kauto Star	185
2008	Denman	184
2007	Kauto Star	175
2006	War Of Attrition	173

fairytale, with Coneygree and his young rider veering off to the right just as multiple Gold Cup winner Ruby Walsh creamed Djakadam into one last attack up the inside.

"Towards the last I could hear them coming," De Boinville says. "After that it was head down, all-out drive and in the lap of the gods. I think they got to within a length of him but he knuckled down and stayed on."

****

THE impossible had become possible. The idea of buying Plaid Maid, the dam of Coneygree and Carruthers, to give John Oaksey "an interest in retirement" had succeeded beyond anyone's wildest dreams and among the tears of happiness there was a tinge of sadness that John never lived to see this day of days.

How he would have loved every detail. Poor De Boinville being nearly incapacitated when a generous Walsh unwittingly smacked the damaged left shoulder in congratulation; Coneygree staying calm through the ecstatic chaos of the winner's enclosure; Mark Bradstock stopping for diesel on the return journey and being asked "didn't you just win the Gold Cup?" as he refuelled; the banners out when they reached Letcombe Bassett; the stable staff and camera crews taking the Gold Cup with them for a late-night pizza in Wantage.

▸▸Golden summer: Coneygree (right) and Carruthers in their paddock at Chicky Oaksey's Hill Farm in July; (below) Nico de Boinville and Mark Bradstock celebrate their Gold Cup triumph

And now here we were in Royal Ascot week with Coneygree in those pyjamas flicking the flies off his older brother. "The rug is very light and breathable," says Chicky Oaksey, John's widow, as she looks a shade wistfully at the two siblings in their arcadian setting. "Without it he gets sores all over from midges. The pair are so peaceful together, it's hard to believe what has happened. John would have adored it all and to think that there could be more to come."

Some sceptics feel that such an alignment of the stars could never happen again and that next year order will prevail and the big training battalions will reassert. But both trainer and jockey feel that Coneygree, still officially rated only 172 compared to the 180 accorded most Gold Cup winners, has not had his due. Having gone for the Gold Cup earlier than most novices, he came out of the race as a fairly youthful eight-year-old with only ten runs on the clock.

"I'm very positive," De Boinville says. "I don't like to down anyone else's horses but I'm really looking forward to the season ahead. Fingers crossed we can stay injury-free and it will be good if everyone else turns up because then we can prove just what we think of our horse."

Découvrez **La Teste.**

Find your next

Royal Ascot winner.

2016 Sales

April Breeze Up Sale

September Yearling Sale

La Teste de Buch

THE REIGN AND THE RAIN

Gleneagles was the miling king of spring and early summer but then came a long run of dashed hopes as the weather scuppered plans time after time

By Nick Pulford

STANDING in the Royal Ascot winner's enclosure after the St James's Palace Stakes, Aidan O'Brien spoke in glowing terms about Gleneagles. "He's very like Giant's Causeway in that he's got the same constitution, but he has more speed. I don't think we've had a miler as good as him. On ratings he's never going to get up there because he'll do only the minimum. But he's a very classy horse."

Gleneagles had just achieved a feat that eluded his close relative Giant's Causeway, the Iron Horse, with a quick-fire Group 1 treble in the 2,000 Guineas, Irish 2,000 Guineas and St James's Palace – bang, bang, bang in the space of six and a half weeks. His famous predecessor at Ballydoyle had won hearts with his toughness and class in turning up for nine consecutive Group 1 races from May to November in the year 2000 – winning five and finishing second, often agonisingly, in the other four – and Gleneagles' early-season hat-trick appeared to be only the beginning for him too.

He seemed the type anyone could fall for. He had that spark, that something extra to mark him out from the crowd, along with a big heart. Yet what had promised to be a summer of love turned out to be a series of missed dates as Gleneagles stood us up time after time. When he did turn up again, back at Ascot four months later, the early fireworks had become a damp squib and once more there was the feeling that racegoers across Europe had been denied something even more exciting after that brief springtime affair.

Most frustratingly of all,

Continues page 54

Gleneagles never crossed swords with Golden Horn even though that prospect was raised on several occasions. That would have been the first clash in 14 years between the 2,000 Guineas and Derby winners and might have pushed both of them to new heights, but it was not to be.

Twice the pair were at the same course on the same day – first for York's International Stakes, then for the Irish Champion Stakes at Leopardstown – but on both occasions Golden Horn raced while Gleneagles didn't. Rain was to blame, easing the ground to good to soft at York – which played a part in Golden Horn's shock defeat by Arabian Queen – and yielding at Leopardstown, where the Derby winner landed a rough race.

From the sidelines at Leopardstown, O'Brien acknowledged the disappointment of missing Irish Champions Weekend, and as the frustration mounted it was decided to take the chance on good to soft ground for British Champions Day, even though the trainer said minutes before the Queen Elizabeth II Stakes that "all the ducks are not in a row".

As O'Brien seemed to half-expect, Gleneagles at Ascot in the wet autumn was not the same as the blistering miler of June and he finished a flat sixth behind Solow.

"We knew it was going to be tough, especially in the ground," O'Brien said afterwards. "Maybe with the benefit of hindsight I shouldn't have run him. But we were conscious of the big day, an important day for racing."

Disappointingly, frustratingly, it was just another big day that passed Gleneagles by.

****

UNTIL the weather intervened to stop Gleneagles in his tracks, he had passed the post first in five consecutive Group 1 contests – the first two as a juvenile, albeit that he lost the second of them in the stewards' room at Longchamp when he was demoted to third in the Prix Jean-Luc Lagardere. The form was strong going into the winter and so were the vibes of early spring as bookmakers reported a plunge on Gleneagles for the 2,000 Guineas and Joseph O'Brien, his regular partner at home, said: "Anything that puts it up to Gleneagles in the Guineas will really be an exceptional horse."

The trials produced nothing of that ilk, although Andre Fabre threw down a challenge to Gleneagles by supplementing Territories. The pair were old rivals from the Prix Jean-Luc Lagardere, where Territories finished third but was moved up to second after Gleneagles was found guilty of interference.

At Newmarket they occupied the first two places in the betting – Gleneagles at 4-1, Territories 5-1 – and both were drawn among the supposedly favoured high numbers. Gleneagles had a new jockey with Ryan Moore taking over from Joseph O'Brien, who as a still growing 21-year-old was fighting an unequal battle with his weight. O'Brien managed to get down to 9st to partner Ballydoyle second-string Ol' Man River, who finished last, but it was already clear Moore would be taking most of the big rides.

Moore had never won the 2,000 Guineas but he set the record straight with a smooth success. He always had everything covered in the stands-side group that came from the high draws and kicked Gleneagles into the lead just over a furlong out to score by two and a quarter lengths from Territories. For O'Brien it was a seventh 2,000 Guineas, equalling John Scott's record from the 19th century.

▸▸ While the going's good: Gleneagles and Ryan Moore score a decisive victory in the 2,000 Guineas at Newmarket; (below) being led back in; (previous page) the pairing land another Group 1 in the St James's Palace Stakes

Newmarket had inserted a cutaway rail three furlongs out in an attempt to prevent the field splitting but, while that measure proved a failure, there was no doubt the best horse won. The biggest danger to Gleneagles had been his own temperament during a nervous few minutes in the parade ring, but he was expertly handled by both Pat Keating, O'Brien's travelling head man, and Moore.

Gleneagles was sweaty and fidgety again at the Curragh but more worryingly the draw and the ground were not in his favour this time. Where the going had been good to firm at Newmarket, it was now good to yielding and it was only the 'good' part that stopped O'Brien scratching him. As for the draw, Moore's berth close to the rail raised the possibility of traffic problems and he was still seventh in the field of 11 at the merger with the round track just over three furlongs out.

▸▸ *Continues page 56*

HORSERAIL

The Future of Equestrian Fencing

Are you ready to replace your broken and worn out fencing?

Horserail is the best solution to the problems associated with traditional timber post and rail, wire, tape and braided rope. Horserail provides an electrifiable, injury free, maintenance free, stylish and affordable fencing sytem with a 30 year guarantee. The average price per meter is just £2.70 per meter per rail and this includes the rail and the fittings. Horserail is available in 3 colours: Black, Brown and White. It is extremely versatile and can be used on a variety of applications such as paddocks, lunging rings, gallops arenas and horse walkers

W: www.horserail.org.uk • E: horserail@mmg.ie • P: 0808 2344766 • P: +353 58 68205

▸▸ Classic tale: Aidan O'Brien talks to the media after Gleneagles' victory in the Irish 2,000 Guineas at the Curragh

The gap came well enough for Gleneagles but, with the ground negating his superior turn of foot, it was a battle to the line. At the post the 2-5 shot was only three-quarters of a length ahead of Endless Drama, while Ivawood – third here as he had been at Newmarket – was almost two lengths closer this time. Having recorded a Racing Post Rating of 124 at Newmarket, Gleneagles dipped to 119 but it was one of those races where winning mattered more than the performance.

"It's hard for a horse to win from so far back at the interchange of the tracks, and Ryan had a good bit to do," said O'Brien after winning his tenth Irish 2,000 Guineas and completing the Newmarket-Curragh double for the third time. "In the last half a furlong Ryan had to say 'come on, I need you again'. He never had to show that kind of courage before, but he answered big time."

O'Brien did not seem seriously tempted to send Gleneagles to Epsom, although the option was left open until Derby week. Instead he stuck to the four-race schedule mapped out in the winter for Gleneagles, all over a mile, and the third leg was the St James's Palace Stakes.

For now, everything was going to plan and Gleneagles was lapping it up. At Royal Ascot he was odds-on again, this time 8-15, and the opposition had shrunk to four rivals, although Fabre had a new challenger with French 2,000 Guineas winner Make Believe. Back on good to firm ground, Gleneagles was far too good, beating outsider Latharnach by two and a half lengths with Make Believe last.

O'Brien had another record – this was his seventh St James's Palace victory, moving him ahead of 19th-century great Mathew Dawson – but he passed on much of the credit for the latest success in a fascinating post-race interview that gave an insight into the Ballydoyle operation and what the future might hold.

"I'm just a small part of a very big team," he said. "The lads are coming on and it's making it a little bit easier. I'm 45 and it's great to see younger people coming along and taking responsibility and the pressure.

"Joseph is with the Flat horses in the morning and with the jumpers in the evening. He's taking my job, slowly. I only look on – I just stand at the top of the gallops and watch the work, which is good for me, and a lot less pressure."

Over the rest of the summer O'Brien jnr would have learned plenty about the frustrations of bringing a horse to concert pitch only for the performance to be cancelled at late notice. Rain clouds got there before Gleneagles every time and he missed the fourth leg of the miling plan, the Sussex Stakes, and then the Prix Jacques Le Marois, followed by the International and the Irish Champion. He did get a run, finally, in the QEII but in far from ideal conditions.

Courage, class, consistency, character; Gleneagles had it all. It was just a shame that an unfavourable summer prevented British and Irish racegoers from seeing those qualities more often.

SHOCK RESULT

Aidan O'Brien followed Gleneagles' Guineas double with more Classic success at Epsom but from a most surprising source.

As usual O'Brien had a multiple entry in the Oaks and the insurance policy paid off as Qualify, the outsider of the field at 50-1, snatched victory after better-fancied stablemates Together Forever and Diamondsandrubies were among those to lose their chance in a dramatic sequence of bumps a furlong and a half out.

Colm O'Donoghue managed to bypass the congestion on Qualify and, after Legatissimo had raced clear with a furlong to run, reeled in the 5-2 favourite to score by a short head. It was a dramatic reversal of form from the 1,000 Guineas, which was won by Legatissimo with Qualify 41 lengths behind in last place.

The general sense of surprise was not shared by O'Brien, who bred Qualify. "We always thought she was very good," he said. "We knew up to a mile and a quarter she would be top class, we weren't sure at a mile and a half. Colm gave her a masterful ride. We always knew she had ability because she worked like a high-class filly."

O'Brien became the first trainer to win the Oaks with a filly he bred himself since Edoardo Ginistrelli in 1908 with Signorinetta, who had won the Derby at 100-1 two days before. Qualify was the joint-longest-priced Oaks winner, alongside Vespa (1833) and Jet Ski Lady (1991).

The trainer added another Classic with Order Of St George's victory in the Irish St Leger, but for the first time in ten years he did not win a Derby in Britain or Ireland. Giovanni Canaletto was his best representative, finishing fourth at Epsom and third at the Curragh.

CHAMPIONSHIPS
FINALS DAY AT LINGFIELD PARK
GOOD FRIDAY 25 MARCH 2016
WITH OVER £1 MILLION IN PRIZE MONEY!

SPONSORED BY
Ladbrokes UNIBET CORAL 32Red

ALL-STARS
ALL-WEATHER
ALL-ACTION!

The Best of British All-Weather Horseracing
29 OCTOBER 2015 - 25 MARCH 2016
EVERY RACE COUNTS!

80% INCREASE
RUNNERS **RATED 90+***

155% INCREASE
RUNNERS **RATED 100+***

39% INCREASE
TOTAL PRIZE MONEY*

FOLLOW THE LEAGUE TABLES EACH WEEK THROUGHOUT THE SEASON ON OUR WEBSITE

awchampionships.co.uk

* Over the first two years of the All-Weather Champisonships

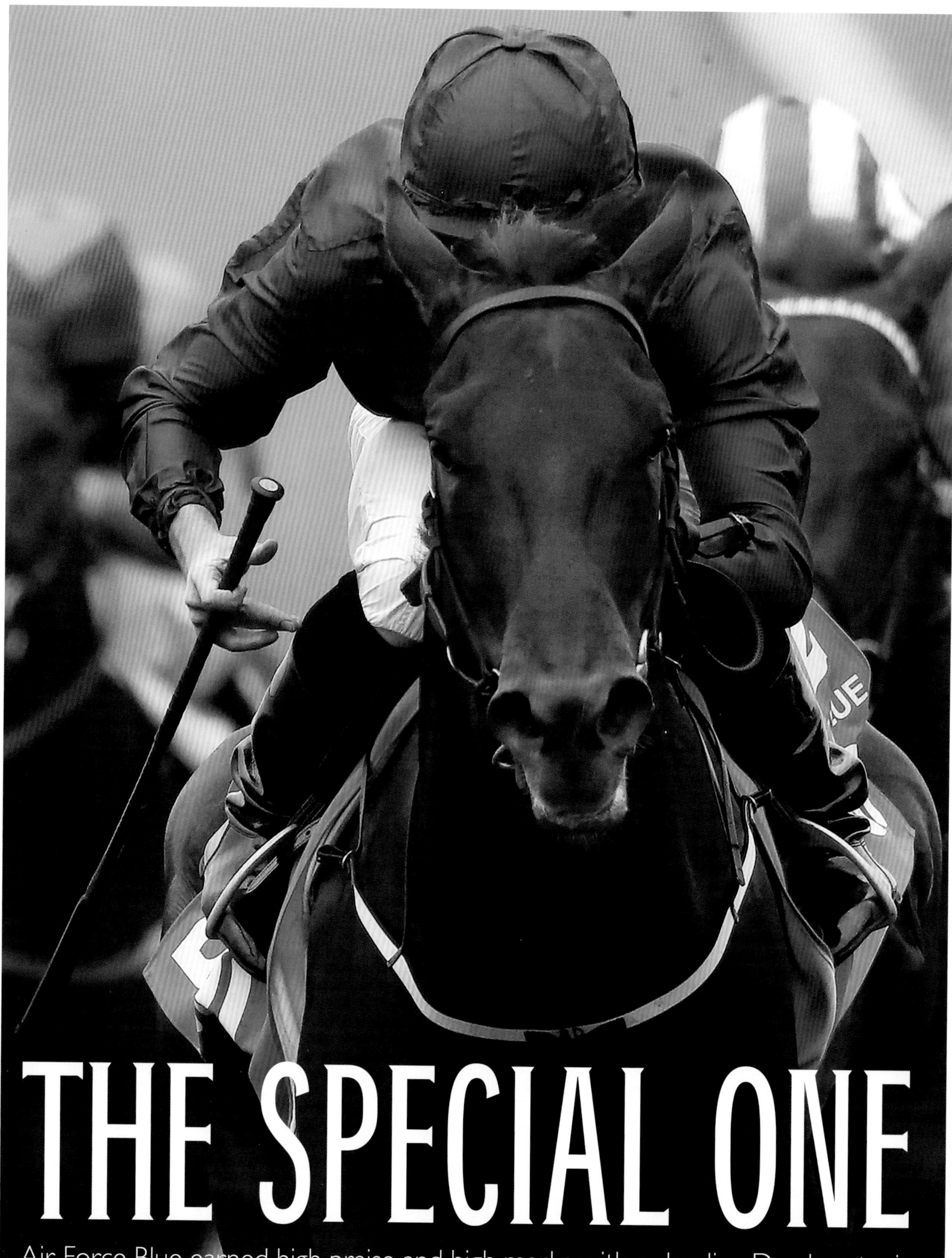

THE SPECIAL ONE

Air Force Blue earned high praise and high marks with a dazzling Dewhurst win

By Nick Pulford

"Every year everyone's looking for the special one," Aidan O'Brien said after Air Force Blue's electrifying success in the Dubai Dewhurst Stakes, before leaving nobody in any doubt that he believes he has found the one. "He's something like we haven't had before."

O'Brien's list of champions sets a stiff benchmark for that claim, and the bar is raised even higher by the storied history of the Dewhurst with its catalogue of greats from 19th-century nonpareil Ormonde in 1885 through Nijinsky and Mill Reef in consecutive years (1969 and 1970) to Frankel in 2010. Air Force Blue is in their company as a Dewhurst winner but that was one small step; now he has to make a giant leap, and O'Brien clearly believes he can.

The previous day the O'Brien-trained Minding had looked pretty special in winning the Dubai Fillies' Mile, giving her clear favouritism for next year's Qipco 1,000 Guineas, but that merely served to strengthen Ballydoyle confidence in Air Force Blue.

In the 24 hours after Minding's victory, the colt shortened from 13-8 to 4-6 and as the Dewhurst runners went to post Michael Tabor – one of Air Force Blue's owners, and of course a veteran of the bookmaking business – put words to the numbers.

"We're very bullish, we think he'll win," he told Channel 4 Racing. "We'll be surprised and disappointed if he gets beat. He looks very special. Minding looks very special, but probably not as special as this horse." There it is again: the S-word.

Tabor's comments and the betting outlined where the story was heading but the denouement was jaw-dropping; even if the hero and the fall guys were obvious from a long way out, the twist was in the manner of victory. Air Force Blue surged through the Dip under Ryan Moore and into a clear lead up the hill, scoring by three and a quarter lengths.

Immediately it was clear that he was a Dewhurst winner of the highest quality. His Racing Post Rating of 125 ranks him joint-second among Dewhurst winners of the past quarter of a century, level with Teofilo and New Approach. Only Frankel, on 126, stands higher in that period.

▸▸ High flyer: (opposite page) Air Force Blue wins the Dewhurst; (left) with jockey Ryan Moore

'In February he was a baby and still head and shoulders above everything'

The visual impression alone would have been enough to leave racing fans eagerly anticipating next year's Qipco 2,000 Guineas, for which Air Force Blue was swiftly cut to even-money favourite, but O'Brien stoked the fires with his bullish post-race comments.

His first telling observation came in relation to Minding's Fillies' Mile success, which earned her an RPR of 119. "Ryan came in and said he'd never ridden anything like this filly and we said to him 'wait until tomorrow'. The reality is that the filly would probably lead this horse [Air Force Blue] to about halfway in his work and then he would blow her away – that's how good he is."

O'Brien was only just getting started. "I'd say there's no doubt he's the best two-year-old we've had. The size of him, the scope of him, the class of him and the way he travels, and when you let him go he delivers."

As usual O'Brien passed on much of the credit for Air Force Blue's development to the backroom team at Ballydoyle, but it was clear the strategy from the war room had been just as important and had been framed with bigger targets in mind. The Dewhurst, for instance, was the end-of-campaign choice because it would teach Air Force Blue about the Dip on the Rowley Mile prior to his return next year for the Guineas.

Another box was ticked on his previous run in the Group 1 National Stakes at the Curragh, where the ground was yielding and O'Brien was worried about running him. Perhaps mindful of the way in which going concerns had stymied plans throughout the summer for Gleneagles, this year's 2,000 Guineas winner, the Coolmore owners decided to take the chance. "They made the decision to run because they said 'if the ground comes up soft when he's a three-year-old, what are we going to do if we don't run and find out?'" O'Brien said.

Air Force Blue answered the question well enough with a three-length victory over Herald The Dawn in a small field, having previously opened his Group 1 account in the Phoenix Stakes. In that he reversed form with Buratino from the Coventry Stakes, his only defeat in five outings. Having finished a two-length runner-up at Royal Ascot, Air Force Blue was two and a half lengths ahead of Buratino eight weeks later in the Phoenix.

This was all part of the development, aimed all the while at making him into a Classic colt. The American-bred with the fast pedigree – by War Chant, a son of Danzig from the age-old Northern Dancer sire line that was the cornerstone of Ballydoyle's success – cost $490,000 as a yearling at Keeneland sales in September 2014, and from the moment he appeared on the Ballydoyle gallops five months later O'Brien and his team realised he was a rare talent.

"In February he was a totally unfurnished baby and he was still head and shoulders above everything," the trainer said. "When he was doing that, at that time of year, in very soft ground, he looked exceptional, but they have to do it [on the racecourse]. You have to see them do it."

Seeing is believing, and there was a multitude of believers after the Dewhurst.

OUT WITH THE OLD IN WITH THE NEW

Richard Hughes signed off at the top as a jockey to face the challenges of life as a trainer – the job he had wanted for so long

By Lee Mottershead

THIS was the year when not one but two reigning champion jockeys quit the saddle. Yet while there was a similarity in the final farewells of Tony McCoy and Richard Hughes, there was also a crucial difference. For McCoy, there was little that was sweet in the sorrow of parting from the job he loved. For Hughes, this was an altogether less painful experience.

Britain's three-time Flat champion walked away at the time of his own choosing. He retired from the weighing room because he

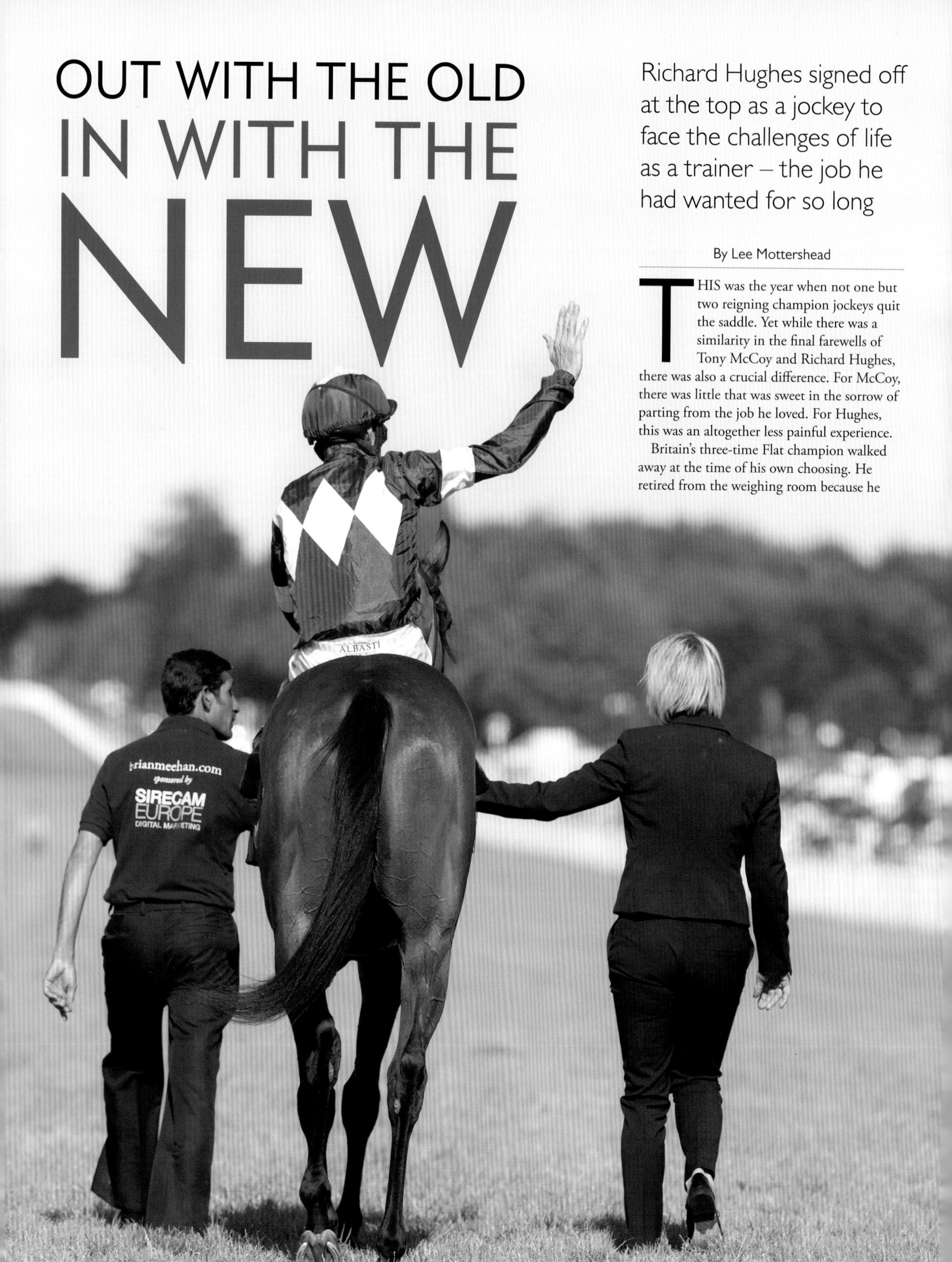

wanted to retire, in the main because there was something else he wanted to do more. Hughes began 2015 as a jockey; he ended it as a trainer.

The announcement that this would be his final year came in early March. At that stage Richard Hannon's stable jockey vowed to ride until the end of the season with the aim of becoming champion for the fourth time. He made a good start to his final year, winning the Group 1 Al Quoz Sprint at Meydan on old friend Sole Power, but as the months passed a realisation hit home to Hughes. He would need to stop sooner rather than later.

In some ways, of course, it was a miracle he had gone on for so long. Not only had the tall, lanky Irishman maintained his body at an unnaturally low weight for a quarter of a century, he had also battled and beaten alcoholism, with which his long fight reached its nadir but also its happy conclusion during seven years as retained rider to Khalid Abdullah. Since then he had worked principally for a Richard Hannon, first his father-in-law, then his brother-in-law, and it was for the latter he enjoyed one of his two successes at his last Royal Ascot in silks. That meant a lot. The jockey cried after Illuminate's victory in the Group 3 Albany Stakes and so did the trainer.

But the Hannon job had changed considerably in recent years, with the yard attracting high-profile Arab owners who wanted to use their own men. So it was that the 42-year-old's regular ally Toormore was lost to him when he contested and won the Lennox Stakes at Glorious Goodwood. By that point the horse had been bought by Godolphin and Hughes had revealed he would bring forward his retirement to the final afternoon of Goodwood's signature festival.

Once the Sussex sojourn is over, trainers begin preparing to move from one of the bloodstock industry's major yearling sales to another, seeking to fill their yards with winners of the future. Hughes knew very well that in his first full year of training the best way of advertising his talents would be to fire in juvenile winners in the way the Hannons have done for so long. To get those juveniles Hughes would need to be active at

⏩ *Continues page 62*

⏩ Stop and start: (opposite page) Richard Hughes parades at Goodwood on Fox Trotter, the final ride of his career; Hughes steps up his training career with an active sales season in the company of (clockwise from top) Richard Hannon and bloodstock agents David Myerscough and Brendan Bashford

LIFE OF A CHAMPION

Full name Richard David Hughes

Born January 11, 1973

First ride Scath Na Greine, 9th at Naas, March 19, 1988

First winner Viking Melody, Roscommon, August 2, 1988

First winner in Britain Scissor Ridge, Wolverhampton, July 23, 1994

First Group 1 winner Posidonas (1995 Gran Premio d'Italia)

Best winner (Racing Post Ratings) Canford Cliffs (130 in 2010 Sussex Stakes, 2011 Queen Anne Stakes)

British Classic winners Sky Lantern (2013 1,000 Guineas), Talent (2013 Oaks)

Irish Classic winner Canford Cliffs (2010 Irish 2,000 Guineas)

Seven winners on one card Windsor, October 15, 2012 (plus a third on eight-race card)

Champion jockey in Britain 2012, 2013, 2014

Most wins in a year in Britain 208 (2013)

the sales. Riding through the late summer and autumn would have been a distraction and so Hughes decided he would ride no longer.

Gibeon ensured a great Goodwood favourite would not end his final festival without a winner when he took the opening race of day three. On day four Belvoir Bay, given a typically confident ride, became Hughes's final career winner and the 2,440th in the land he made home when moving to Britain in 1994. On day five there were six rides and six losers but, as on McCoy's final day, a winner was not needed. The reception, from his colleagues, other racing professionals, friends and racegoers, was enough.

For the record, the last mount, Fox Trotter, finished fourth. Hughes was then paraded on horseback in front of the stands and, finally, inner feelings came to the surface. "I had predicted there would be tears and that is when they arrived," he wrote in his Racing Post column. "I became very emotional and chose to pull down my goggles. By the time I pulled them back up again they were full. But I was ready to stop. There was not an ounce of regret, not for a second. One reason for that lack of regret was because I could eat."

Subconsciously, his mind had been fixated on his weight far more than he had ever realised. There was glee at standing on racecourse scales for one last time, after which he returned to Goodwood's winner's enclosure, where a host of people, led by Frankie Dettori and Francis Norton, covered him in champagne. "I'm relieved," said Hughes. "And wet."

And a jockey no longer. Hughes was by now setting up a training operation on Ken Cunningham-Brown's Danebury estate in Hampshire, once home to Classic winners, Grand National winners and Stockbridge racecourse. It was a place he had first eyed up long ago. Spread out over 310 acres of gorgeous Hampshire countryside, Danebury has gallops options aplenty, roaming deer and a new master who, as an early measure of his commitment to a new life, went to a hypnotist in a bid to quit smoking. The patient subsequently reported he had no real understanding of what the hypnotist did, but whatever she did it worked.

Had Hughes still been a smoker he would have been entitled to nervously get through a considerable number of cigarettes while spending his own money on future Danebury inmates at Deauville, Doncaster, Keeneland, Goffs and Tattersalls. From one sale to the next he was buying horses on spec, just as the Hannons always have, but he was also being promised support, and horses, by the likes of Coolmore, Al Shaqab, Highclere Thoroughbred Racing and Middleham Park.

Those horses duly arrived as yearlings. Come the spring they will be two-year-olds – and it is with those two-year-olds Hughes knows he must make an impression. His first runners started to appear in September but these were, in the main, relatively low-grade performers contesting low-grade races. They were useful sighters for the important business of what is to come from March 2016.

"I worked my arse off to be champion jockey on three occasions for only one reason," Hughes explained. "I felt having the champion jockey tag would be beneficial to my training career. I wanted to use the publicity being a champion jockey would provide in my vital first year as a trainer."

A plan was, and is, in place. Fortunately, Hughes was trained to be a trainer from his days growing up under father Dessie at the family's yard close to the Curragh. Dessie's passing in November 2014 ensured the final year of his son's riding career was even more emotional than it would otherwise have been. All concerned, not least Dessie's widow Eileen, knew someone was missing, but she was there with Richard when he had his first runner at Epsom, just as she had been at Goodwood, proud but tearful, to see him draw the line under a superb riding career.

As Hughes dismounted from Fox Trotter, his great friend and one-time boss Mick Channon shouted to him: "Now your problems begin." There will indeed be problems but Hughes wanted to train every bit as much as he wanted to ride. Given his pedigree, ambition and talent, he should succeed in the role he has chosen.

Thunder bolts to momentous win

THE next generation of the Hughes training dynasty triumphed over adversity in the last jumps season when Sandra Hughes, daughter of Dessie and sister of Richard, took over the family yard on the death of her father and within six months had scored a landmark success in the BoyleSports Irish Grand National.

Thunder And Roses' victory was notable not only for the Hughes family but for its female trainer-jockey combination, with Katie Walsh becoming the third woman to ride an Irish National winner. The first two were Ann Ferris, who rode Bentom Boy in 1984, and Walsh's sister-in-law Nina Carberry, who scored on Organisedconfusion in 2011.

It was an incredibly emotional success for the winning trainer, who was accompanied by her mother Eileen. Hughes was granted a licence after Dessie, the immensely popular trainer and former jockey who sent out Timbera to win the Irish National in 2003, lost his battle with cancer the previous November.

After achieving the biggest win of her short career, Hughes said: "I'm sure Dad was looking down and helping us. It's a huge thrill to have won this race as it was a race he always loved. There were some tough days after Dad passed away but we're not the only people who've had to go through it and you just have to carry on."

Thunder Of Roses relished the soft ground at Fairyhouse to lead home Rule The World in a one-two for the Gigginstown colours of Michael O'Leary. "It's amazing, absolutely fantastic," said Walsh, whose brother Ruby has ridden two Irish National winners and combined with their father Ted to land the prize with Commanche Court in 2000. "It's a great day for everyone, for Gigginstown, for Sandra and Eileen Hughes, as well as me, and they're probably more emotional than me.

"Crossing the line was a magical feeling, fairytale stuff. I remember being here a few years ago when Nina won on Organisedconfusion and wondered if I'd ever get to experience that. I'm a very lucky girl."

THIS IS THE
Ladbrokes
LIFE

WE'VE SWITCHED ON

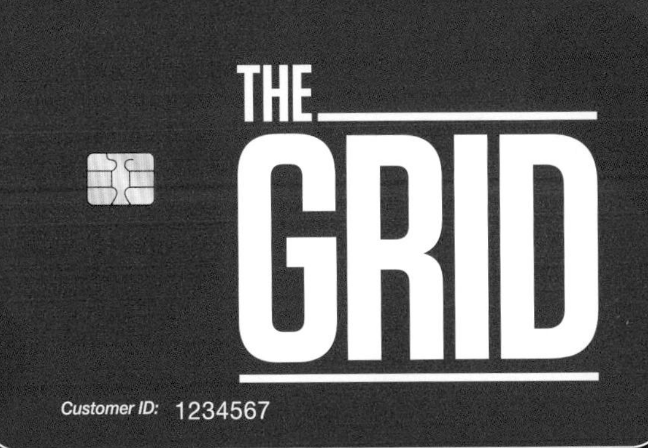

UNLOCK GREAT BENEFITS

- Special racing offers & prices
- Exclusive free bet promotions
- New 'The Grid' app: Track your in-shop bet & cash out wherever you are

JOIN IN SHOP TODAY
THEGRID.LADBROKES.COM

WHEN THE

STOPS

™

gambleaware.co.uk

...kes rules apply. See thegrid.ladbrokes.com/en/thegridtandc PLEASE BET RESPONSIBLY. gambleaware.co.uk Need help? Call the National Helpline free on 0808 802 0133

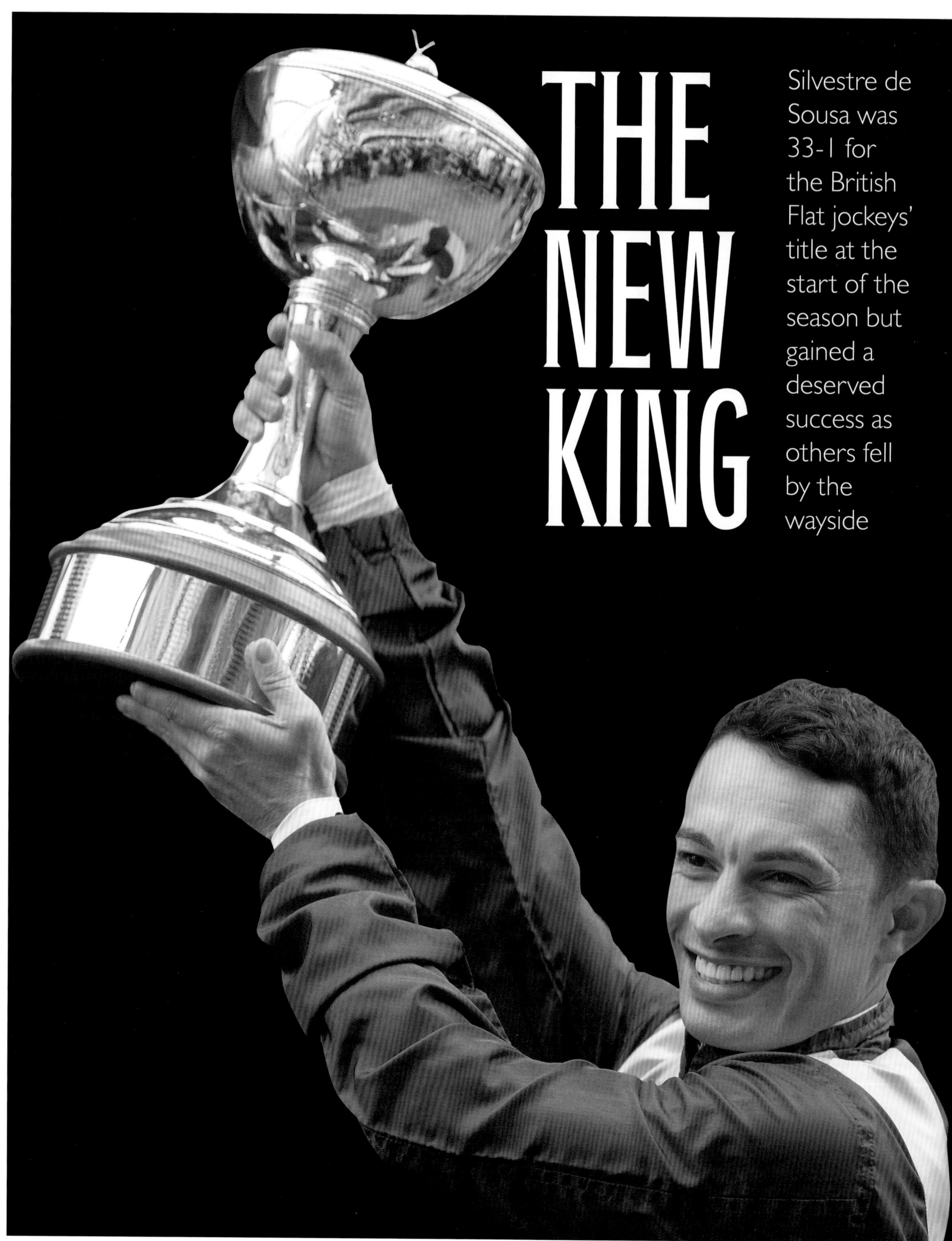

THE NEW KING

Silvestre de Sousa was 33-1 for the British Flat jockeys' title at the start of the season but gained a deserved success as others fell by the wayside

By David Carr

SILVESTRE DE SOUSA'S first British Flat jockeys' title may have come a month early for some tastes but it was a popular and deserved success. After all the arguments about shortening the championship season, the Brazilian let his riding do the talking.

Crowning De Sousa on Qipco British Champions Day at Ascot on October 17 brought more publicity and a sense of occasion than the old low-key end of the turf season in November, but it was far from a universally popular move to miss out chunks of the traditional calendar. In March it was announced that the jockeys' title would be decided only on the period from Newmarket's Guineas meeting at the start of May to Champions Day rather than from the Lincoln Handicap in March to the November Handicap, the traditional Doncaster-to-Doncaster battle.

Eight weeks had gone missing, and one critic likened the move to discounting football results before Halloween and after Easter, or forgetting the first three reds and the final colours in a frame of snooker.

De Sousa, 34, himself said during the year "they should have left it alone" but as things turned out the dates were irrelevant to the outcome of what turned into a one-sided contest once Richard Hughes retired from the saddle and Ryan Moore succumbed to injury once again. The man Godolphin let go in 2014 was unstoppable on his return to life as a freelance, racking up 132 winners to win by 36 from joint runners-up William Buick and Paul Hanagan.

Four years earlier, in a ding-dong battle with Hanagan under the old system, De Sousa had lost by four. This summer he admitted that was the biggest disappointment of his career, and that made victory all the sweeter. "It has been exciting, I'm very proud," he said after picking up the coveted trophy and a cheque for £25,000 – the first time a cash prize had been awarded to the champion. "I've always believed I had the ability to win the championship and I've proved I can."

▸▸Title role: (from far left) Silvestre de Sousa lifts the trophy at Ascot and relaxes in the jockeys' room

Frankie Dettori proved in even more spectacular fashion that there is life after Godolphin and it was ironic that he should have been the victim on the day when De Sousa produced the ride that will be remembered above all others in his title-winning campaign. While there was much talk of a tactical foul-up when Golden Horn was defeated in the Juddmonte International at York, De Sousa's masterful effort on Arabian Queen should not be forgotten. He was always in the right place in a trappily run contest and proved steadfast in the closing stages on a 50-1 chance who won a race she probably shouldn't have – the very definition of a brilliant ride.

That was a rare top-level ride in 2015 for the Brazilian, but the championship remains a numbers game and it matters not a jot that the greatest contributions to his final tally came at places such as Leicester, Chelmsford and Wolverhampton. Nor should De Sousa's achievement be decried on the basis that he was behind in the race until Moore was injured in July and sidelined for 11 weeks. He put in the miles – well over 50,000 of them as he criss-crossed the country – and had the day-in, day-out consistency required of a champion. "Mr Reliable," retiring champion Hughes called him.

De Sousa follows numerous overseas winners in a sport with a long history of embracing foreign stars. The Italian Dettori and America's Steve Cauthen took the crown three times each, and in between them was South African Michael Roberts' annus mirabilis in 1992, while the Aussie Scobie Breasley won four titles between 1957 and 1963.

Further back there were championships for the US pair Lester Reiff (1900) and Daniel Maher (1908), while German-born Otto Madden topped the standings four times from 1898 to 1904.

The first champion from Brazil is just the latest talent to emerge from a country that has also produced Jorge Ricardo, whose 12,000-plus winners briefly made him the most successful jockey in history, Dubai World Cup winner Tiago Pereira and Joao Moreira, whose exploits in the Far East include the Hong Kong title and partnering a record eight winners on the same day in Singapore.

Within days of completing his title success, De Sousa set off for America to try to make it in New York over the winter. That was another criticism levelled at the new format of the jockeys' title – that Britain would see less of its top riders – but for De Sousa it was a fresh opportunity.

Following his dream brought De Sousa, without a word of English, to Ireland 11 years ago and then on to Britain. He has worked his way to the top through a combination of hard graft, resilience and no little talent, and has won the admiration of racing professionals like Lesley White, who has spent years at the sharp end travelling horses for Mick Channon and was a fitting 'dedication' winner at last year's Godolphin Stud and Stable Staff Awards.

Which made White's words on a grey evening at Wolverhampton, a venue for plain speaking rather than flowery prose if ever there was one, all the more memorable. For she was practically wide-eyed with enthusiasm for De Sousa's efforts on nursery winner Breslin, having heard the jockey recommend the maiden juvenile be tried in a visor and then watched him make his occasionally reluctant partner's mind up for him from the off.

"He deserves to be champion," she said. And he did.

MOORE MOORE MOORE

A modern-day record nine winners at Royal Ascot was another bravura performance on the big stage by the peerless Ryan Moore

By Tom Kerr

THE story of Ryan Moore's career has yet to be written, the scale of his achievements remains unknown, but racing historians may well look back to the past 12 months, during which the jockey cemented his reputation as a big-stage performer with a string of global successes, as the turning point when he shifted from a leader of the current generation to a rider for the ages.

If there was one moment that best exemplified the transition, it came amid the pomp and circumstance of Royal Ascot 2015 when Moore toppled the modern-day record for the most winners at world racing's most storied meeting. Lester Piggott and Pat Eddery, two of the all-time greats, were masters of Royal Ascot and now Moore had the same towering presence.

Moore entered Ascot in scintillating form, sitting top of the jockeys' championship with 35 wins from just 158 rides, his 22 per cent strike-rate bettered at the time only by the under-appreciated George Baker. At Royal Ascot, as ultra-competitive as ever, Moore won nine races and recorded an astonishing 31 per cent strike-rate. Never was the phrase 'big-race jockey' more appropriate.

Among those nine winners was a stunning victory on Gleneagles in the St James's Palace Stakes, but what marked Moore's achievement as so remarkable was that many of his winners came on relatively unheralded rides (five of the nine were priced at 5-1 or over and two were double-figure shots) and by small margins (six were by half a length or less). The clear inference was that here was a jockey making the difference between victory and defeat for his mounts.

The longest-priced winner was representative of the virtues that make Moore such a lethal rider. On the 200th anniversary of Wellington's famous victory few beyond coincidence backers could have had solid confidence in maiden winner Waterloo Bridge, a 12-1 shot in the Norfolk Stakes, and when favourites Log Out Island and King Of Rooks engaged in a ding-dong slugfest out front even the most optimistic supporters might have given up hope. Moore, however, had the self-belief to stick to his own pace and launched his charge late, collaring the front pair well inside the final furlong to score by half a length.

Waterloo Bridge was the first of three winners on the Thursday, which ended with Moore having equalled the modern-era royal meeting records of Piggott and Eddery with eight wins. Anyone who might question the validity of Moore's achievement on the basis that Royal Ascot has expanded in recent times would be confounded by the fact that his eight had come from 18 races, fewer than had been available to his great predecessors even in the old days of a four-day meeting.

The following day Moore went one over the eight, and therefore beyond Piggott and Eddery, when

▸▸ *Continues page 68*

Queen's Vase winner Aloft became his ninth of the meeting. Although he was winnerless from then on, which meant he was unable to challenge Fred Archer's record 12 winners at Royal Ascot in 1878, the feat was deeply impressive.

Among those to pay tribute were two retired masters of the saddle, Piggott himself ("Moore is a brilliant jockey, anyone can see that") and Tony McCoy ("He is the best jockey in the world. And he is getting better"). They were an appropriate duo to join the chorus of praise, for it is in their league that Moore is now frequently ranked, not just by the pundits but by the racing public who pick their heroes much as they pick their bank accounts – based on the expected return.

What makes Moore such a dangerous adversary is not his strength in the finish or style in the saddle – although he is not short of either – but how rarely he makes mistakes. His self-confidence and calmness under pressure is allied to a ferocious work ethic; Moore is a regular sight walking the tracks before races and is among the weighing room's most well-informed riders, aware of not just his own mounts' strengths and weaknesses but those of every other horse – and jockey – in a race too.

His decision-making and versatility in races is second to none, as seen to tremendous effect eight months before Royal Ascot when Moore landed one of his most spectacular top-level victories on one of his regular international trips. He was riding Adelaide in the Cox Plate at Moonee Valley, a racecourse that turns and banks like a Nascar track, and having been drawn halfway to Tasmania in stall 13 he appeared to have lost all chance after his mount virtually walked out of the gate. Going against logical instinct, Moore took his mount wide round the field, went into the final corner five-wide and shot out like a firework to take the win in a blanket finish. Locals said it was one of the most audacious and high-octane winning rides ever seen in the Plate, Australia's most important weight-for-age race.

Ten days later Moore was back in

Continues page 70

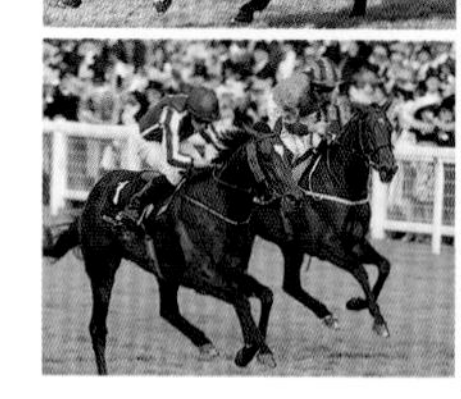

MASTER AT WORK

RYAN MOORE'S NINE ROYAL ASCOT WINNERS – AND WHAT PEOPLE SAID

Gleneagles St James's Palace Stakes 8-15f *Won by 2½ lengths*
"I didn't think Frankie was going to lead on Consort but I know the horse from home and he stays very well, so I made sure to track him. Gleneagles has a very good turn of foot and won really well" (Moore)

Clondaw Warrior Ascot Stakes 5-1f *Won by half a length*
"He was given a fine ride by Moore, who dropped him in on the rail from his wide draw and saved ground until the turn into the straight" (Racing Post analysis)

Washington DC Windsor Castle Stakes 5-1 *Won by a head*
"He's very fast and always travelled very strongly. It's not easy when one goes clear like that and Ryan didn't want to go after her too early" (Aidan O'Brien, trainer)

Acapulco Queen Mary Stakes 5-2f *Won by 1½ lengths*
"She's got loads of pace. I wasn't even quick away. I just cruised up and she had far too many gears for them" (Moore)

GM Hopkins Royal Hunt Cup 8-1 *Won by a neck*
"We were worried the pace wasn't on our side but it was. Ryan rode a beautiful race and covered him up well" (John Gosden, trainer)

Waterloo Bridge Norfolk Stakes 12-1 *Won by half a length*
"He hasn't always looked straightforward in his previous starts but he was partnered by a man in inspired form. Given a patient ride, he picked up very nicely when asked" (Racing Post analysis)

Curvy Ribblesdale Stakes 9-2 *Won by a length*
"Wayne [Lordan] explained to Ryan how to ride her and he carried it out beautifully. It was a very messy race but I was confident that if she got out she'd have a great chance" (David Wachman, trainer)

War Envoy Britannia Stakes 10-1 *Won by a neck*
"Ryan gave him an absolute peach of a ride. He's a marvellous jockey, probably the greatest I'll ever see" (O'Brien)

Aloft Queen's Vase 5-2f *Won by half a length*
"Another top-quality ride by Moore, who resisted the temptation to play it safe and come wide" (Racing Post analysis)

Royal standard: (from top) Gleneagles, Clondaw Warrior, Washington DC, Acapulco, GM Hopkins, Waterloo Bridge, War Envoy, Aloft and (right) Curvy

A RIGHT ROYAL
REFURBISHMENT

* For all bookings made at least 14 days in advance. Offer subject to availability and conditions of sale. Standard rate call.

Australia to claim his first Melbourne Cup, riding Protectionist for German trainer Andreas Wohler, with a masterful waiting ride. The Australians had previously been impervious to Moore's charms – it is reputed that frustrated local hacks dubbed him 'No F***ing Moore' after his fifth-placed finish on the fancied Dandino the previous year – but the next day the Australian papers gushed with praise for such a composed victory at Flemington.

Australia is just one territory in Moore's ever-expanding global empire. Between the Cox Plate and Melbourne Cup he travelled to California for the Breeders' Cup (where, admittedly, he drew a blank) and after Flemington he jetted to Japan for a seven-week stint before stopping off in Hong Kong on his way back to England, where he arrived just in time to spend Christmas with his family.

Moore's international focus is rooted in his desire to focus on quality over quantity. His younger brother Jamie, the accomplished jump jockey, tells the story of Ryan being offered his first ride aged 16 by their trainer father Gary. Most aspiring jockeys would be expected to leap at the chance to make their debut but Moore declined, saying he felt the horse had no chance. If that story casts Moore in an overly cocksure light, it is to be considered that when he came to make his debut in 2000 he won his first three races.

Quality was available in abundance this year. Having signed up with Europe's foremost owners Coolmore in April, creating in the process nothing short of a racing dream team, and in demand with dozens of major British and Irish trainers, Moore had no shortage of potent ammunition. Early in the season there was a stunning five-timer on Lockinge day, followed up weeks later by becoming only the sixth jockey since 1900 to complete the Guineas double at Newmarket, taking the colts' Classic on Gleneagles and the fillies' on Legatissimo.

Less than a month after Royal Ascot, however, Moore's season came to a sudden halt following an innocuous incident at Newmarket's July meeting, where he appeared to bang his head after his mount reared in the stalls. His subsequent absence stretched on and on, during which time he maintained a near-complete media blackout, leading to feverish speculation about when he might be back. A belated – and sudden – return in late September came just in time for the big autumn meetings and Moore quickly set about salvaging what he could from his broken season and laying the foundations for next year.

For Coolmore he rode a trio of juvenile Group 1 winners – Ballydoyle, Minding and Air Force Blue, each more impressive than the last. He also took the valuable Tattersalls Millions Fillies' Trophy on Alice Springs, another promising two-year-old from Ballydoyle. If, as Moore prefers, the horses do the talking next year, the chatter could be pretty loud and incessant.

▸▸ Royal appointment: The Queen presents Ryan Moore with the leading jockey award and Aidan O'Brien with the leading trainer award at Royal Ascot and (below) Moore marks his ninth win of the meeting

Completely free of any self-aggrandisement, the taciturn and modest Moore always insists he owes his good fortune to the quality of horses he rides. At Royal Ascot, he called himself lucky and said, "I get to ride the best horses and that makes a big difference." Yet the winning distances told a different story. Punters, trainers and owners alike know it is the capacity of riders to grind out small margins that separates the good from the exceptional.

Likewise, Moore rejects the tag 'best in the world'. He prefers to focus on his infrequent mistakes and the races yet to be won (the Kentucky Derby is a major ambition) than his countless top-tier victories. He is famously uncomfortable with the trappings of celebrity that attach to leading sportsmen. That is something he will have to come to terms with. Aged just 32, with the racing world at his feet and potential stars like Air Force Blue and Minding lined up for next year, Moore's finest moments are likely still to come.

GO RACING IN IRELAND 2016

Wherever you are in Ireland, you're never far from a race meeting and if you want to understand one of our country's great passions, choose from over 300 race meetings at any of the 26 racecourses around the country. Play the odds, raise a glass and enjoy good times with friends – you'll have a day out you'll always remember. So what are you waiting for?

It's time to go racing... because nothing else feels like this.

2016 RACING FESTIVALS

CORK
Easter Festival
26th - 28th March

FAIRYHOUSE
Easter Festival
27th - 29th March

PUNCHESTOWN
National Hunt Festival
26th - 30th April

KILLARNEY
Spring Festival
15th - 17th May

CURRAGH
Guineas Festival
21st - 22nd May

DOWN ROYAL
Ulster Derby
17th - 18th June

CURRAGH
Irish Derby Festival
24th - 26th June

BELLEWSTOWN
Summer Festival
30th June - 2nd July

KILLARNEY
July Festival
11th - 14th July

CURRAGH
Irish Oaks Weekend
16th - 17th July

GALWAY
Summer Festival
25th - 31st July

TRAMORE
August Festival
11th - 14th August

KILLARNEY
August Festival
17th - 20th August

LEOPARDSTOWN & CURRAGH
Longines Irish Champions Weekend 10th - 11th September

LISTOWEL
Harvest Festival
11th - 17th September

DOWN ROYAL
Festival of Racing
4th - 5th November

PUNCHESTOWN
November Winter Racing
19th - 20th November

FAIRYHOUSE
Premier Jumps Weekend
3rd - 4th December

LEOPARDSTOWN
Christmas Festival
26th - 29th December

LIMERICK
Christmas Festival
26th - 29th December

HORSE RACING IRELAND

To plan your day at the races or for a FREE racing information pack, please call the Marketing Team on **+353 45 455 455** or visit **www.goracing.ie**

facebook.com/goracing **twitter.com/@goracing** **@horse_racing_ireland**

IN THE PICTURE

Buick on top of the world with dazzling win on Prince Bishop

William Buick landed the Dubai World Cup in March in his new job as a Godolphin jockey with an extraordinary last-to-first swoop on Prince Bishop, sparking rapturous scenes on their return to the Meydan winner's enclosure.

Carrying the new cornflower blue colours of Sheikh Mohammed's son Sheikh Hamdan Bin Mohammed Al Maktoum, Buick was five lengths off the field at the end of the first furlong and scrubbing along on Prince Bishop, whose long-standing tendency to break slowly was compounded by his dislike of the kickback when he was behind horses.

Turning for home, however, the eight-year-old gelding was back on the bridle travelling alongside California Chrome, the 5-4 favourite, and he powered clear of the American challenger in the straight to win by two and three-quarter lengths.

"I don't go numb very often, but I can't explain what I feel at the moment," said Buick, three months into his role as a retained rider for Godolphin alongside his good friend James Doyle. "He has a very unorthodox way of racing, so I took him out of the kickback down the back and when I got on California Chrome's tail he started to pick up the bridle and he won well in the end. This is just nuts and a really special moment for me and the whole team."

After five years on Tapeta, the Dubai World Cup returned to dirt in 2015 and that offered some explanation as to why Prince Bishop was able to pull off a 14-1 upset after previous placings of tenth, seventh and ninth in the world's richest race.

The principal reason, however, was the breakneck speed at which the race was run. Reflecting in the summer on his momentous victory, Buick, 27, said: "He'd been beaten before because he gave himself so much ground to make up in races that were steadied up at halfway before the leaders kicked again. I ride him the same way all the time, push the head off him all the time, but in the World Cup the pace was crazy-quick.

"No matter what horse was in front of us they couldn't keep it up and they were already running on fresh air halfway round the last turn. I managed to get a breather in and off he went, the only one staying on.

"There was joy in our camp. Sheikh Hamdan had decided Prince Bishop would run in his new colours and he took a lot of pride in it. Sheikh Mohammed was overjoyed, but it wasn't until I got home and put the trophy away that it sank in. It was a big deal, a huge moment."

Picture: FRANCOIS NEL/GETTY IMAGES

AP McCOY
the farewell tour

PLUS SPECIAL GUESTS
CARLINGFORD LOUGH
UXIZANDRE
GILGAMBOA
JEZKI
DON COSSACK

11 WEEKS
26 COURSES
168 RIDES
35 WINNERS
5 GRADE 1 VICTORIES

Tony McCoy's long goodbye after announcing his retirement in February brought the final memorable moments of his illustrious career

By Nick Pulford

"I said something like 'Er . . .' and all I could hear was Carl Hicks, my producer, in my ear saying 'Keep talking, keep talking'." The biggest scoop of the racing year had just landed in the lap of Rishi Persad, live on Channel 4, after he started a post-race interview with Tony McCoy at Newbury by congratulating the champion jockey on bringing up another double century of winners. This was the cue for the seemingly routine to turn into something extraordinary.

"I'm gonna tell you something else Rishi," McCoy said, "it's gonna be the last time I ride 200 winners because having spoken to Dave [Roberts, his agent] and JP [McManus, his principal employer] I'm gonna be retiring at the end of the season. That's a bit of news for you." The master of the saddle has always been a master of understatement too. This "bit of news" was about to reverberate around the sporting world.

The date was February 7 and the end of the season was 11 weeks away. Suddenly, even though that period would be packed with the Cheltenham and Aintree festivals and the jewels of the jump racing season, it didn't seem long. The AP McCoy Farewell Tour had started.

Unlike many sports stars, McCoy had the luxury of being able to choose the manner and timing of his retirement – albeit a right he had earned through his own brilliance and pre-eminence. He may have been a reluctant retiree, but he was not being forced out through declining popularity among trainers, injury – as fellow top rider Robert Thornton was a few months later – or any diminishing of his powers.

He later revealed that retirement had been on his mind for the past five years and while he could do nothing about the 'if' ("I'm a realist, I know I can't go on forever") he could decide the 'when'. He had started the season aiming to ride 300 winners as "the best way of going out on a real high" but a fall at Worcester in October scuppered that ambition and he readjusted his target to another double century – for the tenth time in his career – and his 20th consecutive British jump jockeys' championship. When he hit 200 with a lead of 71, he felt secure in revealing his plans.

On hearing the news, those in the wider world not entirely familiar with McCoy's curriculum vitae and modus operandi might have supposed that, as a 40-year-old, he must be on the wane and was bowing to the reality of being overtaken by younger rivals. That's what happens to many sporting greats – look at the travails in 2015 of Tiger Woods, 20 months younger than McCoy – but it wasn't the case here. In every respect McCoy was still operating at the highest level.

That was made abundantly clear the day after his announcement when he landed the big race of the weekend in Ireland, the Grade 1 Hennessy Gold Cup, on Carlingford Lough. Fittingly the victory was in the McManus colours and was hard earned in trademark style. McCoy's mount looked one-paced three out and had to be ridden after a mistake at the second-last but he was responding to his rider's urgings, and having been third at the final fence McCoy snatched victory from Foxrock by three-quarters of a length with a typical driving finish.

There was wild acclaim for McCoy, both from the crowd – up 17 per cent from the previous year – and Carlingford Lough's connections. "It was a privilege to have AP on board today. He gave the horse a peach of a ride," said trainer John Kiely, a view that was to be echoed over the following weeks. Meanwhile, Foxrock's trainer Ted Walsh told McCoy: "It's a pity you didn't retire yesterday."

Nor had McCoy's courage or sheer

▸▸ *Continues page 76*

grinding appetite for winning changed. In the first few days after announcing his retirement, he went to all four corners of his world. After Ireland, he rode in England (Catterick), Scotland (Ayr) and Wales (Chepstow), followed by many other workaday places: Fakenham, Carlisle, Exeter, Southwell, Plumpton, Bangor, Ludlow . . .

This was the daily routine that had sustained him for two decades, far from the bright lights of Cheltenham and Aintree, and these latest visits brought him winners at every one of those tracks. After that Grade 1 success at Leopardstown, he was back to accumulating the winners in the bread-and-butter handicap hurdles and chases, maiden hurdles and bumpers that had added up to all those titles.

Yet it was soon evident that something was different. Everywhere he went, he was followed by cameras and greeted by autograph hunters, well-wishers and, quite simply, worshippers. Even before his retirement was announced, McCoy was being tracked by a documentary team making a film about his season – they had a scoop, too, because Being AP would turn out to be the story of his final season told in 90 minutes.

Racecourses were quick to ride the wave of adulation, with many billing McCoy's final appearance on their track as a 'last chance to see'. When the Racecourse Association announced overall attendances in the first six months of 2015 had reached a record figure of almost three million, the McCoy effect was cited as one of the contributing factors.

McCoy had become used to wider celebrity after the landmark vote as BBC Sports Personality of the Year that followed his 2010 Grand National triumph on Don't Push It, but this was on a different level. Huntingdon, for example, had to draft in extra security to help McCoy deal with all the requests for pictures and autographs, and off course McCoy's support team were inundated with 400 interview requests each week.

▸▸ Being AP: (clockwise from top left) McCoy is given a guard of honour by his fellow jockeys on his final day at Sandown; with wife Chanelle and their children Archie and Eve; on his way to victory on Uxizandre in the Ryanair Chase at Cheltenham; winning the Aintree Hurdle on Jezki; signing autographs at Sandown; riding Don Cossack to victory in the Melling Chase at Aintree; with the Ryanair Gold Cup at Fairyhouse after his winning ride on Gilgamboa

> 'Over the last two and a half months people have come out to give me a wonderful welcome and I'm very grateful for that. I thought it would die down but it never really did and those are things I'll remember forever'

The great man himself was overwhelmed by the reception from racegoers. "It's very nice to feel that I have the respect of people up and down the country," he said after the farewell tour was all over. "Over the last two and a half months people have come out to give me a wonderful welcome and I'm very grateful for that. I thought it would die down but it never really did and those are things I'll remember forever."

McCoy left his fans with plenty to remember too, not only in his career highlights but also in those emotional final few weeks. When the Cheltenham Festival loomed in March, everybody was hoping for one

big final hurrah and, although he missed out on Jezki in the Champion Hurdle and Carlingford Lough in the Gold Cup, McCoy graced the winner's enclosure with a Grade 1 scorer after Uxizandre took the Ryanair Chase at 16-1. None of the other 34 winners on his farewell tour started bigger than 7-1, but none was sweeter than this one.

"I got such a thrill riding him," McCoy said after he had seized the race by the scruff of the neck with a brilliant front-running ride. "I'll miss riding horses like this, the ones that run away with you and jump like stags. I was actually thinking I wouldn't mind riding him in next year's Champion Chase. It's nice. Cheltenham is all about winning, isn't it?"

The moment was even more special for being shared with members of his family, not only wife Chanelle but also father Peadar, brother Colm and three of his four sisters, Kelly, Jane and Anne-Marie. Chanelle said there had been an air of melancholy about

Continues page 78

RECORD BREAKER

Full name Anthony Peter McCoy

Born Ballymena, County Antrim, May 4, 1974

Parents Peadar McCoy (breeder of Thumbs Up) and Claire McCoy

Apprenticeship Billy Rock 1987-89, Jim Bolger 1989-94, Toby Balding 1994-95

First ride Nordic Touch, 7th on Flat at Phoenix Park, September 1, 1990

First winner Legal Steps on Flat at Thurles, March 26, 1992

First ride over jumps Riszard, brought down over hurdles at Leopardstown, March 17, 1994

First winner over jumps Riszard over hurdles at Gowran Park, April 20, 1994

First ride over fences No Sir Rom, fell, Galway, July 30, 1994

First ride in Britain Arctic Life, 2nd over hurdles at Stratford, August 13, 1994

First winner in Britain Chickabiddy over hurdles at Exeter, September 7, 1994

First winner over fences Bonus Boy, Newton Abbot, October 4, 1994

First Graded winner Brave Tornado (1995 Finesse 4-Y-O Hurdle, Grade 2)

Grand National winner Don't Push It (2010)

Cheltenham Gold Cup winners Mr Mulligan (1997), Synchronised (2012)

Champion Hurdle winners Make A Stand (1997), Brave Inca (2006), Binocular (2010)

Queen Mother Champion Chase winner Edredon Bleu (2000)

Triple Cheltenham Festival winner Albertas Run (2008 Royal & SunAlliance Chase, 2010 & 2011 Ryanair Chase)

Other Cheltenham Festival winners Kibreet (1996 Grand Annual Chase), Or Royal (1997 Arkle Chase), Champleve (1998 Arkle Chase), Unsinkable Boxer (1998 Gold Card Hurdle Final), Edredon Bleu (1998 Grand Annual Chase), Cyfor Malta (1998 Cathcart Chase), Blowing Wind (1998 County Hurdle), Hors La Loi (1999 Supreme Novices' Hurdle), Majadou (1999 Mildmay of Flete Chase), Royal Auclair (2002 Cathcart Chase), Liberman (2003 Champion Bumper), Well Chief (2004 Arkle Chase), Reveillez (2006 Jewson Novices' Chase), Black Jack Ketchum (2006 Brit Insurance Novices' Hurdle), Wichita Lineman (2007 Brit Insurance Novices' Hurdle, 2009 William Hill Trophy Chase), Noble Prince (2011 Jewson Novices' Chase), Alderwood (2012 County Hurdle, 2013 Grand Annual Chase), At Fishers Cross (2013 Albert Bartlett Novices' Hurdle), Taquin Du Seuil (2014 JLT Novices' Chase), Uxizandre (2015 Ryanair Chase)

King George VI Chase winner Best Mate (2002)

Irish Hennessy Gold Cup winner Carlingford Lough (2015)

Welsh National winner Synchronised (2011)

Scottish Grand National winner Belmont King (1997)

Irish Grand National winner Butler's Cabin (2007)

Irish Champion Hurdle winners (Punchestown) Brave Inca (2005), Jezki (2014)

Irish Champion Hurdle winner (Leopardstown) Brave Inca (2006)

1,000th British/Irish win over jumps Heros Fatal, Cheltenham, November 14, 1999

2,000th British/Irish win over jumps Count Tony, Market Rasen, November 20, 2003

3,000th British/Irish win over jumps Restless D'Artaix, Plumpton, February 9, 2009

4,000th British/Irish win over jumps Mountain Tunes, Towcester, November 7, 2013

Fastest 100 in a British season August 21, 2014 (Arabic History, Newton Abbot)

Fastest 200 in a British season December 20, 2002 (Chicuelo, Ascot)

Most wins in a calendar year 307 in 2002 (305 jumps in Britain, 1 jumps in Ireland, 1 Flat in Britain)

Most wins in a European season 290 in 2001-02 (289 in Britain, 1 in Ireland); beat Peter Schiergen's record of 271 in 1995

Most wins in a British season 289 in 2001-02; beat Gordon Richards' record of 269 on Flat in 1947; champion by margin of 157 over Richard Johnson

Most prize-money in a British season £2,753,453 in 2001-02

Richest win £521,052 (Don't Push It, 2010 Grand National)

Champion conditional rider 1994-95

Champion jump jockey 20 times

Total wins over jumps 4,348 (4,204 in Britain, 144 in Ireland); 9 wins on Flat (3 in Britain, 6 in Ireland)

Last winner Capard King, Ayr, April 17, 2015

Tony McCoy with the jockeys' championship trophy is lifted up by David Casey (left) and Andrew Thornton

the champ as he left the house that morning. "For me this felt different from any other winner because I knew what it meant to him to have a winner this week and how desperately he wanted a winner. More so than ever I have seen him before," she said. "He wanted one more time to ride a winner at Cheltenham, to soak up the atmosphere and not finish his career without one more winner. He wanted that feeling one more time."

Inside the weighing room was Chris Maude, a former rider who had been with McCoy at Martin Pipe's yard and, after retiring, his valet for the last 14 years. "I don't think anyone fancied Uxizandre much but rides like that didn't really surprise us any more. It was extraordinary," Maude recalled in the summer. "I was too busy to go out on to the weighing-room steps to watch him come in, but we all knew what it would mean to him. He was very quiet afterwards and everyone just left him to his thoughts. Let it all sink in. I think it hit us all hard afterwards – that this was probably it so far as Cheltenham was concerned."

Indeed, that was to be the 31st and last of McCoy's festival winners. In the final race of the four days, renamed in his honour as the AP McCoy Grand Annual Chase, he was fourth on Ned Buntline. He rode back up the walkway to an ovation that sent shivers up the spine and continued all the way to the paddock and winner's enclosure, where he took his place on the podium to hand out the trophies for his race. When the applause finally subsided, he told the audience: "The crowd here are amazing, racing people are amazing. I'm always a person who has looked forward but I'll have to start looking back because I've nothing to look forward to now. I'm going to miss being a jockey here, that's for sure."

There was still more to come. At the Fairyhouse Easter meeting he won the Grade 1 Ryanair Gold Cup Novice Chase on Gilgamboa and Aintree later that week brought his induction into the course's Hall of Fame as well as a Grade 1 double on Jezki in the Aintree Hurdle and Don Cossack in the Melling Chase. The memories were piling up, but there was not long

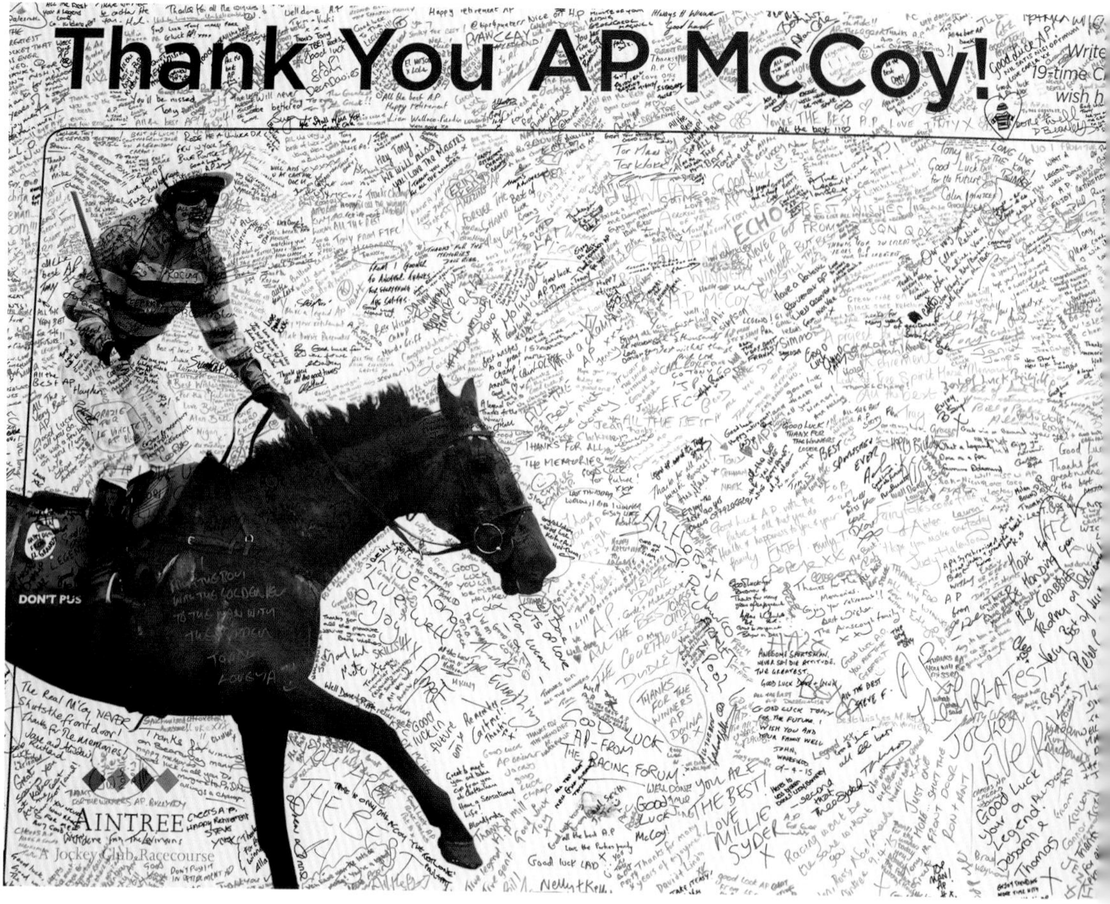

WORLD OF DIFFERENCE

In September Tony McCoy talked to Alastair Down about life out of the saddle

In the last five months I've had more holidays than in the previous 40 years. I've been to sporting events I've always had to miss, been to dinners that have been declined in the past, done Q&A evenings and even a bit of after-dinner speaking with some coaching from Rob Nothman.

Of course there are big differences. I used to speak to Dave Roberts every day without fail and although we still talk now I have to make an appointment.

My regime is different without the hot bath and no longer worrying all the time about what I'm eating. If I feel my jeans are getting tight then it's time to go for a run.

When I retired I received a wonderful letter from perhaps the most intelligent and influential man in racing which included the line "at the end of it all keep looking forward" and that is just what I am doing.

▸▸ Writing's on the wall: (above) the McCoy appreciation wall at Aintree; (below) Racing Post front pages after his retirement announcement and on his final day

RACING POST ON SUNDAY
PRICEWISE
MOORE BIG-RACE SUCCESS
McCoy bombshell: I'll retire at end of season
Newcastle, Man Utd & Barcelona 11/2
RACING POST
THANK YOU & GOODBYE
MONEY BACK AS A FREE BET

left now. Two weeks and counting to that fateful last day at Sandown.

Except that now there might be a change of plan. If Shutthefrontdoor could give him a second Grand National triumph, McCoy declared he would hang up his boots there and then. The 2014 Irish National winner had solid form and, with public sentiment behind McCoy, there was never much doubt he would start favourite, with bookmakers predicting he would carry one-fifth of all National bets.

The fairytale result belonged to the bookmakers – "We were cheering every runner apart from Shutthefrontdoor," said a Ladbrokes spokesman – and not to McCoy, who confessed afterwards to being "gutted" at finishing fifth on his 20th and final ride in the National. "I really thought for a long way he could win," he said.

The boots would have to stay on a little longer. There were only three more stops on the roadshow – Cheltenham, for the very last time, Ayr and Sandown – and by now the

▸▸ *Continues page 80*

Graham Budd
AUCTIONS

THE LEADING SPECIALIST AUCTIONEER OF SPORTING MEMORABILIA IN THE UK

All sales held at Sotheby's New Bond Street saleroom, London

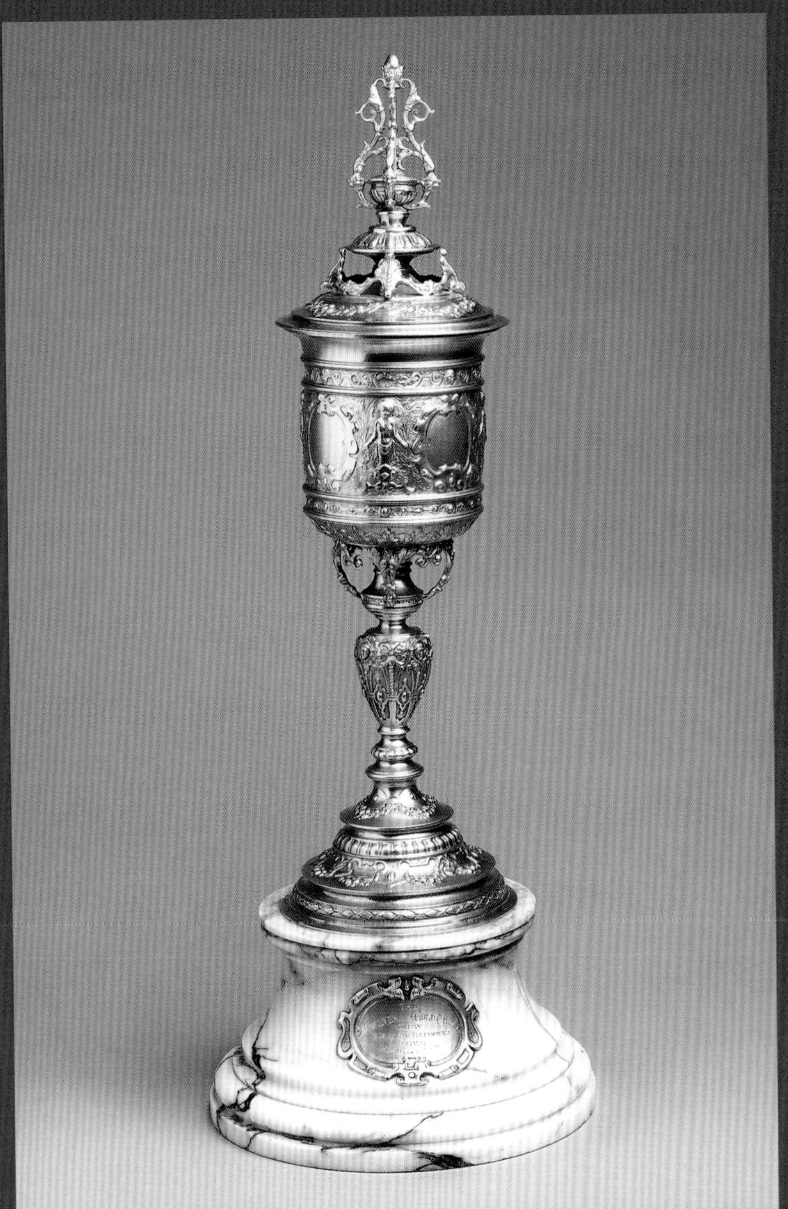

The 1926 Cheltenham Gold Cup. Sold for £18,000.

Graham Budd Auctions Ltd, PO Box 47519, London, N14 6XD
Tel: 020 8366 2525 E-Mail: gb@grahambuddauctions.co.uk
web: www.grahambuddauctions.co.uk

enormity of his decision had hit home. "I honestly never really thought about retirement until after Aintree," he said in a Racing Post interview published on April 25, the day of that last Sandown meeting. "It was only after Shutthefrontdoor was beaten that the reality set in. It was the first time I thought to myself, 'This is the end.'

"I suppose I felt it most when I left Cheltenham last Thursday. Driving home that evening was the first time I did feel a bit emotional. I had a few tears to myself."

There were more tears at Sandown, not because neither of his two mounts could give him the perfect send-off but simply because this was the end, once and for all. It was an extraordinary day, witnessed by a bumper crowd and a peak audience of 1 million viewers on Channel 4 (up 38 per cent on the previous year), and marked by presentations, a guard of honour from his fellow jockeys, another race named in his honour, rousing cheers and emotional interviews. "I feel I've lived the dream," McCoy said. "I wouldn't rather be anything other than a jump jockey in terms of adrenaline rush, the thrill of it, the people you meet, the whole sport. I've been so blessed, I wish I could do it all again."

Once was enough for McCoy to rewrite the record books and redefine what was humanly possible in this most demanding of sports. His three epoch-making records for a jump jockey are for the most wins in a career (4,348), the most wins in a season (290) and the greatest number of championships; he was champion in all his 20 seasons as a full professional, easily eclipsing the old record of eight titles, including one shared, by Peter Scudamore.

Whoever becomes champion jump jockey next April, they will not get their hands on McCoy's prized possession. The trophy he lifted this year was commissioned in 2007 and it was 'retired' with him, being presented for him to keep permanently in recognition of his 20 titles. Just one more small but significant acknowledgement of what he meant to racing.

Injury forces Thornton to retire

THE jump jockeys' weighing room lost another high-profile member in September when Robert Thornton, 14th on the all-time list, announced his retirement at the age of 37 after a long battle with injury.

Popularly known as 'Choc', Thornton had not ridden since fracturing vertebrae in his neck and back in a fall at Chepstow in April 2014, and despite concerted efforts to return to the racetrack the injuries resulted in complications that made retirement inevitable.

Thornton partnered 16 winners at the Cheltenham Festival, including three of the four major championship events – the Champion Hurdle on Katchit in 2008, the Queen Mother Champion Chase on Voy Por Ustedes (2007) and the World Hurdle on My Way De Solzen (2006), all for his long-time mentor and boss Alan King. He was the festival's leading jockey in 2007 and is joint-ninth on the all-time list at the meeting.

His career total of 1,123 wins over jumps in Britain and Ireland (plus six on the Flat) ranks him 14th on the all-time list of most successful jump jockeys. Only Richard Johnson, Ruby Walsh, Barry Geraghty, Paul Carberry and Timmy Murphy have won more races over jumps among current jockeys.

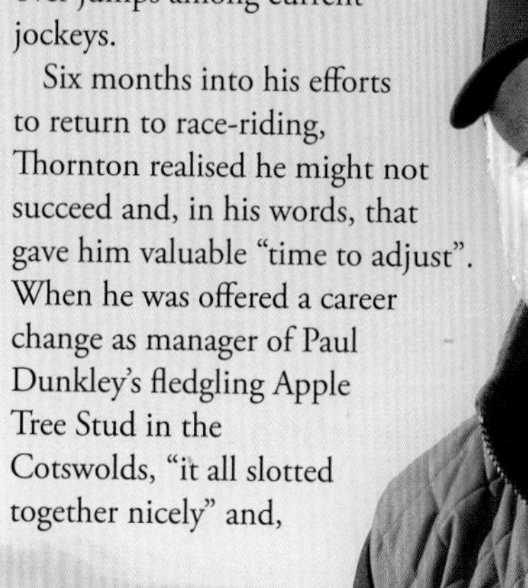

Six months into his efforts to return to race-riding, Thornton realised he might not succeed and, in his words, that gave him valuable "time to adjust". When he was offered a career change as manager of Paul Dunkley's fledgling Apple Tree Stud in the Cotswolds, "it all slotted together nicely" and, while he admitted the move into Flat racing was a culture shock, he made a good start.

"We sold our first horse at Doncaster in August and I'd say I was never that scared in all my race-riding career," he said. "We liked him, we prepared him well, and I'd have been devastated if he'd made no money, so I was delighted when he was knocked down to Brian Ellison for 70 grand."

Thornton will also serve as racing manager to Dunkley and his business partner Danny Reilly – best known as the owners of Medermit, a Grade 1-winning chaser under Thornton – and to the stud, which has eight two-year-olds in training with James Fanshawe, Jamie Osborne and King.

Other career avenues were less appealing. "Training wasn't a route I was interested in because I think it takes a very brave man with plenty of money behind him to start up a yard. I thought about the natural progression of maybe being a BHA starter, but I could never be a stipendiary steward. No offence to them, but that's crossing the line, going over to the dark side."

Perhaps, too, officialdom would not suit such a competitive personality. In his new job, just like the old, Thornton is aiming for the top. "I know it can be a perilous game, and it's going to sound ridiculous, but the aim is to breed a decent-quality horse and the dream is to breed a Classic winner. That might be impossible but I'll be giving it everything."

Just like he always has.

All gut problems respond well to Happy Tummy® Charcoal!

BHRA & FEI compliant

01600 712496

www.finefettlefeed.com

THE NEXT

By Steve Dennis

SOME sportsmen have had their career defined by not winning things, which is after all the very antithesis of sporting endeavour.

The French cyclist Raymond Poulidor – nicknamed 'The Eternal Second', which must have grated on those long winter evenings – finished on the podium of the Tour de France eight times without ever wearing the yellow jersey for even one afternoon. Jimmy White was beaten in the snooker world championship final on six occasions, frequently flirting with victory but always ending the night alone with his thoughts.

It was Poulidor's bad luck to compete against the great Jacques Anquetil and Eddy Merckx, it was White's misfortune to play through the eras of Steve Davis and Stephen Hendry. Yet their tales of subordinate anguish pale in contrast to that of Richard Johnson, who has finished runner-up in the jump jockeys' championship 16 times, always behind AP McCoy, always the bridesmaid, the compiler of a magnificent career but one always overshadowed by a miraculous one.

Now, of course, McCoy is an ex-jockey and Johnson has his chance at last, at the age of 38. It is an opportunity he grasped with both hands, piling on the winners from the start of the season, setting a McCoyesque pace at the head of affairs, reaching his century by mid-October with a lead of 33. Unshackled by the absence of McCoy, Johnson has been working in leaps and bounds.

"I have always wanted to be champion jockey, right from the age of 16, even when I didn't think I'd ever make it as a jockey," he said last season, before McCoy's retirement plan was known. "I'd be happy to be champ once – I know how hard it is to achieve, and I know it would be the best thing I could achieve. Is it going to happen? I'm still trying."

Johnson has always been a trier, has always conducted himself in exemplary fashion, and in riding almost 3,000 winners – a mesmerising feat, one that puts him as far ahead of Richard Dunwoody and Peter Scudamore as he is adrift of McCoy – he has forged a career of the highest standard. There are very few big races he has not won – the Grand National is a notable omission from his record – and from any viewpoint Johnson has been an outstanding success as a jockey. He admits as much himself, in his almost abashed, self-deprecating style that sits easily with this man who would be king if only he could.

"I'll look back on my career and realise I was very lucky to do what I did for as long as I did, just lucky that I had the opportunity to ride so many horses, so many good horses," he said in the same interview.

Johnson started very young, rode his first winner at 16, learned his craft with one of the titans of the game in David Nicholson, has spent much of his career as first jockey to Philip Hobbs, a stability that illustrates his reliability, his steady nature, his loyalty. He rarely displays the all-consuming single-mindedness that characterised McCoy's career, although that lack should not suggest any shortfall of commitment, rather a slightly healthier attitude to the occupational slings and arrows that go with being a jump jockey.

And, as you'd expect, McCoy and Johnson became brothers in arms, sitting at adjacent pegs in the weighing room, the elder statesmen of the game with auras to match. On his

'I have always wanted to be champion jockey, right from the age of 16, even when I didn't think I'd ever make it as a jockey'

IN LINE

Tony McCoy's retirement started the search for his successors as champion jockey and JP McManus's retained rider. Richard Johnson and Barry Geraghty were quick to step forward

emotional retirement McCoy expressed the hope that Johnson would succeed him as champion, succeed in his lifelong ambition to be top of the pile.

It would be a thoroughly popular outcome. Poulidor and White were arguably the most well-loved practitioners of their professions at the time despite their lack of ultimate success. Their tenacity in picking themselves up and beginning again, their good nature in the face of defeat, their generosity of attitude as their dreams were shattered again and again won them hearts if nothing else.

Is it better to be remembered with affection or remembered as a winner? Perhaps Poulidor and White might have swapped their usual roles, just once – but now it looks as though Johnson will be fortunate enough to manage both, as long as he avoids serious injury. If he should take over at the top from McCoy it will be a continuation of the same values, the same commitment, the same reliability, yet at the same time there will be a different sensation at the end-of-season festivities.

There will be the sense of justice done, of the crown prince finally taking over from the king, of the amiable Johnson being rewarded for a lifetime of excellence.

They say nice guys finish last; that isn't true. Nice guys often finish second. This time one might finish first.

FOR years, every time racegoers saw green and gold hoops they thought of AP McCoy in his role as first jockey to owner JP McManus. Not any more.

One of the main consequences of McCoy's retirement was the vacancy as McManus's man, one of the most sought-after jobs in jump racing, a guarantee of good horses to ride and big races in which to ride them. Indeed, McManus has so many horses spread across so many trainers that his main jockey can't hope to ride them all, but when it comes to cherry-picking time at the big festivals the incumbent can expect a rich harvest.

As soon as McCoy announced his decision to retire, speculation began about his replacement. Several names were in the frame but the broad consensus – and the bookmakers' choice – was Barry Geraghty. He ticked all the boxes, as the cliche goes – a top-class jockey, a big-race specialist, an Irishman, a fount of experience. He seemed the chosen one before the choosing had even started, but was reluctant to discuss the possibility in interview, preferring to wait until the decision had been made.

When the decision was made, it was Geraghty. Few raised an eyebrow. With McCoy gone and Ruby Walsh secure with Willie Mullins, there are few other riders around with the necessary heft for the McManus job – Geraghty is one of the few. The only obvious point to be made is that at 36 he is not a long-term appointment, but his sheer suitability outweighs that drawback. At 36 he's a family man too, which was a key factor for Geraghty.

"It's a great job to get and I'm

▸▸ *Continues page 84*

thrilled," he said when the news broke. "I'll be in England a few days a week but not there all week, which works well. When you have a young family it's hard on the kids when you're saying goodbye to them on Wednesday and not seeing them again until Sunday. It's fine for one week, but that can happen week after week. I would imagine I won't be spending as much time in England. That's the big attraction for me. When it came to the crunch, this job offered me the chance to spend more time at home. That was the incentive."

So Geraghty relinquished his job with Nicky Henderson, a role epitomised by the success he enjoyed with the great Sprinter Sacre. It won't be the last time he rides for Henderson, though, as McManus has several horses in training at Seven Barrows including Champion Hurdle runner-up My Tent Or Yours, who was ironically McCoy's choice of McManus's runners in the 2014 race. His discard was Jezki – who won the race with Geraghty in the saddle.

Thus the continuity prevails, which will appeal to Geraghty and to Henderson alike. In recent years it has appeared that Geraghty was the natural replacement for McCoy in any case – he also won the 2014 World Hurdle on McManus's More Of That when McCoy preferred At Fishers Cross – and now he'll get to make these decisions himself.

As well as those two horses, Geraghty can look forward to riding Grand National contender Shutthefrontdoor, crack three-mile chaser Carlingford Lough and hugely promising novice chaser Minella Rocco, among many others. Those he doesn't ride will be available to Mark Walsh and Richie McLernon, among others, who will play the same roles now as they did when McCoy was the top man.

McCoy's influence lingered into the appointment of his successor – "AP was a great help in guiding me through the decision-making process," Geraghty said. "He was a good confidant to have all the time we were in discussions" – and he will continue his association with Geraghty if he adopts a role within the McManus machine. Now, though, the change has been made and Geraghty is the man in the hotseat.

He can expect little reduction in his rate of big-race accumulation and will find that he can count on a deep resource of young, promising stock – as well as the occasional mid-season big-name purchase for which his new boss is renowned. For his part, McManus will relish the continuity of another major player at his call, one already aware of the way things are done, one already familiar with many of the horses and the trainers involved.

In this respect, *plus ça change, plus c'est la même chose.* The name has changed, but the process has not and neither will the rate of success. For Geraghty, though, the change brings a vivid new plot twist to the final chapters of his career, one that he will relish.

▸▸ Fresh start: (clockwise from top left) Barry Geraghty in the JP McManus colours on his first ride as retained jockey at Limerick in July; Richard Johnson in the jockeys' line-up at Sandown on the day Tony McCoy retired; Johnson and Geraghty together; Geraghty and his former boss Nicky Henderson

'When it came to the crunch, this job offered me the chance to spend more time at home. That was the incentive'

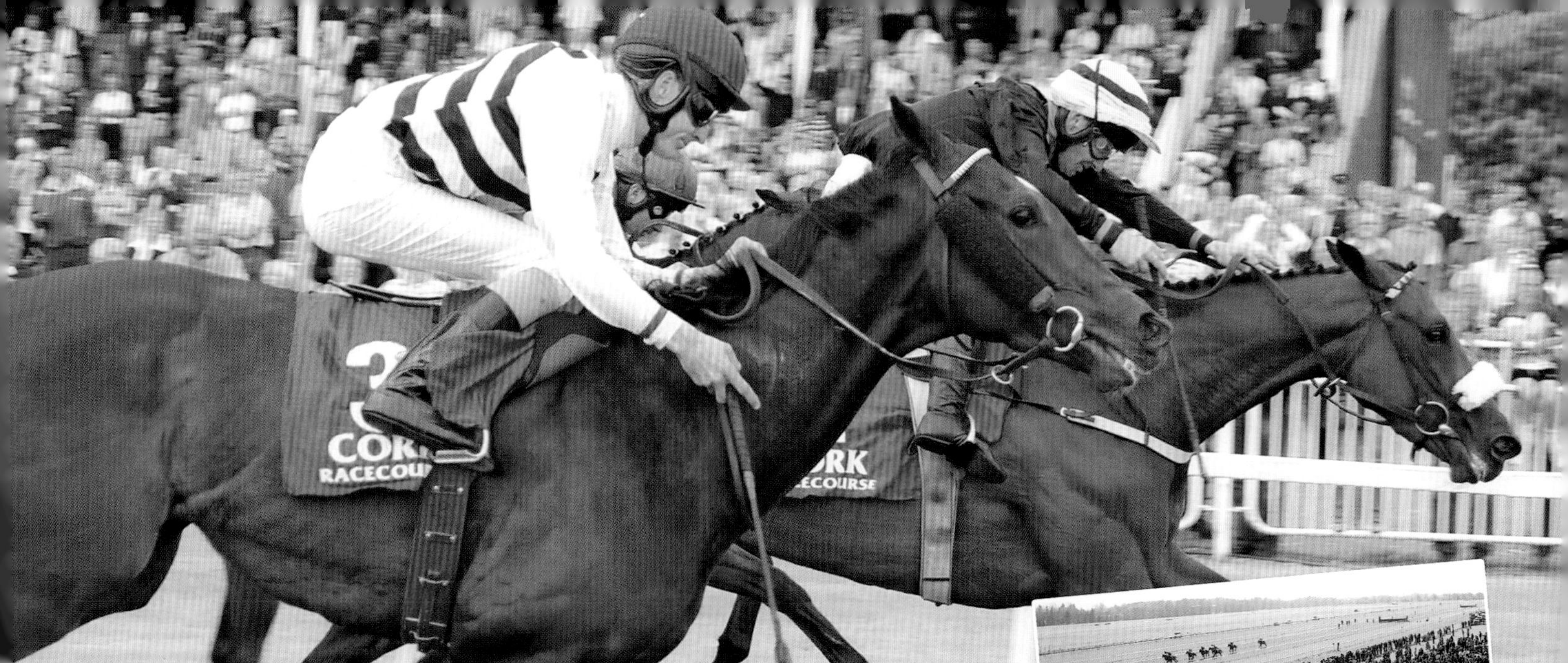

2016 Racing Dates

ATURDAY 2nd JANUARY (NH)

ork's REDFM STUDENT RACE DAY
ONDAY 14th MARCH (NH)

ACING HOME FOR EASTER FESTIVAL
ATURDAY 26th MARCH (F)
UNDAY 27th MARCH (NH)
ONDAY 28th MARCH(BH) (M)

ATURDAY 16th APRIL (F)

RIDAY EVENING RACING - BBQ
RIDAY 6th MAY (E) (NH)
RIDAY 20th MAY (E) (F)

UNDAY 12TH JUNE (F)

BQ
RIDAY 8th JULY (E) (NH)

ONDAY 1st AUGUST (BH) (NH)
UESDAY 2nd AUGUST (E) (F)

UNDAY 28th AUGUST (NH)

ATURDAY 15th OCTOBER (F)
UNDAY 16th OCTOBER (NH)

E PADDYPOWER CORK NATIONAL
UNDAY 6th NOVEMBER (NH)

UNDAY 20th NOVEMBER (NH)

E KERRY GROUP HILLY WAY CHASE
UNDAY 11th DECEMBER (NH)

Get your heart racing...

- Premium Level Restaurant Package
- Premium Level Barbeque Package
- Social Package
- Premium Level Admission
- General Admission
- Children go FREE

Book your tickets today

www.corkracecourse.ie

t: +353 22 50207

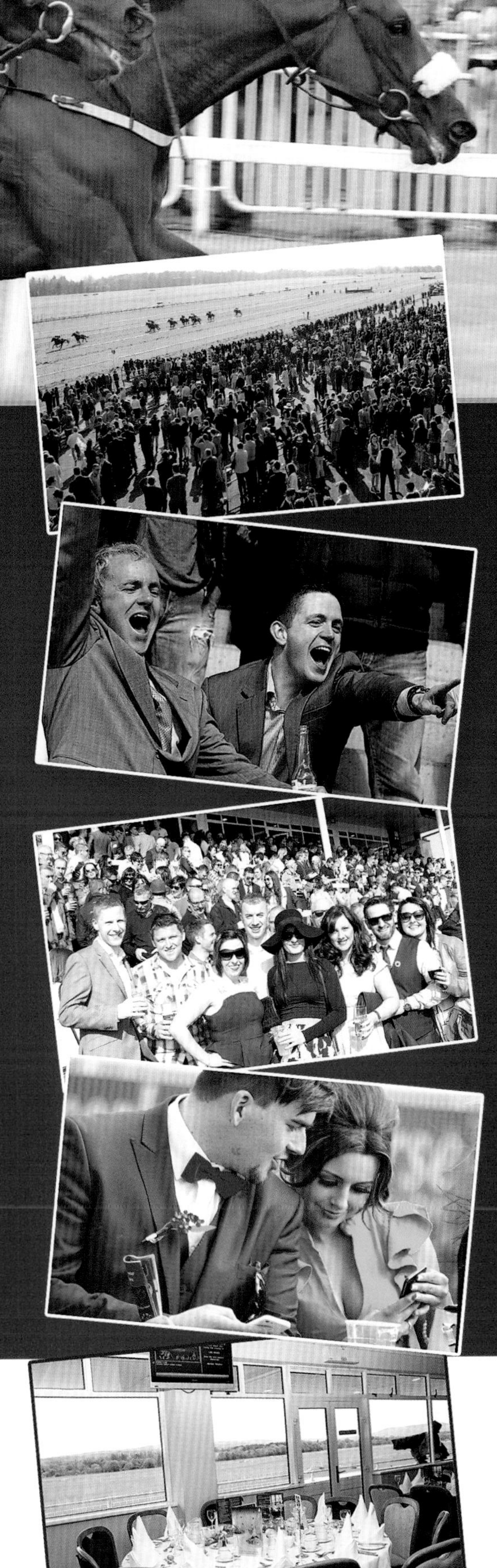

corkracecourse.ie

@corkracecourse

facebook
Cork Racecourse Mallow

END OF THE ROAD

AP McCoy was by no means the only jump jockey to retire last term. Four lesser-known former riders tell their stories

TOM SIDDALL, 38

AFTER 19 years in the saddle, Tom Siddall did not exactly go out in a blaze of glory: his final ride, the 13-year-old novice chaser Westwire Toby, was sent off at 50-1 before finishing a distant last of three at Bangor in March. So ended a career spent largely away from the major stages in which Siddall partnered 163 winners over jumps in Britain, his best tally of 27 coming in 2008-09, the season before he broke his neck in the Grand National.

After that, the numbers dwindled – with good reason, as Siddall was juggling riding commitments with a flourishing equine-dentistry business, and the latter was taking up the bulk of his time. "It was a gradual process but the two were clashing until there was no way I could keep riding because I was so busy with the teeth," he explains.

"It's grown and grown and I'd have customers booked in for a day, then suddenly I'd get a ride and had to let people down. But I started riding less and less and it wasn't going anywhere. We've been flat out since I stopped riding and now I don't have to miss appointments because I've got to go to Uttoxeter for one ride."

Based in Broadway in the Cotswolds, Siddall numbers Dan Skelton, Martin Keighley, David Dennis and Kim Bailey among his clients. There has also been an addition to the family in recent months, wife Laura having given birth to daughter Dolly in May to join Siddall's stepson Rocky in the clan.

"With a couple of kids to support, from a financial point of view it was difficult to earn a living with the stage I'd got to," Siddall says. "I needed a second income and that's how the dentistry played in, but I was making more money doing that than I was riding, so it was a bit of a no-brainer to stop."

Looking back on his career as a jockey, Siddall says his proudest moment was riding Mendo to win a handicap hurdle at the Cheltenham November meeting for his friend Noel Chance; his biggest win came on Songe in Haydock's Champion Hurdle Trial in 2009.

"I've got to admit you don't get the same buzz doing a horse's teeth as you would riding a winner over fences. The buzz of riding a winner cannot be matched, but the satisfaction is short-lived; you can pull up or have a fall the next day.

"In being a dentist, I have the satisfaction of building my own business, knowing I'm good enough at my job to make a difference and providing stability for my family. Plus I get Sundays off."

HADDEN FROST, 25

WHEN Hadden Frost reflects on a 135-winner career that featured Cheltenham Festival success on Buena Vista in the 2010 Pertemps Final, the now former jockey can't help quoting an old number-one hit single. "When people talk about it, I always start singing the Specials song Too Much Too Young," he chuckles.

Perhaps that's why Frost retired in April aged just 24, browned off with life as a jump jockey and keen to explore other opportunities in the equine world. "It was the hardest decision I've ever had to make but it wasn't an impulse decision," says the son of Champion Hurdle-winning jockey Jimmy Frost. "I've got lots of happy memories but I'm not gonna lie, towards the end I wasn't doing it for fun."

Frost reached the conclusion he could not make a decent living as a jump jockey. "You're all holding on to the idea of winning that big race but it's very fickle if you aren't a fashionable name," he says.

Then there was the ever-present worry about serious injury; in February, Frost left Exeter in the Devon Air Ambulance after being knocked unconscious in a fall.

"If you start to think it might not be worth it, then you shouldn't be doing it. I might have retired a little bit early but I didn't want to retire a little bit late. I'd had my shot at it and it didn't quite work out. I felt I was just bumbling along and I'd have a go at something else."

In part at least, that 'something else' means a return to his roots in the showjumping arena, plus HJF Saddlery, an artisan leatherware business making belts, bags and bridle accessories on commission at his workshop in Wickham, where he lives, near Newbury.

The main focus of Frost's day-to-day working life since he quit the saddle, however, is pre-training young horses, both potential racehorses (at premises in Letcombe Regis) and showjumpers at the prestigious Oakingham Stud. "I love the challenge and satisfaction of working on a horse one-on-one and seeing the improvement," he says.

"My idea is not just to break them in but to teach them to jump as well. I want to send them back doing their pole work impeccably so that trainers only have to practise and get them fit."

Frost is also rather pleased about

▸▸ Different lives: (from left) Tom Siddall; Hadden Frost; Barry Keniry with wife Stef and daughter Annie; and Davy Condon

having bowed out with a 25-1 success on Ocean Venture in an Exeter novice hurdle. "They say you're as good as your last ride and you can't say I stopped because I wasn't good enough if you watch that one!"

BARRY KENIRY, 36

THERE were no hard feelings when Barry Keniry called time on his career in January. "I lived the dream for 20 years," he says. "I had a good 20 years and I got out in one piece. I didn't do any work – and now all of a sudden I do have to do some work."

Former jockeys usually admit to having pangs of longing for the old days once their time in the saddle is over. Not Keniry, however; not yet, anyway. He simply hasn't had time. Not only has he been "flat out" with his pre-training business based at Richmond in North Yorkshire, there was the small matter of getting married in August, swiftly followed by the birth of daughter Annie the following month.

"There's been a lot going on," laughs the older brother of Flat jockey Liam Keniry, with a trace of understatement. "I've also started on my courses to get a training licence and hopefully I'll start training in the next year or so."

Keniry's first winner was Marlonette for Willie Mullins on the Flat at Clonmel in 1996, while his first in Britain was Taufan Boy in a handicap hurdle at Ascot in 1998 for Toby Balding, with whom he was based for six years. Another 279 jumps winners in Britain followed, among them a handful of Grade 2 scorers including French star Kasbah Bliss, aboard whom he won the Rendlesham Hurdle in 2008.

His best season brought 34 successes in 2010-11 but recently he had found himself focusing more on the pre-training business he runs with his wife Stef. "We've constantly been kept busy and it got to the stage where I was too busy to go racing," Keniry says. "That last winter we had plenty of horses in and I was going racing when I didn't really have time to go racing. Something had to give."

DAVY CONDON, 30

IT is a chilling fact of life for jump jockeys that, unlike AP McCoy, they do not always have the luxury of choosing the date of their own retirement. Davy Condon was one of the unlucky ones: when Portrait King fell three out in the Crabbie's Grand National, it signalled the end of his career.

"He was really enjoying it, jumping away, and I was getting a great feel from him," recalls Cork-born Condon. "I knew he'd stay and I thought he had a good chance of being placed."

Then, in a couple of seconds, it was all over. Condon sustained such severe spinal injuries in the fall that he was left temporarily paralysed; he was told it was too dangerous to carry on as a jump jockey owing to the risk of permanent paralysis. Yet while the news could hardly be anything other than devastating, Condon says he was not entirely surprised as the injury came on top of a spinal concussion and broken vertebrae he had sustained in a fall at Cork the previous August.

"I have come to terms with what happened. It's not something I was ready for but I had that fall in August and I was warned then, so I kind of half-knew I wouldn't be able to ride again when it happened at Aintree."

One of Ireland's leading jump jockeys, Condon began his career with Willie Mullins, for whom he rode Holy Orders in the 2003 Melbourne Cup at the age of 18. His biggest successes included Cheltenham Festival victories on Ebaziyan and Flaxen Flare, plus wins in the Fighting Fifth and Christmas Hurdles on Noel Meade's top hurdler Go Native. He won last year's Ladbroke Hurdle at Ascot on Bayan. "I had a pretty good 14 years," he says.

Condon, who lives in County Meath, was taken to Fazakerley Hospital in Liverpool after the National fall, which left him lying on the Aintree turf for more than ten minutes. Although the initial prognosis suggested Condon would never even be able to sit on a horse again, he received a boost after an operation to remove the disc between the C3 and C4 vertebrae in his neck that was causing his problems.

"My spinal cord is okay and I'll be going back to Gordon Elliott to start riding out again in the new year. I won't be doing any schooling but I'll be riding out six mornings a week."

Before then, however, Condon set off on a two-month backpacking trip around Asia with his girlfriend Louise. "It's something I've always wanted to do. As a jockey, you never get more than a week off here or there, so this was the perfect opportunity."

Interviews by Nicholas Godfrey

IN THE PICTURE

Casey handles the pressure to bow out a winner at Listowel

David Casey was given a guard of honour at Listowel in September before ending his riding career on a winner provided by Willie Mullins, for so long his comrade in arms.

Casey, 39, was applauded by his weighing-room colleagues before his final ride on novice hurdler Long Dog, who was long odds-on to beat three much inferior rivals and scored by nine and a half lengths to give the jockey a perfect send-off.

"I've ridden Cheltenham winners and Hennessy winners but, I'll tell you something, I've never felt so much pressure in all my life," Casey said. "It was the fact I was on a bloody 1-6 shot that made it worse."

It was fitting that the final winner came for Mullins, just as Casey's first had done 20 years earlier when he scored on If You Say Yes in a claiming hurdle. The following year he rode Mystical City to win the Galway Hurdle, providing Mullins with one of his early major wins as a trainer, and the pair continued to combine regularly for big-race success.

"David was always there when I needed him and he'll be a great addition to me going forward," said Mullins, who prompted Casey's decision to retire when he offered him the chance to travel to Australia with Max Dynamite to supervise his preparation for the Melbourne Cup.

"Opportunities were getting harder and harder to come by. When Willie asked me to go to Australia with Max Dynamite I felt it was a great opportunity and too good to turn down," Casey said. "After that I suppose my role will be helping Willie and helping out the yard in any way I can. Anything that needs doing, I'll be throwing my hat at it. I'm looking forward to the new challenge."

Casey rode two Cheltenham Festival winners – Fadoudal Du Cochet for Arthur Moore in the 2002 Grand Annual Chase and the Mullins-trained Rule Supreme in the 2004 Royal & SunAlliance Chase – and his big-race victories in Ireland included the Hennessy Gold Cup at Leopardstown on Rule Supreme and Kempes, both for Mullins, and the Thyestes Chase on three occasions.

"I've been very lucky to ride for some great trainers," he said. "Willie was great to me and Arthur [Moore] gave me some great opportunities, as did Charlie [Swan] and Mouse [Morris]. It's hard to pick a highlight. The Cheltenham wins were great but maybe winning the Hennessy on Rule Supreme two days after I came back from a broken leg was the one I'll remember most fondly."

Picture: PATRICK McCANN (RACINGPOST.COM/PHOTOS)

ZERO OPTON
Kieran
KÜSCHALL

BRIGHT NEW STAR

Faugheen answered all the questions with a front-running Champion Hurdle triumph that confirmed him as the dominant force in what had seemed a competitive division

By Steve Dennis

ASTRONOMERS scanning the skies frequently locate hitherto undiscovered heavenly bodies. There then follows long and forensic examination to decide which category this new find belongs in – is it a new star, is it a barren and rocky satellite, is it simply a cloud of dust? Only then is it accorded its true worth.

And so it was with Faugheen during 2014-15. We knew we'd found

▸▸ *Continues page 92*

RACING UK

something truly interesting, but it seemed to take an awfully long time to accord him the status he deserved as one of the brightest stars in the racing firmament. Sometimes we in racing move too soon, pronounce some horse as 24-carat on the basis of a little glitter before more stringent testing reveals only iron pyrites. Sometimes we move too tardily, and so it was with Faugheen.

It was only his sparkling success in the Stan James Champion Hurdle, darting away from the field between the last two flights and drawing easily a length and a half clear of stablemate Arctic Fire, that finally, conclusively made up our minds. What took us so long? Some called him a talking horse; perhaps we just weren't listening properly.

Faugheen emerged from his novice season with a reputation that appeared subordinate to that of his stablemate Vautour, the member of Willie Mullins' team of all the talents who really seemed to have it all. Indeed, Faugheen's final outing as a novice, in the Grade 1 Herald Champion Novice Hurdle at Punchestown, came when sent in as pinch-hitter for the absent Vautour over a two-mile trip that seemed insufficient for his needs. He nevertheless strolled home by 12 lengths, but the Racing Post's analysis writer Justin O'Hanlon summed up with the words "to label him as a genuine Champion Hurdle contender on evidence such as this is premature".

****

IT WAS only in the autumn, after Vautour was committed to a novice chase campaign, that Faugheen took on the mantle of Champion Hurdle contender. "I thought he should go novice chasing," Mullins told Johnny Ward in the Racing Post. "Then we analysed everything we had and what he was doing; that he hadn't been beaten.

"Everyone was keener for him to go back hurdling. I thought 'let's do it' – to have a Champion Hurdle winner or one with the potential is huge for a yard. We thought Vautour could possibly win the Arkle and maybe become a Gold Cup horse some day, and we weren't as sure about Faugheen doing that."

▸▸Chilling out: a relaxing walk for Faugheen at Willie Mullins' Closutton base during the triumphant season that took him to the top of the hurdling tree

Almost by default, then, Faugheen was directed down the path so memorably trodden by another stablemate in Hurricane Fly. Faugheen did nothing wrong when winning at Ascot in November, making all, hacking up after a couple of sticky jumps in the early stages, but although that performance made him market leader for the Champion Hurdle there was still a constituency who considered he hadn't done all that much right either. For all that headline writers with a soft spot for a rhyme exhorted us to think of Faugheen as a machine, it was easier to consider him as the kind of machine that needed a couple of well-placed thumps to induce it to perform.

"What did he beat?" was the cry. Not very much, came the answer, and despite Faugheen's swaggering victory in the Christmas Hurdle at Kempton, when he thrashed Elite Hurdle winner Purple Bay by eight lengths after proving amenable to restraint in the initial stages of the race, there was still no evidence of unconditional acceptance that we were witnessing the procession of a new champion towards his rightful place. The bookmakers trimmed his price, but without any great display of conviction.

For there were others to consider. The British challenge for the two-mile crown was led by The New One, arguably unlucky not to have won the Champion Hurdle the previous season and busy cementing his credentials further with a string of comfortable victories over second-division rivals. It was exactly what Faugheen was doing, and after The New One's victory at Cheltenham in December his trainer Nigel Twiston-Davies made his opinion plain. "Faugheen was impressive at Ascot but most of his form is over longer distances. Will he have the turn of foot this horse has? I think we can sit behind and overtake going to the last."

For all his evident brilliance over two miles, Faugheen was still perceived as a stayer dropping down

▸▸ *Continues page 94*

'I thought 'let's do it' – to have a Champion Hurdle winner or one with the potential is huge for a yard'

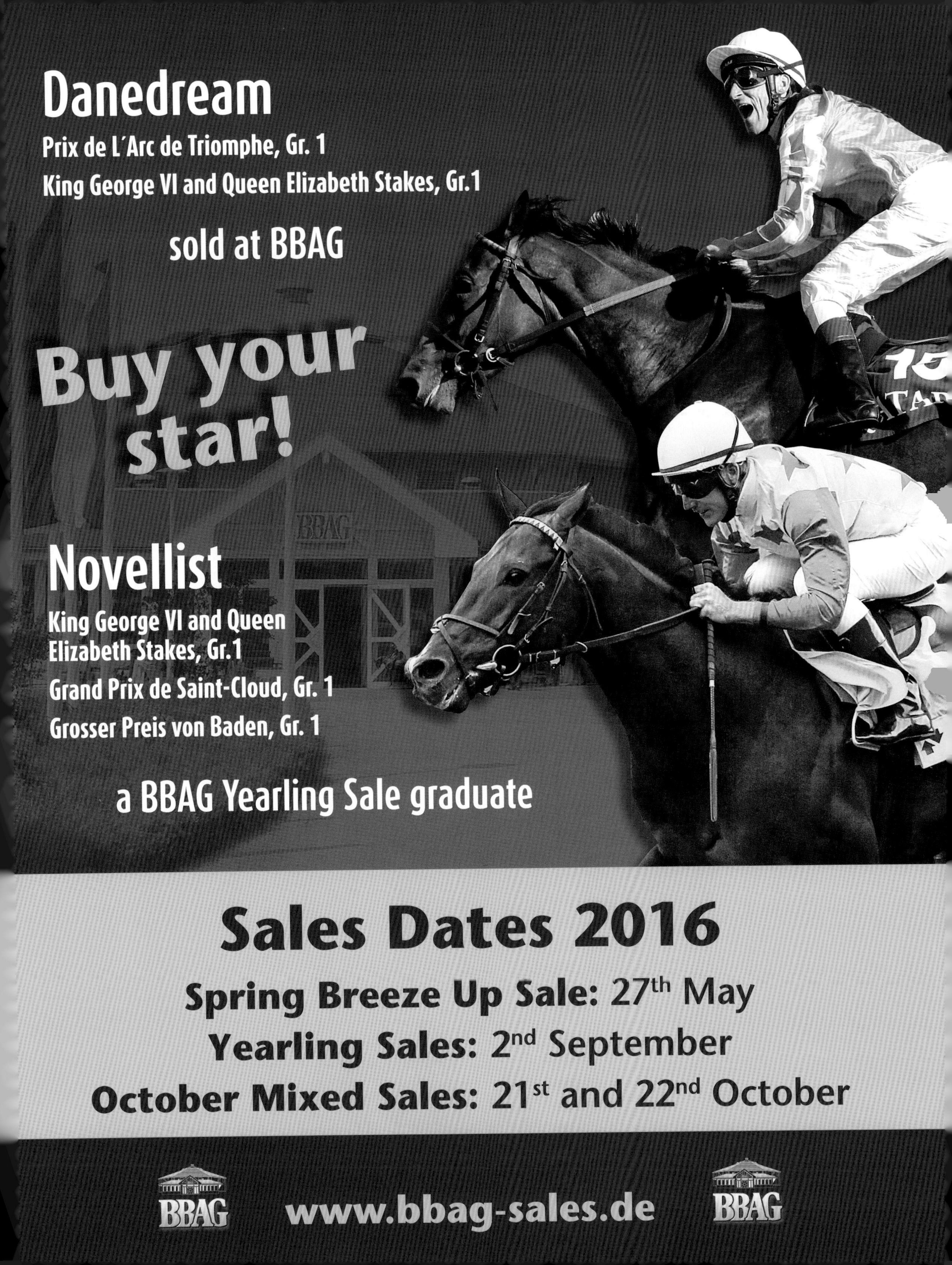

Danedream

Prix de L´Arc de Triomphe, Gr. 1

King George VI and Queen Elizabeth Stakes, Gr.1

sold at BBAG

Buy your star!

Novellist

King George VI and Queen Elizabeth Stakes, Gr.1

Grand Prix de Saint-Cloud, Gr. 1

Grosser Preis von Baden, Gr. 1

a BBAG Yearling Sale graduate

Sales Dates 2016

Spring Breeze Up Sale: 27th May

Yearling Sales: 2nd September

October Mixed Sales: 21st and 22nd October

www.bbag-sales.de

in trip to fill the gap left by a more talented stablemate. Make that plural if you wish, because the wonderful Hurricane Fly was staking his claim for a third Champion Hurdle with a series of heartwarming victories at Punchestown and Leopardstown, defying the advancing years and the younger generation but, nevertheless, doing so in conditions that were unlikely to be replicated at Cheltenham in March.

There was much talk as the year turned about whether Ruby Walsh would remain loyal to the old-timer or put his faith in Faugheen, another conversation that did little to reinforce Faugheen's position as the one to beat. Walsh, a hard-nosed operator if ever there was one, surely wouldn't let sentiment colour his decision, but the fact that he was linked with Hurricane Fly until the last few days before the festival was another reason to temper faith. If Ruby couldn't commit, then how could anyone else?

And then he did. He stacked his chips on Faugheen pink instead of Hurricane Fly blue, and sounded relieved that the choice had been made while still open to the possibility that it had been made wrongly. "I think the younger legs might be the difference but there's every chance I'm wrong," he said. "I just feel Faugheen is in really good form and he's the one I want to ride."

It was hardly a convincing case, but suspicions that Walsh had known his own mind much earlier came in the aftermath of Cheltenham glory. Mullins intimated that Walsh had talked tactics a month before and produced a gameplan that might propel the seven-year-old to victory in what was a particularly strong renewal of the race.

Here he was, then, short-priced favourite for the two-mile title, seemingly a six-of-one choice for his jockey, a flat-track bully of inferior opponents now climbing into the ring to face a bunch of seasoned sluggers. Hurricane Fly seemed almost as good as ever, the reigning champion Jezki was winless in three starts but was notable for peaking on spring ground at Cheltenham, The New One – unbeaten in four – seemed firmly on course to erase the unhappy memories of 12 months earlier. Did Faugheen have what was required?

After the confirmation that Walsh would ride, Faugheen's odds contracted further, yet there was still no feel of foregone conclusion that

THE FLY'S EQUAL

How Faugheen ranks on RPR

"I'm not going to say he's as good as Hurricane Fly in his heyday but he's a very good horse and over hurdles the second best I've trained," was Willie Mullins' verdict on Faugheen in the Cheltenham winner's enclosure after the Champion Hurdle.

By the time Faugheen added Punchestown's Champion Hurdle to his roll of honour in May, bringing his record under rules to a perfect ten, he was the equal of Hurricane Fly on Racing Post Ratings.

In extending his superiority over stablemate Arctic Fire from a length and a half at Cheltenham to eight lengths at Punchestown, Faugheen achieved an RPR of 173 – a mark reached three times by Hurricane Fly, most notably in his second Champion Hurdle win in 2013.

Punchestown was an improvement on Faugheen's 170 at Cheltenham, which made him only an average winner of the Champion Hurdle – six of the previous ten winning performances had rated higher on RPR – but with clear potential to rate higher given a true pace and top opposition.

There is some way to go if Faugheen is to join the pantheon of great two-mile hurdlers, with the bar set high in recent times by three-time Champion Hurdle winner Istabraq. His best RPR was 181 at Punchestown in 1999, one of four occasions when he exceeded a mark of 173, although his best at Cheltenham was 174 in his first Champion Hurdle win in 1998.

▸▸ Class act: Istabraq sets the recent standard among two-mile hurdlers

might be associated with the usual odds-on chance. The Mullins factor ensured that strong support was inevitable, but doubts were still being raised right up to the point where the tapes went up and Walsh put his tactical plan into operation.

Conscious of Faugheen's proven stamina and his amenability to front running, Walsh set a steady, tactical pace on the white-faced favourite. "Ruby told me a month ago what he was going to do and how he was going to do it – and he did it," Mullins said. "It was just too good to be true. I wasn't ever concerned."

It was slowish stuff but utterly compelling. As the field swept away from the stands it soon became clear that Walsh had his rivals precisely where he wanted them, and when he kicked Faugheen on as they turned for home he soon put the result beyond doubt – as well as the ability and status of his gallant mount. The strong field floundered in his wake, and although Arctic Fire closed on the hill the winning margin flattered him. Hurricane Fly kept on for third, for an unparalleled Mullins trifecta. Told you so, said the talking horse.

Faugheen's chasing career is, one suspects, on permanent hold. There seems no earthly reason why any of those behind him in the Champion Hurdle should deny him in 2016 – The New One has arguably regressed and Jezki may now be better suited by a longer trip, while Hurricane Fly has been retired. The best two-mile novice of last season, Douvan, has the Arkle Chase as his objective. The Triumph Hurdle graduates – Peace And Co, Top Notch, Hargam, to skim the cream from Seven Barrows – have considerable improvement to find.

No-one doubts him now. The only question worth asking is the one about how high Faugheen's rating might climb over the next 18 months, although the suspicion remains that he will need to beat a rival almost as good as himself in order to push his mark towards the 180 that would herald a champion for the ages.

Hindsight, of course, makes clarity of all, but as Faugheen came back in through the jammed-in and joyful Cheltenham crowds, we now knew exactly what a beast of a horse he was.

Sometimes we go looking for the wrong things in the wrong places, and sometimes the dazzling star in the centre of the telescope lens really is just a dazzling star.

▸▸In the pink: (clockwise from far left) Faugheen leads Arctic Fire and Hurricane Fly in a 1-2-3 for Willie Mullins at Cheltenham; Ruby Walsh celebrates as he reaches the winning post; and again in the winner's enclosure; Mullins and Walsh with Faugheen; Walsh kisses his trophy; owners Rich and Susannah Ricci (right) join the celebrations; Walsh after the third Champion Hurdle win of his career; (below) Mullins with the trophy

EASY AS 1-2-3

Mullins makes history

Willie Mullins fielded as many runners in the 2015 Champion Hurdle as British trainers combined and his trio proved vastly better, filling the first three places as Faugheen was followed home by Arctic Fire and Hurricane Fly.

No trainer had previously swept the first three places in the Champion Hurdle, while Aidan O'Brien in 1998 and 1999 had been alone in welcoming back the first two.

"This is beyond our wildest dreams," said Mullins, whose feat rivalled Michael Dickinson saddling the first five home in the 1983 Cheltenham Gold Cup.

"I was hoping one of them might win, but to be 1-2-3 is just fantastic. We jokingly talked about it but we were only hoping, no more than that."

IN THE PICTURE

Monumental triumph as House that Jack built opens to riders

The Injured Jockeys Fund reached another milestone in its 51-year history with the opening of Jack Berry House, a jockeys' rehabilitation and fitness centre for the north of England.

The £3.1m centre in Malton, North Yorkshire, which features a state-of-the-art gym, hydrotherapy pool and respite units, is the sister facility to Oaksey House in Lambourn, Berkshire, which has been a great success since its opening in 2009.

The official opening ceremony in Malton on June 2 was performed by HRH The Princess Royal, the IJF's patron, although the centre first opened its doors on April 20 and has been busy ever since.

The facility is named in honour of Berry, vice-president of the IJF and the driving force behind the original idea of a jockeys' rehabilitation centre, from which Oaksey House was born. Berry, 78, a former top trainer who broke 46 bones in falls during his own riding career, received an MBE in 1996 for his tireless fundraising efforts on behalf of the IJF.

"The opening of Jack Berry House is one of the proudest moments of my life," said Berry (*main picture*), whose contribution is also marked by a life-size bronze statue, complete with Berry's trademark red shirt, outside the centre. "I'm so grateful to the many generous people who made it possible through their donations and legacies. We've been rattling cans for three and a half years to try to get the funding and, now it has come to fruition, words can't say how I feel."

Berry said his "pride and joy" is the 4ft 6in heated hydrotherapy pool, one of only three in Britain. The others are at Sport Wales in Cardiff and Manchester United Football Club. Also on site at the centre, which is managed by Jo Russell, are physiotherapist Gemma Darley, gym and fitness manager Danny Hague, a nutritionist, a Jockeys' Employment and Training Scheme (Jets) representative and a sports physician.

One of the fundraising initiatives at Jack Berry House involved more than 2,000 bricks (sold at £50 a time) being inscribed with human and equine names before being used in the construction.

Paying tribute to Berry, The Princess Royal said: "This is a remarkable achievement and it really does deserve your name bricked in, which is entirely appropriate on the basis of the way you managed to raise all that money. To everybody who made this day possible, a very big thank you but this is Jack Berry's house."

Pictures: EDWARD WHITAKER (RACINGPOST.COM/PHOTOS), LOUISE POLLARD

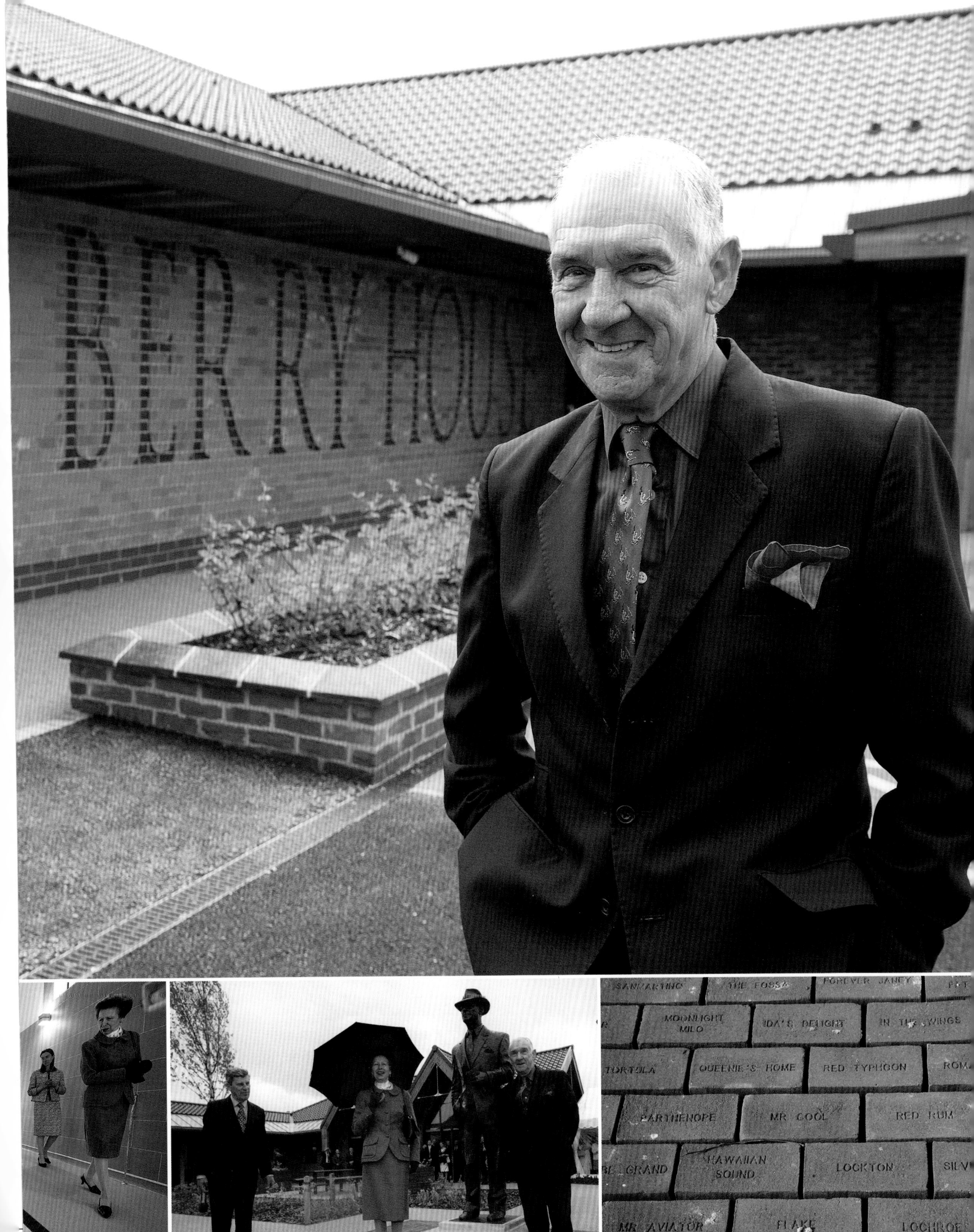

THE FOSSA
FOREVER JANEY
MOONLIGHT MILO
IDA'S DELIGHT
QUEENIE'S HOME
RED TYPHOON
PARTHENOPE
MR COOL
RED RUM
HAWAIIAN SOUND
LOCKTON
MR AVIATOR
FLAKE
LOCHROE

made the difference, not just the new gallop," Nicholls says. "The three times he won he had a tongue-tie on, which we'd never been able to get on him before, but mentally he was able to take that last season. You never stop learning about these horses. You have to get to know everything about them to get the best out of them on the track. Even with Kauto I think he was at his best at 11 because we just did different things. Dodge came right and kept on improving. The improvement in him was phenomenal."

Dodging Bullets was not the only one. The Nicholls string was on a roll for most of the season, clocking up notable winners on 21 consecutive Saturdays stretching from November 1 to March 21. That extraordinary run started just as the sand ring was completed, which was no coincidence according to Nicholls, and created a buzz around the yard.

"It was a very good season once we got up and running. The horses kept on improving, they kept on winning. Having those 21 winners was awesome. We kept looking at the paper and saying 'we've got no chance today' and then a horse like Rebel Rebellion would run a career-best and win. It was good for the whole team."

****

THE team has taken on a more youthful look with Sam Twiston-Davies as number-one jockey, backed up by Nick Scholfield, champion conditional Sean Bowen and Jack Sherwood, another promising claimer. This season Harry Derham, the former stable conditional who quit the saddle last year at the age of 19, has started as pupil assistant in preparation for taking over next term from Tom Jonason, Nicholls' current assistant.

"To see those lads do well is exciting," says Nicholls, who has praise for all of them and is deeply impressed by how Twiston-Davies, still only 23, has coped with the demands of his high-profile position. "It's a high-pressure job for him, it's a high-pressure job for me. I got a bit of flak for taking Sam on the year before but I always said it was an investment for the future. You have to say he did incredibly well and he's only going to go onwards and upwards. He's a big addition to the team."

The accent on youth is also evident in Nicholls' squad of 125 horses, which includes his other two Wednesday winners at the Cheltenham Festival – Aux Ptits Soins, the highly regarded Coral Cup winner, and Fred Winter scorer Qualando – as well as Saphir Du Rheu, second in the World Hurdle and winner of a Grade 1 novice chase at Aintree on his final two starts of last season.

"Saphir Du Rheu is my great white hope. He's a true stayer, a lovely, big horse with plenty of improvement to come. It might be a year too soon to go for the Gold Cup, we might just want to mind him a bit and it might happen the year after, but he'll tell us."

The Gold Cup is likely to be off the agenda for Silviniaco Conti, who was dominant again in the King George VI Chase last season but beaten for a third time in the Cheltenham showpiece. "Even I was trying to convince myself he'd be all right at Cheltenham but he doesn't seem to run his race there, it doesn't seem to suit him," Nicholls says. "Kempton and Aintree suit him better. I've learned in this game never to say never – he might run [in the Gold Cup], he might not. I wouldn't want to rule it out but I think this season's Gold Cup is going to be very hot."

Failure at Cheltenham should not diminish Silviniaco Conti's achievements at Kempton any more than it did for three-time King George winner Wayward Lad in the 1980s. "Cheltenham's not the be-all and end-all" is a new mantra around Manor Farm Stables.

"We all love Cheltenham and we want to aim horses for that, but there are plenty of races to be won either side of that," Nicholls says. "I need to be more selective about what to run at Cheltenham and save some of the horses for other races they can win."

The Cheltenham Festival is the cup final but, as Nicholls knows, championships are won over a whole season. When Saturday comes, he will have his team primed and ready every time.

Kauto Star leaves golden legacy

KAUTO STAR, the greatest steeplechaser since Arkle, was put down in June after sustaining injuries as the result of a fall in his paddock at Laura Collett's eventing yard in Lambourn, where he spent his final years following his retirement from racing in 2012. He was 15.

The Paul Nicholls-trained superstar won 23 of his 41 races, including the King George VI Chase a record five times (2006-09 and 2011) and the Cheltenham Gold Cup twice, becoming the only chaser to regain the crown when he followed his 2007 victory with another in 2009. In all he won 16 Grade 1 races, from two miles to the three miles two and a half furlongs of the Gold Cup.

"I'm very lucky to have trained such a great horse. He was a champion of all champions," Nicholls said after Kauto Star's death was announced. "I'm sure his record of winning five King Georges will stand the test of time. On his day, when we had him right, he was unbeatable."

Jockey Ruby Walsh also paid tribute, saying: "He was a one-off, the horse of a lifetime and definitely the best chaser I have ever ridden or am likely to ride."

Putting Kauto Star's achievements into perspective, Racing Post historian John Randall said: "Kauto Star's awesome display in the 2009 King George, when he triumphed by 36 lengths, was the greatest performance by any chaser since Arkle, and earlier that year he had won his second Gold Cup with the best performance in the race since Arkle."

Kauto Star's later years were shrouded in controversy after Nicholls and owner Clive Smith fell out over retirement plans and the owner sent him to Collett to be retrained for a dressage career. The acrimony resurfaced after his death, with Nicholls complaining he had not been given the opportunity to see Kauto Star before he was put down.

Smith later announced that some of Kauto Star's ashes would be placed under the statue of his chaser at Kempton, scene of those King George triumphs. "Kauto Star had everything – speed, class and stamina," the owner said. "He was the complete racehorse."

SPOTTER

TAKE CONTROL OF THE NIGHT

Operates with Zero Ambient Light
400+ metre Range
20x Optical Zoom

Ideal for :-
Security
Pest Control
Animal Search

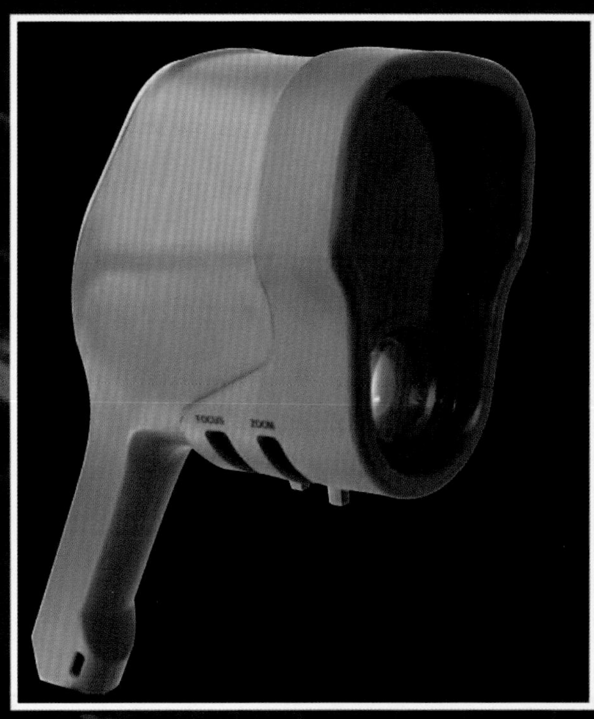

Supplier of NiteSite Spotter

MANS LOCATION SERVICES LTD

+44 (0) 1249 816 181 sales@mansls.co.uk

www.mansls.com

A series of electrifying novice-chase victories marked out Un De Sceaux as a two-miler with exceptional promise

SO FAR SCEAUX BRILLIANT

By David Jennings

ROBBIE POWER was in mischievous mood. "I had him covered," the jockey said, tongue firmly embedded in his cheek. He had just won the Killinan Beginners Chase on a nippy November afternoon at Thurles on Mr Fiftyone but, for most of the journey, all he could do was admire a chasing debut he had never before seen the like of.

"That was something else, lads," Power told the scatter of press on duty. He went on to describe what he had just experienced. "I was flat out from the word go. We went quicker than they will go in the Arkle next March. I can never remember going as quick as that in a beginners' chase before. That was mental."

That was only one way of describing Un De Sceaux's first appearance over fences. Breathtaking was another, or perhaps thrilling, electrifying or exhilarating – any of those adjectives would have been apt descriptions of what we witnessed. For ten of the 13 fences, the Willie Mullins-trained novice was foot-perfect. He attacked every fence with relish and, with three left to jump, he held a 20-length advantage over Mr Fiftyone with Ruby Walsh just using the steering wheel and not bothering with the accelerator, brake or clutch.

But the risks attached to backing a favourite on his first start over fences, even a 1-8 favourite, soon surfaced as Un De Sceaux didn't sort out his landing gear at the third-last and sprawled on landing. He may have fallen but we had seen enough prior to the departure to know that something special was brewing.

Un De Sceaux had been pretty special over hurdles. He had won seven out of seven, two at Grade 2 level and another at Grade 3, and had an average winning distance of more than 17 lengths. But there was always a suspicion that he could be even better over fences if he could negotiate the larger obstacles at the same speed.

The Thurles tumble raised questions, but by the end of April they had been answered. After a beginners' chase success by 12 lengths at Fairyhouse, he won the Frank Ward Solicitors Arkle at Leopardstown in January, the Racing Post Arkle at Cheltenham in March and the Ryanair Novice Chase at Punchestown in April. Three Grade 1s, all won in his customary front-running style. Un De Sceaux zooms out of his driveway in sixth gear and doesn't bother moving down the gears until his destination is reached.

"You're just on auto-pilot when you hop on Un De Sceaux," explains Ruby Walsh, the man entrusted with negotiating a safe landing. "He wears his heart on his sleeve and only knows one way of running. That's the beauty of him. He would be a nice ride around Sandown in the Tingle Creek, but he does need soft ground to be at his best."

That was the worry going to Cheltenham last March. Yes, he had clobbered Clarcam and Gilbamboa on yielding to soft ground at Leopardstown. Yes, his cruising speed was sensational. Yes, he was nimble over his fences. But he had never encountered anything as quick as the good to soft surface

'You're on auto-pilot when you hop on Un De Sceaux. He wears his heart on his sleeve and only knows one way of running. That's the beauty of him'

for the opening day of the festival. Those fears saw his price hover around even-money in the weeks leading up to the Arkle before the big hitters got stuck in just before the off after Mullins had sent out Douvan to win the Supreme Novices' Hurdle half an hour earlier. Un De Sceaux started at 4-6, with Vibrato Valtat closest to him in the market at 7-1.

Dunraven Storm and Sail By The Sea battled with Un De Sceaux for early supremacy. They really shouldn't have; both were pulled up. The experienced God's Own gradually closed him down and got within two lengths over the last. But Un De Sceaux was only teasing us. He scooted clear again up the hill to win by six lengths. "He has a very high cruising speed," Walsh said afterwards. "He's a bit like an 800-metre runner, he just keeps going."

Un De Sceaux's dominance of the two-mile novice chase division continued at Punchestown, where he was more workmanlike than magical in the Ryanair Novice Chase. Yielding ground was blamed for his failure to wow like he had in the devastating displays at Fairyhouse, Leopardstown and Cheltenham that defined his first season over fences.

"I'm probably more nervous watching him than any of the others, even though they all have their own pressures. He's a tough horse to watch with his style of running," Mullins admitted.

The rest of us couldn't take our eyes off Un De Sceaux and the prospect of him moving from novice company into the top Grade 1 chases was cause for palms to be rubbed together. Even as a novice he was close to the current best of the two-mile division, with his Racing Post Rating of 169 in the Arkle matching Dodging Bullets' winning figure in the Queen Mother Champion Chase, although before that Dodging Bullets had been slightly better in victory at Ascot.

The division is crying out for a new star and many believe Un De Sceaux, with his fearless fencing and breathtaking speed, is the one. He looks special. Sceaux special.

THE CRYING GAME

Warren Greatrex left no doubt about what it meant to land his first Cheltenham Festival success with Cole Harden in the World Hurdle

By Peter Thomas

THERE are times in a winner's enclosure when it's hard to know quite who the winners are. Familiarity can breed something close to contempt for the joys of being a successful owner, and it's not every jockey or trainer that knows how to crack a smile when it's what the watching world would most like to see.

Perhaps there will come a time when Warren Greatrex can remain similarly aloof from the unbridled joy of success at the races, but if the evidence of this year's Cheltenham Festival is anything to go by, that time is a long way off.

Perhaps he may learn to tone it down a fraction, though, for the simple reason that if he were to have too many more Grade 1 winners accompanied by celebrations like the one that greeted the Ladbrokes World Hurdle success of Cole Harden, he might spontaneously combust and cut off a burgeoning training career in its prime.

The big meeting has rarely seen blubbing like it from a licensed professional, but the crowd loved Greatrex even more for the rarity value of his emotional breakdown. It was a first win at the festival and at the top level for the former jump jockey, with a supposedly unsound horse who had been snapped up by Greatrex and his bloodstock agent wife Tessa for less than £30,000 and passed on to loyal owners Robin and Jill Eynon, so the tears were thoroughly justifiable, and although he spent the precious moments between winning post and prize-giving urging himself to "be cool, be cool, be cool", his coolness was the first thing that deserted him.

Winning jockey Gavin Sheehan, also enjoying his first festival success, went so far as to call his boss "a big girl" – reasoning, no doubt, that you're not going to get the sack when you've just delivered a peach of a ride to land one of the biggest races in the calendar – and Greatrex himself was a little bashful once he had regained his composure. Yet the scenes provided one of the great highlights of the four days and came as no great surprise to paddock watchers who had witnessed Greatrex's pre-race pep talk to the young rider being groomed for great things at the famous Uplands yard in Upper Lambourn.

Greatrex had seen his prodigy "fall off" the stable's Seedling in the Supreme Novices' Hurdle and reckoned he needed a confidence boost; the young man from Cork saw things rather differently, recounting the tale of a "slightly crazy" man and recalling how, by the end of the adrenaline-fuelled outburst, "I thought I was going into the boxing ring rather than on to a racecourse". Whatever the truth of the matter, it certainly didn't do any harm.

Greatrex, 40, three years into life at Uplands after nine years as assistant to Oliver Sherwood and three working for major owner Malcolm Denmark, went into Cheltenham believing he had a serious horse on his hands but knowing that the beast named after a Wild West movie hero (the son of Westerner has the name of a character played by Gary Cooper in the film The Westerner) would need everything to go right if he were to win this shootout.

The six-year-old had been revitalised by a wind operation after flopping on his previous run; the 22-year-old Sheehan had been psyched up whether he needed it or not; all of which meant Greatrex had done all he could and now had to leave it to horse and rider to get it right on the track.

He needn't have been concerned

about either of them. Sheehan had already shown an aptitude for drawing the best from a willing horse and it was an ability that stood him in good stead when Greatrex urged him to "go hard and leave nothing out there".

Encouraged by two racecourse gallops and the considered views of head man Graham Baines, Sheehan felt empowered to take Cole Harden to his outer limits and ensure that any rival wanting to pass him would have a pain barrier to contend with. He set off in front, daring the others to go with him, shrugged off mistakes at the seventh and eighth hurdles to re-establish a clear lead, met the final three obstacles in his stride and stretched for home.

"After the second last, I thought we were going to get swallowed up," admitted Sheehan, "but I felt him stick his head down and then we were going for gold."

Saphir Du Rheu tried hard to bridge the gap and Zarkandar plugged on gamely, but Cole Harden had been delivered "on the money" by his rising star of a trainer and ridden with verve by a gifted man with the confidence of youth on his side, and had enough wind left in his sails to prevail by three and a half lengths.

As the crowd cheered the new champion staying hurdler back into the enclosure, a well of emotion was about to erupt, reassuring all those present that winning at the Cheltenham Festival really does matter.

RISING STARS

Uplands pairing on the up

Cole Harden's Ladbrokes World Hurdle win was the highlight of another upwardly mobile season for Warren Greatrex and stable jockey Gavin Sheehan.

Greatrex, who moved into Upper Lambourn's historic Uplands yard with 15 horses three years ago, is now operating at full capacity of 75. Last season he was 18th in the trainers' table after recording a seasonal-best 51 winners, more than three times the total in his first campaign at Uplands.

A key contribution has been made by Sheehan, whose star has risen in unison with Greatrex's growing success. The 22-year-old from County Cork won the British conditionals' title with 50 winners in the 2013-14 season, his first with Greatrex, and last season jumped to 71, putting him eighth in the jockeys' table.

"We've got a good partnership and a good understanding," Greatrex said early last season, which turned out so well for them. "I know how I like it done and he's fitted into that well. Tactically he's very good, he's very good from the front, he's very strong, very good over an obstacle, he's very self-critical, he's hungry.

"We're both hungry, we're going up together and neither of us wants to let the other down. We're competitive and it drives both of us on."

The drive and ambition, as well as Sheehan's front-running acumen, was crystal clear at Cheltenham.

▸▸On top of the world: (clockwise from left) Warren Greatrex in the winner's enclosure; Gavin Sheehan crosses the line; the pair together after their first festival win; Sheehan is congratulated by Daryl Jacob

1914 – 1919
1939 – 1945
TO THE MEMORY OF
THE MEN OF THIS PARISH
WHO LAID DOWN THEIR LIVES
IN THE GREAT WAR:

THE BIGGER PICTURE

Nick Devenish, vicar of Cartmel Priory and chaplain to the racecourse, says a special prayer after Sunday service to bless the horses racing at Cartmel on August bank holiday Monday. Pictured is May's Boy, ridden by his lass Charlotte Jones and led by trainer Jimmy Moffatt's wife Nadine. Unfortunately May's Boy unseated the next day, but he was unhurt and Moffatt still won the race with Captain Brown

JOHN GROSSICK (RACINGPOST.COM/PHOTOS)

Grand National hero Many Clouds put trainer Oliver Sherwood back in the big time and brought more Aintree glory for jockey Leighton Aspell and owner Trevor Hemmings

MANY HAPPY RETURNS

By Peter Thomas

THE result of the 2015 Grand National will appear as a neat and unwrinkled line in the record books: first Many Clouds, owned by Trevor Hemmings, trained by Oliver Sherwood and ridden by Leighton Aspell, the distances were a length and three-quarters and six lengths, the price of the winning horse was 25-1.

The bare facts will tell nothing like the true story. The online form book won't mention the resolutely old-school trainer who had gone out of fashion with the mullet and the SodaStream; the jaded jockey who had retired and crossed over to the dark side of Flat racing; the weary horse who was packed and ready for the summer holidays when his undaunted owner took fate into his own hands.

This being the Grand National, however, the tale, having been played out in front of a TV audience of 500 million people, will pass into legend and be recounted whenever the world's favourite race leaps spring-heeled into the consciousness. "That's what the National brings to the sport," Sherwood, 60, reaffirms with a smile. "There's always a story and this one changed my life."

The story of Many Clouds – at least the part of it that was scripted – began at Christmas 2013, when the promising son of Cloudings won a novice chase at Wetherby that had the Upper Lambourn trainer making uncharacteristically bold predictions about his future. "I said then that if we looked after him, he could be a proper Hennessy horse," he remembers. "That was a plan, but it was the only bit we planned. The rest of it just happened."

Even then, fate wasn't averse to intervening, when Many Clouds was brought down in the RSA Chase at the 2014 Cheltenham Festival. From the outside it may have looked like a deathly blow to

» *Continues page 110*

CRABBIE'S
2
CRABBIE'S
MANY CLOUDS

the team at Rhonehurst, but Sherwood looks back on it as the prelude to greater glory. Few could have predicted that such an inglorious afternoon would be followed by a season that was to bring the greatest public honour jump racing can bestow, but Sherwood, admittedly with the assistance of hindsight, appreciates the first twist in the tale.

"If he'd stayed on his feet that day, he would have had to be in the first three," he says, "and that would have been the Hennessy out of the window from a handicapping point of view. It was a blessing in disguise." Defeat at Aintree the following month was quickly dismissed as a course-related blip and a reappearance victory at Carlisle seven months later was duly followed by a Hennessy win that sparked tumultuous celebrations. The epicentre may have been at Newbury but the reverberations were felt the length and breadth of National Hunt country.

Here was a trainer who had been schooled in the old-fashioned arts by Arthur Moore and Fred Winter, announced himself on the scene with festival victories for the likes of Rebel Song and The West Awake in the 1980s, continued the success through the 1990s with Large Action, Young Pokey and Berude Not To, then disappeared into the wilderness of the Noughties with an efficacy that would have made Lord Lucan look like a shameless self-publicist.

His popularity among his peers never waned, but his fame and fortune decamped as the game changed around this staunch champion of outmoded concepts such as the store horse and the long haul. Where others might have been tempted to change their ways, however, Sherwood waited out the lean years, resisted the temptation to ignore the lessons of his tutors and gradually put together a small group of young horses who could take him back to the big meetings with some live chances.

****

ALONGSIDE Sherwood was Aspell, 39, another man on a second coming. Worn down by the hard yards on the motorways of Britain and lean times that had included a six-winner season and a losing streak of 138 rides, the jockey had packed in the game eight years earlier and taken up a job with his local trainer John Dunlop in West Sussex. The man from Kildare started to plan for life as a trainer, until realising the error of his ways and performing a sheepish U-turn, back into the welcoming arms of his old guv'nor Sherwood, with whom he enjoyed a glorious mutual resurgence.

The only complication was that, while Sherwood was busy planning a spring campaign for Many Clouds, Aspell was anticipating the renewal of his acquaintance with Pineau De Re, his partner in a memorable Grand National success the previous year.

For a while, it seemed as though the point was purely an academic one. Many Clouds ran a minor stinker in the Cheltenham Gold Cup, with his lacklustre sixth in stark contrast to his trial win over course and distance two months earlier.

Sherwood was dejected, clinging to the belief that it was the run of a tired horse rather than an outclassed one, ready to send the eight-year-old off for a well-earned summer break. Aspell was seemingly reduced to a choice of one for his National ride, but the horse and his owner had other ideas.

Hemmings, cloth cap-wearing businessman, property tycoon, fixture on the Sunday Times Rich List, owner of Preston North End, had already won two Nationals, with Hedgehunter in 2005 and Ballabriggs in 2011, and thus had every right to his opinion about Many Clouds. He wasn't insisting, of course, but he was keen, and when his racing manager Mike Meagher went to Rhonehurst in the aftermath of Cheltenham, it was with the treble very much in mind, and as a counter-balance to the trainer's natural tendencies.

"Was I being over-cautious?" Sherwood asks himself. "Probably. We've all got weaknesses and one of mine is that I'm over-cautious, but my natural concern was that I didn't know what had happened in the Gold Cup, and I still don't know to this day what happened, and we'll probably never know.

"He'd disappointed us that day. In our heart of hearts we knew he hadn't

▸▸ Growing force: (from left) Many Clouds and Leighton Aspell (right) make their way to the Lambourn schooling grounds in March; the Oliver Sherwood-trained chaser (right) scores his first big win of last season in the Hennessy at Newbury; another major success for Many Clouds (centre) in the BetBright Cup Chase at Cheltenham

'Deep down I was terrified something terrible would happen at Aintree and I wouldn't get the horse back, which is natural with a trainer with a small amount of horses'

run his race and I felt it was a year too soon to go for the National, but we did a few tests and he was fine, I did nothing with him for two weeks bar a little hack here and there, and Nathan Horrocks, who rides him every day, insisted he was fine.

"We had it in our minds that he'd possibly had one race too many and may have gone over the top, but two weeks after the race he did a little bit of light work, and I said to Mick, 'he's fit and healthy, what do we do?'

"Mick said if he was fit and well, he'd run in the National. It was either that or out in the field – the National or nothing. Deep down I was terrified something terrible would happen at Aintree and I wouldn't get the horse back, which is natural with a trainer with a small amount of horses, but I utterly respect and adore Trevor, so I said 'we've nothing to lose, go on, have a crack'."

For Aspell, the temptation to stick with Pineau De Re was outweighed by his loyalty to Sherwood and his belief in Many Clouds. "We'd planned to wrap him up and go for some big races next year," he confesses, "so it was a surprise he still had the energy for the race after the year he'd had. Everybody's admiration for him trebled, quadrupled, and for me there was really no choice."

HEAVY HITTER

With 11st 9lb Many Clouds carried the biggest weight to victory since Red Rum shouldered 12st to win the second of his three Grand Nationals in 1974. Although the 2015 winner was raised 7lb in the official ratings after his Aintree success, he cannot carry more than the 11st 10lb topweight limit if he returns to defend his title.

Phil Smith, the BHA's chief handicapper, was so impressed he felt the eight-year-old's performance was at least the best since 1998. "He's won off 160 and he's the highest-rated horse to win the National since Red Rum," Smith said. "It's a tricky one in terms of the best performance because in 1998 Suny Bay was second off 170, which was a fantastic performance.

"It should be an encouragement to the owners and trainers of those better horses, it's not necessarily going to be the weight that stops you. The most he can carry next year is a pound more. That's the maximum topweight but you never know, there might be something better than him entered in the race next year.

"The key thing is going to be the relativity of horses and how many pounds he is going to be giving other horses. If Many Clouds runs a couple of stinkers next year I'll ignore them because he's got the runs on the board. I know what he's capable of achieving on that ground in early April."

Weight for it: winning jockey Leighton Aspell

****

GIVEN the circuitous, nay helter-skelter, nature of the horse's route to Aintree, it would have been no surprise to see the resurgent trainer, the re-employed jockey and the insistent owner endure all manner of turmoil on the big day itself. Had Many Clouds dived into the Water or stopped for a rest in the Chair, connections would hardly have batted an eyelid, but with a firm grasp of the irony of the situation, he turned the race itself into the only straightforward part of the journey.

Aspell recalls sitting in the weighing room with pals Paul Moloney (fourth on Alvarado) and Wayne Hutchinson (pulled up on Godsmejudge) and plotting a middle-to-inner course that would hopefully keep them out of trouble.

He remains wide-eyed with incredulity as he relives the traffic jams on his outer, the "panoramic view" he had of the first half-dozen

Continues page 112

fences and the good fortune he enjoyed in evading loose horses and missing the carnage at the Canal Turn. Even when The Druids Nephew fell five from home and left Many Clouds in front, Aspell had on his side that priceless asset of equine courage. "He'd run into a concrete wall if I asked him," says the rider, but all that was required was for the bold beast to dig ever deeper as Saint Are laid down a late challenge, and the job was done.

In proving himself a modern master of Aintree, Aspell became the first jockey to win back-to-back Nationals since Brian Fletcher on Red Rum in 1973 and 1974, and the first to double up on different horses since Bryan Marshall on Early Mist in 1953 and Royal Tan in 1954.

In the owners' and trainers' stand, Sherwood grew ever more agitated as events unfolded. Normally a "good watcher of a race", he was turned by the National into a quivering wreck.

"Wherever he went, he had a clear run all the way round," remembers Sherwood. "I couldn't tell, I'd never had a horse finish the race, let alone win it, but after three or four fences it was clear he'd taken to it like a duck to water, and going out on the second circuit I thought 'hello, we're in with a squeak here'.

"I watched it with people I didn't know and who didn't know me, through my binoculars on the big screen. I picked him up early on and didn't move for four miles, but when we were still in front two out I started trembling, and after the last I just turned my back, listening to the commentary and shaking like a leaf at what was happening.

"It's a very emotional sport and if you can't get emotional about winning a Grand National then you shouldn't be in the bloody game. That's what we all do it for and I'm a very lucky man."

It was a third National for Hemmings, two in a row for Aspell and a defining moment for Sherwood.

▸▸ Heading for home: Many Clouds takes the final fence of the Grand National ahead of Saint Are

"Wherever I go, I still get people coming up to me and saying 'well done'," he beams, enjoying the deluge as thoroughly as he had previously endured the drought.

"I buy horses you've got to give a bit of time to, and it was a long time coming, but if you've got the right owners, with the patience and the bank balance to give them time, it will pay off in the end."

****

ONCE again, the Grand National passed by without fatality and with a reaffirmation of public affection for it, but for a few brief moments after the race there were fears that Many Clouds, having gone to the bottom of the well for Aspell, was tottering and on the point of collapse.

The rider appreciated the horse's efforts more than anybody but was unperturbed by the wobbles that followed. "He was incredibly brave and gave me every last bit of energy, as you could see afterwards," he says.

▸▸ *Continues page 114*

CUSHION TRACK™
EQUESTRIAN SURFACES
Cushion Track™ has a proven track record
Cushion Track is a recognised product which has been supplied at national and international racing and training tracks.
Cushion Track is a product which is entirely manufactured in the UK, its synthetic make up rendering it virtually indestructible. This ensures the Cushion Track surface is consistent in all weathers. This consistency allows for safer training and racing throughout the year, allowing the horse to grow in confidence after every run, transpiring into winners.
Cushion Track is the only surface which is manufactured to ISO 9001 UKAS accredited standards, thus guaranteeing YOU a quality, consistent product.
Charlie Mann, Racehorse Trainer
"Since installing Cushion Track Premier in 2006, the surface has become widely known as the best surface in Lambourn. Younger horses can work for longer, without soreness and we are able to use it 365 days of the year."
TO VIEW OUR FULL RANGE OF SURFACES VISIT OUR WEBSITE
Tel: 0800 652 0810
www.equestriansurfaces.co.uk
Equestrian Surfaces
@ESurfaces

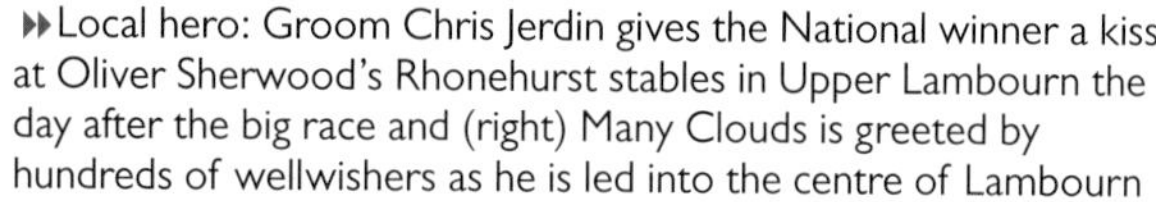
▸▸Local hero: Groom Chris Jerdin gives the National winner a kiss at Oliver Sherwood's Rhonehurst stables in Upper Lambourn the day after the big race and (right) Many Clouds is greeted by hundreds of wellwishers as he is led into the centre of Lambourn

"He just got a bit hot but he was fine once they got the cold water on him and his temperature came down.

"I was really pleased in the press coverage that nobody made a meal of it. It's an extreme distance wherever you run it and an extreme test once a year, but I don't think it's unfair. They're very fit, well-trained animals doing what they're bred for on decent ground."

"He's in his prime," confirms Sherwood, "and he loved the post-National celebrity status, being horse of the year, meeting the Queen at Newbury, being patted all the time. I'll never forget what he and the great race did for me."

THREE TIMER

Trevor Hemmings became the joint most successful owner in Grand National history when Many Clouds added to the tycoon's earlier victories with Hedgehunter (2005) and Ballabriggs (2011).

He is the fourth owner to win the race on three occasions and only the second in the past 100 years after Noel Le Mare's famous hat-trick with Red Rum in the 1970s. The other two on the list – like Hemmings – won with three different horses, but Hemmings stands alone in sharing his success with three trainers. Along with Many Clouds' trainer Oliver Sherwood, Hemmings has also won with Willie Mullins (Hedgehunter) and Donald McCain (Ballabriggs).

Hemmings, 80, whose love affair with the National grew out of the 1971 success of his mentor Fred Pontin with Specify, was delighted with his latest victory. "This race captured my heart and it's such a lovely feeling to win it again. I always dreamed of winning the Grand National and then we won it. Then we won it again and it was something special, but now the third comes along. I just can't believe it. It's an amazing feeling."

Six weeks after Many Clouds' Aintree success, Hemmings celebrated a rare sporting double when Preston North End, the football club he has supported since boyhood and now owns, won the League One playoff final to secure promotion to the Championship.

"Preston was where I grew up and when the club got into difficulties, I was asked if I could help and I did. I kept financing it and became the owner," he said. "We've been very fortunate to win the Grand National and get promotion all within a couple of months. It can't get much better than that, can it?"

OWNERS WITH THREE GRAND NATIONAL WINS

James Machell Disturbance 1873, Reugny 1874, Regal 1876; **Sir Charles Assheton-Smith, previously Charles Duff** Cloister 1893, Jerry M 1912, Covertcoat 1913; **Noel Le Mare** Red Rum 1973, 1974 and 1977; **Trevor Hemmings** Hedgehunter 2005, Ballabriggs 2011, Many Clouds 2015

WELCOME TO 2016

- One of only 3 fully floodlit courses in the UK
- Currently listed in top 15 courses in terms of prize money
- Recently re-waxed and up-graded Martin Collins polytrack surface
- Left handed, one mile round course
- Highly acclaimed stable facilities and stable lads canteen area
- Exclusive Owners & Trainers area with further expansion planned
- Two à la carte restaurants
- Regular post-racing entertainment

JANUARY

[illegible]	Saturday	AFT
[illegible]	Sunday	AFT
[illegible]	Wednesday	AFT
[illegible]	Thursday	TWI
13	Wednesday	AFT
14	Thursday	TWI
16	Saturday	AFT
21	Thursday	TWI
24	Sunday	AFT
28	Thursday	TWI

FEBRUARY

4	Thursday	TWI
7	Sunday	AFT
11	Thursday	TWI
18	Thursday	TWI
25	Thursday	TWI

MARCH

3	Thursday	TWI
10	Thursday	TWI
11	Friday	TWI
17	Thursday	TWI
31	Thursday	TWI

APRIL

7	Thursday	TWI
14	Thursday	TWI
28	Thursday	EVE

MAY

4	Wednesday	EVE

JUNE

1	Wednesday	EVE
15	Wednesday	EVE
16	Thursday	AFT

JULY

11	Monday	AFT
19	Tuesday	EVE

AUGUST

2	Tuesday	EVE
7	Sunday	AFT
15	Monday	AFT
20	Saturday	EVE
21	Sunday	AFT
23	Tuesday	EVE

SEPTEMBER

1	Thursday	TWI
8	Thursday	TWI
11	Sunday	AFT
15	Thursday	TWI
22	Thursday	TWI
29	Thursday	TWI

OCTOBER

6	Thursday	TWI
13	Thursday	TWI
20	Thursday	TWI
22	Saturday	TWI
26	Wednesday	AFT
27	Thursday	TWI
29	Saturday	TWI

NOVEMBER

3	Thursday	TWI
5	Saturday	TWI
10	Thursday	TWI
17	Thursday	TWI
21	Monday	AFT
24	Thursday	TWI

DECEMBER

1	Thursday	TWI
8	Thursday	TWI
15	Thursday	TWI
19	Monday	AFT
22	Thursday	AFT

find us at ChelmsfordCRC

AFT = AFTERNOON TWI = TWILIGHT EVE = EVENING

follow us @ChelmsfordCRC

Chelmsford City Racecourse, Moulsham Hall Lane, Great Leighs, Chelmsford CM3 1QP

www.chelmsfordcityracecourse.com Telephone: 01245 360300

Clerk of the Course: Andy Waitt • General Manager: Fraser Garrity

CENTRE STAGE

Nick Luck joined an illustrious list of presenters when he fronted coverage of the Grand National for the first time

By Lee Mottershead

FROM the first televising of the Grand National in 1960 just five individuals had greeted mainstream television viewers prior to this year's race. David Coleman, Frank Bough, Desmond Lynam, Sue Barker and Clare Balding had all done the coveted job during the long BBC era, with Balding also taking the helm for Channel 4's first two runnings of the world's most famous horserace. In 2015 Nick Luck became the sixth presenter to join that small and select group.

The multi-award-winning Luck became a contender for the job as a

'About 15 minutes before the race, when the national anthem was played and the intensity started, it did begin to hit me'

result of Balding's decision to anchor the Boat Race on the BBC, which for the first time also included live coverage of the women's event.

With Balding having limited her racing workload to just the Cheltenham Festival and Royal Ascot, various names were touted for the Aintree hotseat. This was perhaps inevitable after Channel 4 said Luck would lead the team when Balding was not present but left open the question of the biggest job of all by delaying the announcement of its Grand National squad. John Inverdale was seen as an obvious candidate, while avid racing fan Jeremy Kyle was suggested by some. Luck waited. The wait was worthwhile.

"I'm not sure if any of the really outlandish suggestions ever made it past first base," Luck says. "Channel 4 look at the broadest possible picture for what is their biggest event in terms of prestige and audience figures. Clearly I wanted to do it, and I'm lucky they had the faith in me to let me do it. It was a real honour to have been able to front the Grand National."

Reflecting on his part in bringing the triumph of Many Clouds to a peak audience of 8.8 million, Luck, 37, says: "You can stick the magnitude of the event and the knowledge so many millions are watching to the side of your mind, but about 15 minutes before the race, when the national anthem was played and the intensity started, it did begin to hit me. By that time we'd been on air for three hours, so it's not a bad thing to find yourself being stoked up a bit. You need that extra bit of adrenaline to push you to the end. But I felt good through it and I enjoyed it, I really did.

"Through the race I was listening as much as watching, taking on board the observations the production team were making in my ear. Carl Hicks [the executive producer] is very good at picking out stories, either good or bad, while at the same time observing the sensitivities that apply to the Grand National, and the obvious one this year was Balthazar King. As soon as he went down at the Canal Turn I was thinking, how are we going to deal with this after the race? He had finished second last year and we had done a story on him before the race, so this was a key point to get clarity on. We wanted to get something factual out as quickly as possible.

"Then as soon as Many Clouds passed the line he started to wobble. Fortunately we had Alice Plunkett on the track as senior reporter. She was passing messages back through the gallery that I was able to relay to Oliver Sherwood. We were asking him to be euphoric at the greatest moment of his career while also reassuring him that his horse was all right.

"Everyone on our production team was happy with the programme and to be part of it was a real thrill. As a group I think we got it pretty much where we wanted it this year."

Only two months after Aintree there was another first for Luck when he took over from Balding at Epsom, where she had anchored the Derby, first for the BBC and then Channel 4, from 2001. While Channel 4 has managed largely to keep pace with BBC ratings for the Grand National, there has been a significant decline of viewers for both the premier Classic – even with the Frankie Dettori factor this year – and Royal Ascot. Luck is sanguine about the situation. "Viewing figures for major events rest on the sort of media exposure they receive in the lead-up. On Monday morning of Grand National week you flick on a radio station and someone is talking about it. It retains its position in the national psyche but the Derby has slightly lost its position.

"I would be quite surprised if more people don't watch it next year because of this year's result. It might give it a bounce, but I'm not sure there's much more we, as the racing media, can do."

It is impossible not to connect the fall in viewers with the switch of channels. In the first quarter of 2016 racing's rights holders must decide which channel will screen racing's biggest days from 2017 onwards. Luck, understandably, makes a strong case for the IMG-produced Channel 4.

"I'm pretty sure the programmes have got better through the contract," he says. "As a team we're making some good TV, especially at those big events. I think people would struggle to say it's not well-made television but that's not to say anyone at Channel 4 or IMG is resting on laurels.

"Channel 4 is an incredibly committed partner for the sport and in a TV age where those sorts of partnerships are not exactly commonplace, it's one the sport would have to think very carefully about placing under threat.

"The level of interest in racing at Channel 4 comes from the very top. That is something that isn't perhaps wholly appreciated."

Clearly appreciated more than ever before by Channel 4 is Luck himself. Due to Channel 4 commitments he had to scale down his visits to America but he was still part of NBC's team for the Breeders' Cup, while for his main employer he also hosted the Arc and Qipco British Champions Day for the first time.

Luck says: "I don't think my standing has massively increased but I guess gradually the job has become more high-profile. However, you can get bogged down in the minutiae of your own career progression. Who does what on TV is always a source of disproportionate fascination. You have to balance your ego against the opportunities you know you're lucky enough to get. There would be many who would give their right arm to be in my position and I understand that.

"While I really enjoyed fronting the Grand National and the Derby, and would love to do them again, I'm very fortunate to be main-hosting or co-hosting every big racing event.

"If you said to me, do I want to be fronting the Grand National next year, the answer is self-evident: of course I do. And do I want to be doing it in perpetuity, of course I do. But you have to accept there's always a multitude of factors to take into account."

Not in doubt is that Luck will most regularly welcome viewers to Channel 4 Racing in 2016. He will do so having excelled in the most important year of his career so far.

RESCUE ACT

Many feared the worst when Balthazar King crashed out of the Grand National but he was saved by prompt medical attention and the love and care of his connections

By Steve Dennis

THE Grand National is a famously searching test of its competitors, and a soul-searching test of those watching from the sidelines. The world's greatest race – it seems a fair appellation – is also the world's most scrutinised race, and during its ten-minute span we hold our breath that those we counted out will match those we count back in.

Adaptations to the race after the 2012 running were focused firmly on the safety angle and they were considered hugely successful given that the next two renewals were joyously free from any equine-related disaster, the likes of which are keenly anticipated by the more lunatic strands of the animal-rights fringe, for whom an anguish-free National seems a distinct disappointment. But last season's race was third time unlucky, especially for the Philip Hobbs-trained Balthazar King.

The popular 11-year-old, runner-up in the National 12 months earlier behind Pineau De Re, was third favourite to go one better and was bowling along happily in mid-division under Richard Johnson when fate intervened at the eighth fence, the Canal Turn first time. Balthazar King seemed to take off half a stride too soon, crashed through the top of the fence and went sprawling. Given the number of runners still in contention at that early stage it was odds-on that his flailing legs would bring down someone, and Ballycasey was the unlucky horse to be knocked over. The collision was a heavy one.

Ballycasey got to his feet and ran off; Balthazar King lay ominously still, a brown puddle of horseflesh in the background of the picture, quickly surrounded by green screens. The field rolled on over the next fence and our attention inevitably went with it, but all the time a little alarm bell was ringing in the back of the mind. The incident looked like a heart-breaker. Anatomically at least, it was thereabouts.

After the race, after the head count, Balthazar King was missing, down at the Canal Turn, still down. The impact with Ballycasey had broken several of his ribs and he received treatment on the course before being moved to the University of Liverpool's Philip Leverhulme Equine Hospital. At hand was Dr Ellen Singer, the university's senior lecturer in equine orthopaedics.

"During the Grand National there's a vet at every other fence, so Balthazar King received immediate treatment on the course," she told the Liverpool Echo a few days later. "It was lucky that he came here so quickly by horse ambulance and has responded well to treatment, because if a decision had been made to just monitor his condition for an hour or so at the course we could have had a very different outcome.

"Since being here he's been given oxygen and a lot of pain relief and we've been closely monitoring his breathing. He's still got an IV line in and a bandage around his chest to keep him stable. We're just doing what we can to make sure he's comfortable.

"The first couple of days he was very quiet, but now he's quite bright and eager to eat, which is a good sign."

Every pet owner knows that the inclination to eat is a crucial turning point in recovery, and upbeat bulletins were soon being eagerly absorbed by the gelding's legion of fans and the wider world in general. Six days after the fall there was a photo in the Racing Post of Balthazar King wearing a bright red bandage around his

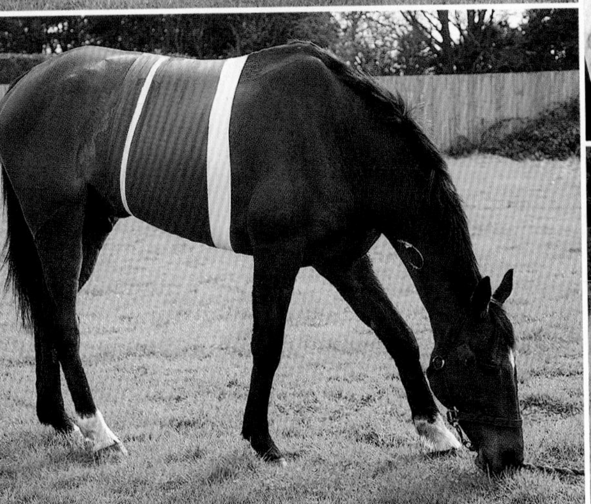

▸▸ National health service: (from far left) Balthazar King exercises on Philip Hobbs's gallops last season; at the University of Liverpool's Equine Hospital the week after his fall in the Grand National; with his get-well-soon cards; and out at summer grass

midriff, a horse in a crop-top beginning his convalescence, accompanied by encouraging news that he'd been led out for a pick of grass.

The worst was over; there would be no 'worst' as far as Balthazar King was concerned. Given his status as a much-loved elder statesman of jump racing, relief shone through on social media. It was that invigorating brand of sincere, heartfelt relief from the sport's devotees that can be imagined being accompanied by a brief fist-pump and a barely stifled 'yessss'. Someone else's horse? No, ours.

We all know the dangers inherent in the sport, we all strike an occasionally uneasy bargain with circumstance, we all wear our hearts on our sleeves in the certain knowledge that one day they may be broken. But not this time. Not by Balthazar King. Steadily, his condition improved.

By the end of May he was back on his joint-owner's farm in Hampshire, ready for a few months of sunshine, looking over a stable door papered with get-well-soon cards, that bizarre yet heartwarming manifestation of our anthropomorphism towards our four-legged friends.

"We have put him in a barn with his two mates, Roalco De Farges and Pateese. He loves it up there," said David Rees. "We just want to get him fit and well again. He's been a marvellous horse and owes us nothing, but hopefully we'll get him back racing. If it's not to be then he'll always have a good home here on the farm.

"He's been in the wars before and bounced back, as he broke a cheekbone when kicked in the face after being carried out in a cross-country event at Cheltenham in December 2011, so we know he's very tough.

"We desperately want to return to Cheltenham, where we've won eight races with him, but I can't imagine he'll ever run in the Grand National again. I don't think our wives would allow that."

That was the burning question – would Balthazar King race again? Broken ribs are no great impediment when compared with tendon injuries and the like, and although most people would stand four-square with the aforementioned "our wives" in preferring Balthazar King to steer clear of Aintree in future, a return to action was eminently possible. At his stable open day at the end of August, Hobbs offered a bright prognosis of his veteran's prospects.

"Balthazar King is still with his owners but had some x-rays done last week, along with some tests on his lungs, and I understand they all came back very positive," Hobbs said.

"The plan, if all goes well, will be for him to come back into training some time in December with a view to running in the cross-country chase at the Cheltenham Festival, which is now a conditions race and not a handicap.

"Whatever happens it's brilliant news for the horse and much more positive than it looked a month or so after the accident, as things were definitely not great for a while."

Things were definitely not great when Balthazar King was lying in a heap at the back of the Canal Turn. Enough tears have been shed in sorrow at Aintree in recent years, fortunately, thanks to the skill of the vets and Balthazar King's sturdy constitution, this wasn't the time for them. Should Balthazar King win the cross-country chase for a third time at Cheltenham next March and walk back in triumph before the seething grandstands, tears of joy instead will be sprinkled liberally among the cheers at this happiest of endings.

IN THE PICTURE

Walsh an Australian National hero as he scores on Bashboy

Ruby Walsh added an unusual entry to his glittering roll of honour in August when he made a flying visit across the globe to win the Australian Grand National on Bashboy, giving him a fifth different National following his victories in the English, Irish, Scottish and Welsh versions.

In a dramatic, emotion-charged finish, Walsh (pictured jumping the last) galvanised the 12-year-old to score by half a length in the A$250,000 (£120,000/€170,000) race over two miles, six and a half furlongs at Ballarat racecourse, an hour north-west of Melbourne. The Ciaron Maher-trained Bashboy became the first horse to win the race three times, carrying the highest weight (11st 10lb) to victory since 1957.

Walsh, riding in Australia for the first time, was overcome with delight as he returned to a rousing reception. "What a horse," he said. "The horse on my inside nearly fell at the second-last and I almost came off, but when I got him back on an even keel he started rallying and I knew I had a good shout. It's a pleasure to ride such a wonderful horse. He's a bloody good jumper."

The ride on Bashboy arose by pure chance. The race had been scheduled for July 26, but with Sandown – which normally hosts the Grand National – undergoing renovations, the meeting was transferred to Ballarat. However, wet weather forced a postponement and, in the meantime, Bashboy's regular jockey Steve Pateman incurred a careless riding ban, which ruled him out.

Maher came up with the idea of asking Walsh, who said the approach to partner Bashboy had come in "a very unexpected phone call".

Walsh's surprise appearance created excitement in Australia and the Ballarat Turf Club offered free entry for what it billed as a once-in-a-lifetime opportunity for jump racing fans to see Australia's "best steeplechaser of recent times together with the world's best jump jockey".

An estimated 3,000 racegoers, more than ten times the usual crowd for a provincial Sunday meeting, turned up, and among them was Jim Flanagan, a jumps enthusiast who had made the two-hour trip from Warrnambool. "I haven't slept since I heard he was coming, I honestly haven't slept," he said. "I said to my daughters, 'if there's any person I'd rather have come, I can't think of them'. This is as good as it gets for someone like me."

Walsh was just as pleased to have made the trip. "As a jump jockey you don't get many opportunities to ply your trade abroad. I'm over the moon I was asked to come, even happier he won. I really enjoyed the experience."

Picture: VINCE CALIGIURI/GETTY IMAGES

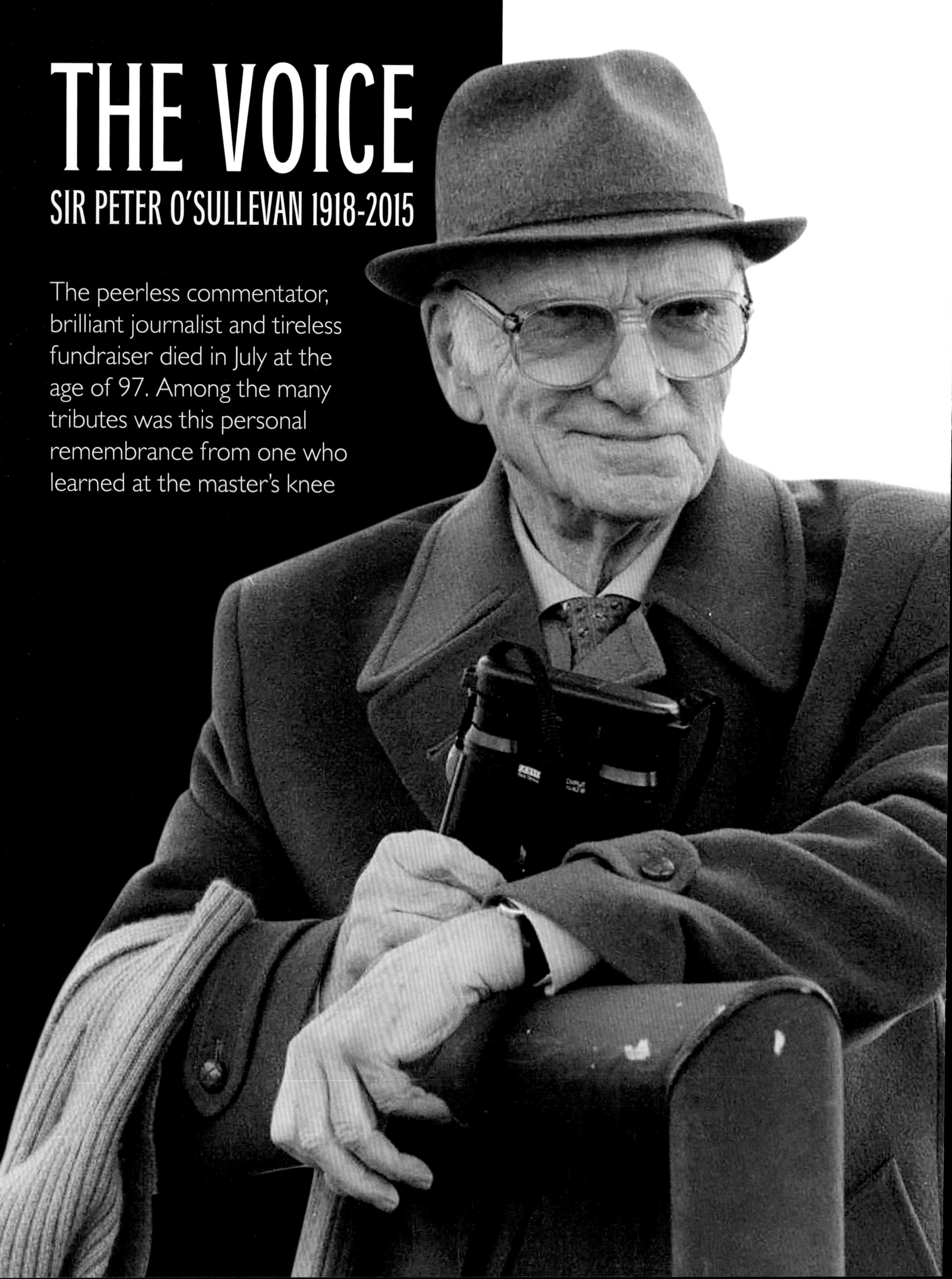

THE VOICE

SIR PETER O'SULLEVAN 1918-2015

The peerless commentator, brilliant journalist and tireless fundraiser died in July at the age of 97. Among the many tributes was this personal remembrance from one who learned at the master's knee

By Brough Scott

IN the early days Peter O'Sullevan was more famous for his column in the Daily Express than for broadcasting on the BBC, where betting was still taboo. A sense of news from the inside has always been addictive stuff. O'Sullevan, with his unfeigned friendships with everyone from Aly Khan to his ubiquitous 'Bert From The Garage', with his travels to the strange distant racing land that was France, with his ante-post coups and genuine scoops, was the most addictive there ever was or ever will be.

Of course the voice was too. For me it had been there almost from the beginning. At the very start there had been the frenetic radio mastery of Raymond Glendenning, but once the arrival of TV had revealed old Raymond as half a furlong behind the action, it was O'Sullevan behind the pictures. That honeyed mix, somewhere between Noel Coward and Michael O'Hehir, became a central part of the great occasions. It was racing's good fortune that it was the most skilled, passionate and eloquent of any voice in any sport.

In 1952 I had the good luck to be ill and at home during the Cheltenham Festival. It was the first time I had seen racing on TV. The flashy young chestnut Mont Tremblant won the Gold Cup, the super professional Sir Ken took the Champion Hurdle. The set was black and white. Sir Peter put the colour in.

But it was only half of O'Sullevan. He was no 'look-at-me' TV host and you hardly ever saw him in vision. Away from the screen he was a reserved figure who steered clear of the press pack, a wolf who liked to walk alone but also a gourmet who valued good friendship as much as fine wine. He was a perfectionist with an art-lined flat in Chelsea but was never afraid of the hard miles on the open road.

It had been with Peter on the BBC that I had made my first broadcast at Newbury. As my throat tightened in terror he gave out the most generous and gentle of verbal baton passes and somehow there was my voice saying something fairly unintelligible about how Joe Mercer rode horses to the start.

Continues page 124

Life's work: (clockwise from top left) Peter O'Sullevan on his last day as BBC commentator for the 1997 Hennessy Gold Cup at Newbury; the Queen Mother receives a bronze casting of O'Sullevan's binoculars for her lifetime contribution to racing; O'Sullevan with Be Friendly after victory in the Vernons Sprint Cup at Haydock; O'Sullevan with his wife Patricia at Buckingham Palace after he was knighted in 1997

GREATNESS SHARED

Sir Peter O'Sullevan was not the only commentating legend to pass away in 2015; three months before his death the world of sport had mourned Richie Benaud, widely regarded as the voice of cricket.

While he was still a player with Australia, Benaud was planning for a later career in broadcasting and in 1956 he went on a course specially devised for him by the BBC, which involved watching and learning from the best sports commentators of the day.

One was O'Sullevan, and Benaud later acknowledged his debt to his fellow titan of the commentary box.

"He was the best-organised man I ever saw," Benaud, who died in April aged 84, told BBC Radio 5 Live. "I went with him to Newbury races and saw exactly how to organise for a television day. The producer said to me 'just trail around on his coat-tails'. We were introduced and Peter said, 'Walk behind me, say nothing. Make your notes, at the end of the day we'll have a few beers and we'll see what you've got.'

"That, in itself, taught me something – that's why it's not unusual for me to be first into the commentary box a couple of hours before the start of play, checking everything, making sure I've got the right books and references. That goes straight down to Peter O'Sullevan and his organisation."

▶▶National treasure: (clockwise from top left) Peter O'Sullevan with his beloved Attivo; next to a bust at Aintree honouring his 50 years as a racing broadcaster; at his annual awards lunch with Lester Piggott; jockeys lead a minute's applause for O'Sullevan at Goodwood the day after he died

A FULL LIFE

Full name Peter John O'Sullevan

Born March 3, 1918, Newcastle, County Down

Died July 29, 2015, Chelsea, London

Educated Charterhouse, Surrey; College Alpin, Switzerland

Married 1951 to Patricia Duckworth (died 2009)

Print career Racing correspondent for the Press Association 1945-1950, Daily Express 1950-1986, Today 1986-1987

Broadcasting career BBC television and radio 1946-1997; commentated on more than 14,000 races, including 50 Grand Nationals; 1949, first TV commentary at Kempton Park; 1953, became first regular BBC TV commentator to operate without a race-reader; 1960, first TV Grand National; 1980, commentated on first race transmitted by satellite from New York; 1997, final TV commentary on the Hennessy Cognac Gold Cup

Best horses owned Be Friendly (won Vernons Sprint Cup 1966 and 1967, King's Stand Stakes 1967, Prix de l'Abbaye 1968), Attivo (won Triumph Hurdle 1974, Chester Cup 1974, Northumberland Plate 1974)

Honours Appointed OBE in 1976 for services to broadcasting, CBE in 1991 for charity work, knighted in 1997 (the year of his retirement from broadcasting)

Elected to Jockey Club 1986

Charitable work 1983, embarked on fundraising for the International League for the Protection of Horses (also supported the Brooke Hospital for Animals and Thoroughbred Rehabilitation Centre among others); 1997, established the Sir Peter O'Sullevan Charitable Trust, raising more than £4m for six animal-related charities

In the years that followed he remained the staunchest of supporters no matter for whom I was working, no matter where we were. Even on the hairy occasion at the 1987 Irish Derby when he, I and Michael O'Hehir were left isolated on the grandstand roof while the crowds were evacuated because of a bomb scare. "What price," said O'Sullevan in the driest of tones, "they know something we don't?"

You will imagine the irony when we found ourselves at Aintree in the same circumstances ten years later. I was there not to broadcast, but to write an article about his 50th and final Grand National. We had climbed the 107 steps to the tin hutch of a commentary box for the earlier races. But when the evacuation order came we were down at the weighing room for one more check on the jockey colours adorning that giant, personalised racecard that for so long was his Grand National lifeline.

O'Sullevan was insistent we should climb the stairs again. "The captain should be on the bridge," he grumbled, "to tell everyone what is happening to the ship." It took three police inspectors to stop him.

"An even £100 it's a hoax," he said as we shuffled out of Aintree. "If we live, you pay. If we get blown to bits, I owe you a century." And with that he repaired to the hotel with Tony O'Hehir to yarn the night away with stories as magnificent as they were well lubricated.

Then, at the age of 79, it would have been reasonable to assume that is all he would do. But not a bit of it. The establishment of the Peter O'Sullevan Charitable Trust and the millions it raised for horse and human welfare charities has been one of his most astonishing achievements. For it makes you remember the real anger in his voice when he talked of those who sold stallions (not to mention food horses) into terrible conditions abroad.

You recall the firm but relentless way, starting with a column he wrote on a muddy day at Fontwell, in which he persuaded non-believers (including me) that we needed to do something about the whip.

A final memory comes from one clear, sunny and mercifully mild morning at the beginning of March last year. Trainers Jack Berry and Ian Balding and I were gathered at the Carlton Tower for the Godolphin Stable Staff Awards and felt we ought to walk across to Chelsea to pay our respects.

Peter and the flat were as elegant and welcoming as ever, with the familiar oils on the walls and the framed Sunday Times Best Seller list in the loo with the O'Sullevan autobiography Calling The Horses topping a field that included tomes by Denis Healey, Robin Day, Stephen Hawking and Prince Charles.

The day before had been his 96th birthday and there was a magnum of pink champagne already opened on the table with four fluted glasses waiting for their bounty. With rather pathetic over-eagerness I offered to pour and promptly let the bubbles froth over the top of the O'Sullevan flute. "No, no," chided the great perfectionist, taking the bottle from me and finishing the job without spilling a drop.

When the task was completed he sat down, raised a glass and said "Salut" to us. Then and now, it is we who should salute.

South Africa's Innovative Thoroughbred Sales Company

Cape Thoroughbred Sales

Founded in 2011, Cape Thoroughbred Sales has become South Africa's paramount bloodstock auction company in just 4 years.

The CAPE PREMIER YEARLING SALE, which takes place in January, is now considered South Africa's most important yearling sale.

January 2016 sees the inaugural running of the CTS MILLION DOLLAR for qualifying graduates of CTS yearling sales. CTS sponsors racing in the extent of R20,000,000 in South Africa.

SALES DATES 2016:

CAPE PREMIER YEARLING SALE
CTICC, Cape Town
21 - 22 January 2016

CTS MARCH YEARLING SALE
Durbanville, Cape Town
19 - 20 March 2016

EMPERORS PALACE SELECT YEARLING SALE
Emperors Palace, Johannesburg
16 April 2016

CTS AUGUST 2-Y-O SALE
Durbanville, Cape Town
August 2016

EMPERORS PALACE READY TO RUN SALE
Inanda Club, Johannesburg
October 2016

CTS READY TO RUN SALE
Durbanville, Cape Town
November 2016

VARIETY CLUB (SAF)
TIMEFORM 131

SOFT FALLING RAIN (SAF)
TIMEFORM 129

VERCINGETORIX (SAF)
TIMEFORM 124

It's A Lifestyle

Contact **Adrian Todd** (COO) **E**: adrian@cthbs.com or **Amanda Carey** (Sales Manager) **E**: amanda@cthbs.com
T: +27 (0) 21 873 0734 **M**: +27 (0) 82 465 4020 **W**: www.capethoroughbredsales.com
European Representatives: **Hermione Fitzgerald** **E**: hermionefitzgerald@gmail.com **M**: +44 (0) 78 3349 8373
Mick Flanagan **E**: mick@townleyhallbloodstock.com **M**: +353 86 609 8119

IN THE PICTURE

Young amateur rider Ferguson somersaults to instant celebrity

The most spectacular fall of the year had to be amateur rider Lewis Ferguson's somersault over the final fence after being fired off Merrion Square at Wincanton in April.

Ferguson, 18, was having his first ride over fences on the 4-9 shot and looked sure to win the 3m1½f hunter chase as he approached the final fence more than a length clear.

But a few strides before the fence, Merrion Square jinked before ejecting his rider, who was sent spinning after hitting the fence chest first. A gasp went up from the crowd as Ferguson landed heavily from the high-speed spin. However, within 20 seconds he was on his feet and happily he walked back into the changing room with nothing more than a graze to the bridge of his nose.

The following day Ferguson was elevated to sudden celebrity status after the photo and TV pictures of the fall made the national media, including the front page of the Racing Post.

"My Twitter and Facebook accounts have been going mad with everybody wishing me well and hoping that I'm okay. It's a bit different to see yourself all over the newspapers, but I don't suppose the publicity can do me any harm," said Ferguson, who developed his riding talents through pony racing in his home town of Hawick in the Scottish Borders and had joined champion trainer Paul Nicholls only five weeks earlier.

Ferguson, who had schooled Merrion Square in the week leading up to the Wincanton race, added: "He was hanging left coming to the last fence as if he was going to run out. He changed his legs and became unbalanced, then ducked right and I came out of the side door. I hit the fence chest-on and then somersaulted, but I stood up straight afterwards and I was fine."

Sam Twiston-Davies, Nicholls' stable jockey, watched the fall on TV in the Wincanton weighing room. "The atmosphere in there changed quite a lot when it happened," he said. "When we first saw it, it went very quiet. The minute we heard the commentator say Lewis was okay it went from worrying about how he was to saying things like 'we'll only give him a seven for that somersault as he didn't land on his feet'. Everyone, including Lewis, was able to look at the funny side of things, which I think is great.

"What I was impressed with was how Lewis walked straight into the weighing room after the fall with his head up. He took the incident on the chin and didn't throw a strop. He didn't go quiet, he just came in and spoke to us about it and was very good about it all."

Main picture: MATTHEW WEBB; screen shots: RACING UK

FIGHT TO THE FINISH

Controversy followed Postponed as he lost a bitter battle but then won the war in the King George

By Steve Dennis

IF THE course of 2015 resembled that of true love as far as Postponed and trainer Luca Cumani were concerned, there was at least the consolation of one day in the summer sun that would forever warm the long winter evenings. Cumani no longer has Postponed, but he'll always have Ascot.

It wasn't the highest-quality King George VI and Queen Elizabeth Stakes ever run, but it was certainly one of the most dramatic. And as Postponed inched out Eagle Top at the last gasp, it was easy to forget that the drama had not been confined solely to the last two furlongs of Ascot's short straight.

Five weeks earlier, Eagle Top and Postponed had finished second and third in the Hardwicke Stakes at Royal Ascot behind Snow Sky, which is where the saga started. After the race, Eagle Top's trainer

▸▸ Day of reckoning: (opposite page) Postponed (Andrea Atzeni, left) beats Eagle Top (Frankie Dettori) by a nose in the King George VI and Queen Elizabeth Stakes; (above) Postponed and Atzeni are led into the winner's enclosure; (below) Luca Cumani described his first win in the great race as "immensely pleasurable" but later came the bitter pill of having Postponed removed from his yard

John Gosden was evidently unhappy with the riding of Postponed's jockey Adam Kirby, sparking as catty a spat as you'll find at racing's top level.

"A certain jockey spent the whole of the race riding our horse, which we hadn't employed him to do. It's not clean racing and it's not intelligent," Gosden said. "This boy did not begin to keep his line from the start. He came across and cannoned into us. In my opinion it's unacceptable."

Then Cumani tossed in his two penn'orth, saying: "I think Frankie [Dettori, on Eagle Top] was as much at fault as Adam. Frankie was trying to keep Adam out and Adam was trying to get Frankie to go in. I think John's comment was fair from his point of view but could be replicated from our point of view."

It was clear that there was an undercurrent of bad feeling between the two Bury Road behemoths, and it was reported that Dettori and Kirby were no longer on speaking terms as the rematch in the King George approached. Of course, during the build-up, Eagle Top and Postponed were regarded as no more than supporting acts behind the top-of-the-bill Derby and Eclipse winner Golden Horn, who was widely expected to add Ascot's midsummer showpiece to the other jewels in his crown.

However, the fickle nature of an English summer meant the ground was considered too soft for the son of Cape Cross, who was withdrawn on the morning of the race. His absence diminished the contest considerably – the seven remaining runners could muster only three Group 1 wins between them, with two of those gained by the outsider Dylan Mouth in uncompetitive races in Italy. With no three-year-olds taking part, the race eventually resembled little more than a re-run of the Hardwicke. Not with identical personnel, though.

Kirby's place aboard Postponed was taken by Andrea Atzeni, who had ridden the colt to victory at Hamilton and York the previous summer. No reason for the switch was given by owner Sheikh Mohammed Obaid Al Maktoum – none needed to be – apart from the indication that Atzeni and Postponed had clearly worked well together before, so why not try it again?

Why not indeed? Postponed, at home on the sticky ground, was always in the vanguard and Atzeni committed him for home at the quarter-mile pole. Down the outside came Eagle Top, with Dettori on board again having switched from the absent Golden Horn, and battle was joined as they approached the furlong marker, with Eagle Top's smooth, sustained challenge soon taking him into the lead.

But then, in echo of the celebrated Grundy v Bustino showdown 40 years earlier, Postponed rallied courageously in the last 100 yards and – with Dettori perhaps less animated than ideal for a crucial few strides – Atzeni dropped his nose back in front right on the line. It was a wonderful finish, the sort of duel that lives long in the collective memory, and it had the pleasing outcome of providing Cumani with his first victory in the great race and with his first domestic Group 1 for a decade.

"It was immensely pleasurable to win," he said. "The King George is one of the major races of the year, a championship race, a defining moment in a horse's career, and a trainer's. I've been lucky enough to have the occasional good horse."

Although Postponed may have ridden his luck to find such an ordinary renewal of the race he was now a King George winner and the manner of his victory was thoroughly memorable. After such a kitchen-sink drama, it was the perfect punchline.

Not the perfect ending, though. In September, Sheikh Obaid announced he was removing all of his 35 horses from Cumani's yard – as well as Postponed, their number included Oaks third Lady Of Dubai and Group 2 winner Connecticut – and sending them to be trained by Roger Varian. Cumani took the blow stoically, no doubt privately wondering what more he might have done for an owner than win one of Britain's greatest races with a horse whose body of form did not entitle him to it, or, indeed, to win a Derby as he did with High-Rise in 1998.

The owner calls the shots, though. Cumani will rebuild without Postponed, but with the memory of one of his finest hours hopefully undimmed by the shock to the system that followed.

NOT SO SIMPLE

The story of the St Leger started with a thrilling finish and went to the stewards' room and BHA headquarters before Ralph Beckett's filly Simple Verse finally got the verdict

By Steve Dennis

ONE man had his head in his hands. Another had his heart in his mouth. A third had his eyes on the prize. And somewhere in the middle of the anatomical detail a thrilling, gripping race was won and lost. For pure edge-of-the-seat theatre, the St Leger had it all.

The oldest Classic is frequently regarded as something of a lame duck, but this rendition took flight as the seven runners bore down on the two-furlong pole. The race itself was thoroughly memorable, but what came after made it utterly unforgettable. And it all started when Andrea Atzeni found himself short of room aboard Simple Verse, and did something about it. One domino falls, and nothing can stop the chain reaction.

As the race began to resolve itself Simple Verse could be seen travelling strongly behind Fields Of Athenry and Storm The Stars, but she had nowhere to go, not with Bondi Beach going equally

▸▸Before the storm: Simple Verse and Andrea Atzeni in the winner's enclosure at Doncaster – but soon all hell would break loose

well on her outside. Atzeni had to do something, an instant decision, the race to win; he decided to go right hand down a bit and Simple Verse swiftly made room to deliver a challenge, elbowing her way past Bondi Beach and into the clear. It was quite a substantial bump.

Then the two front-runners began to run out of steam and Simple Verse and Bondi Beach poured on the coal, Colm O'Donoghue on the latter going to the whip again and again without being able to drive his willing partner's head past the tough filly. The colt rolled in slightly, the filly rolled out slightly, half a dozen of one and six of another, and they came together again. It was not much of a collision, but it happened.

And then Simple Verse put her head down and battled to the line, holding off Bondi Beach, a head in it, the sort of finish that makes you hold your breath and then let it out in a gust of relief and recognition of a great race.

Stewards' inquiry.

All those still tingling from the drama of the race's denouement had something else to think about now. What about those bumps? And Simple Verse had shoved her way out of that pocket. Hmmm. But, you know, nothing short of savagery induces the stewards to alter the result these days. This isn't France, old chap, or the US. The jockeys would get a telling-off, sure, maybe a few days' suspension, but the result would stand. Wouldn't it?

Would it? The first hint of the impending storm came when Atzeni, under the usual benign cross-examination on Channel 4 Racing, seemed a little less than sure of himself. It might have been because of the race's prestige but Atzeni did not react like a man with a clear conscience, and a few minutes later the storm began to break about his head.

The practice of televising the stewards' inquiry adds a sharp new angle to the process, the mysteries of the inner sanctum no longer concealed, the veil lifted on the human face behind the dry deliberations. Inside, Atzeni and O'Donoghue prepared to put their side of the story. Outside, Simple Verse's trainer Ralph Beckett and owner Sheikh Fahad Al Thani were waiting for the presentation ceremony, the elation still coursing through their veins, the prize close enough to touch. Inside, Atzeni could feel it slipping through his fingers.

The Sardinian, working in his second language, was an earnest witness but not as convincing as O'Donoghue, who, with nothing to lose and everything to gain, rose to the occasion with a virtuoso display of courtroom theatrics, filleting the debate to its bare bones with a few pithy phrases.

"Has an incident occurred? Yes. Has it took me off a straight course? Yes," he said, asking himself the salient questions and providing suitable answers. Atzeni could only mumble something along the lines of 'well, he did it as well, so there', and if the stewards were willing to be led then O'Donoghue was shepherding them in his direction. By this stage, with time passing, Beckett began to get the heebie-jeebies. He was aware something was up.

"The longer the stewards' inquiry went on the more worried we became," he said. "By the time it was announced I was prepared for it, we were just standing around waiting for it to happen."

The crowded parade ring must have been a lonely place, Beckett simply waiting for the axe to fall, knowing there was nothing he could do to arrest its descent. Far lonelier, though, was the place Atzeni had found for himself, sitting on a chair outside the stewards' room next to O'Donoghue, like two naughty boys waiting to see the headmaster. As they waited, and waited, under the gaze of the television cameras, Atzeni put his head in his hands in desperation. O'Donoghue stared icily back at the camera. A few yards away, Beckett walked in circles, willing the announcement

» *Continues page 132*

to come for better or for worse, anything to end the torture. Everyone's nerves were at breaking point – and then the silence was broken.

"The placings are revised as follows . . . "

O'Donoghue stood up, clapped his hands briskly, strode back into the changing room. Atzeni slumped in his chair, slowly rose, his face crumpling with disappointment. The camera followed him into the changing room, on the one hand needlessly intrusive, on the other hand a compelling witness as Atzeni threw his whip at the wall, threw down his kit, broke down in tears and was consoled. Sometimes we forget that our sportsmen demigods are no more than young men; Atzeni reminded us.

While Atzeni sobbed, Beckett raged. The camera sought him out, a man boiling with fury, a man with just enough grip on his emotions to prevent them overwhelming him.

"We lose the race when clearly, whatever way you look at it, both horses leaned on each other. Can you honestly say that it was entirely her fault? Could you put your hand on your heart and say it was her fault in the last half a furlong? I don't think I can answer that question – can anybody else? One thing is for certain, we'll appeal this. That's all I've got to say on the matter."

As O'Donoghue lifted the trophy – some moronic racegoers shouted 'cheat' at him – the first act of this absorbing passion play drew to a close.

Two weeks later, in a private committee room at BHA headquarters, the appeal was heard and upheld. The interference was now deemed to be insufficient to have affected the result, and Simple Verse was once again the St Leger winner; Beckett and Atzeni were wreathed in smiles, while Bondi Beach's trainer Aidan O'Brien took the reverse with immaculate good manners.

It was the second appeal of Beckett's summer. His Secret Gesture – also owned by Sheikh Fahad – had been disqualified for causing negligible interference when winning the Grade 1 Beverly D Stakes at Arlington Park and, owing

▸▸One way or another: (clockwise from left) Simple Verse (right) and Bondi Beach do battle in the Leger; Andrea Atzeni in the winner's enclosure with Simple Verse; after the reversal of placings Colm O'Donoghue lifts the trophy; (below) Ralph Beckett, Simple Verse's trainer, won the race back on appeal

to the inflexibility of US regulations, his appeal was subsequently dismissed, but in the circumstances he was inclined to look on the bright side.

"In any other jurisdiction, Secret Gesture would have kept the race. But look, if I had to lose one appeal I'm happy it was that one rather than the St Leger.

"It isn't as much fun to win the St Leger in a committee room in the middle of London. But it doesn't really matter. The fact we had to win it twice is okay – look, I'm in the record books, the only trainer to win the St Leger twice with the same horse."

On the heels of Simple Verse's 'dual' Leger success came another Group 1 triumph, this time at Ascot on Champions Day when she underlined her superiority over the majority of Europe's middle-distance fillies by dashing home for a decisive victory in the Fillies & Mares Stakes.

The happy ending had become even happier.

FLOWN BY IRT
With over 40 years experience transporting horses around the globe and offices in the UK, Germany, USA, New Zealand and Australia, IRT is the world leader when it comes to the international movement of horses.
With our global network of offices, IRT offers a one stop shop solution, offering peace of mind that your horse couldn't be in better hands.
To find out how we can help you and your horse contact IRT today.
Parranda
Winner of the 2015 G1 CECF Singapore Cup
Acapulco
Winner of the 2015 Queen Mary Stakes (Group 2), Royal Ascot
Super One
Winner of the 2015 Singapore Golden Horseshoe Series, IRT Juvenile Stakes
Undrafted
Winner of the 2015 Diamond Jubilee Stakes (Group 1), Royal Ascot
IRT
Your horse. Our passion.
www.irt.com
IRT UK & Europe: Tel +44 1638 668 003
IRT Germany: Tel +49 171 784 7447
IRT Australia: Tel +61 3 9643 3000
IRT New Zealand: Tel +64 9297 2022
IRT North America:
Chicago: Tel +1 630 513 0312
LA: Tel +1 310 306 0262
LONGINES
1:09.5
RACE 5
13
ROYAL ASCOT

THE POWER OF LOVE

A first Classic victory with Covert Love gave Hugo Palmer a year to remember but the trainer's impressive progress was about more than one horse

By Nicholas Godfrey

HUGO PALMER likes to set himself targets. In 2014, he set out his stall to earn £200,000 in prize-money and train a Group winner. He won more than £400,000, with a couple of Group-race victories, so he thought he had better set himself a stiffer challenge for 2015: he'd go for £500,000 plus a Group 1 winner.

At the end of a breakthrough season, Palmer had smashed through the money barrier with more than £1m in Britain alone, even before sizeable coffer boosts from overseas were taken into account. Moreover, he had saddled top filly Covert Love to win a pair of Group 1s among no fewer than seven Pattern-race successes, three of which were provided by a high-quality string of two-year-olds that augurs particularly well for 2016.

All this for one of Newmarket's youngest trainers – he turns 35 in December – who started up just five years ago with 11 syndicate horses. Whichever way you cut it, Palmer seems to be on the fast track. "I'm absolutely delighted with how it's gone," says the trainer, who married long-term girlfriend Vanessa Webb in July. "We've almost exactly doubled the targets I set myself at the start of the year but the more important thing is that we've made progress year-on-year since we started training. In fact we've doubled prize-money every year – we can't carry on doing it forever, I suppose, but we'll be trying."

Even though Palmer was optimistic about the prospects of his Kremlin Cottage team for 2015, he could hardly have imagined what was to transpire.

▸▸ Love is all around: (clockwise from left) Hugo Palmer celebrates with Pat Smullen after landing the Irish Oaks with Covert Love, the trainer's first Group 1 and Classic winner; in the winner's enclosure at Longchamp on Arc day after another Group 1 success in the Prix de l'Opera; Covert Love holds on by a head from Jazzi Top in the Opera

"When I looked around my yard in the spring I thought they were a better bunch of horses than I'd had before and there were more of them as well. But while that helps it's not necessarily a recipe for immediate success. My team works extremely hard to keep them healthy and we had a lot of luck on our side but they haven't been healthy for 12 months of the year. We barely had a winner in August, for example, but we've been really fortunate to have fantastic horses and got it right on the right days."

Undoubted star of the Palmer show was a wonderful three-year-old filly in the shape of Covert Love, whose progress was something to behold as she improved rapidly from a Chelmsford maiden victory in May to record Palmer's first Classic victory in the Darley Irish Oaks and then produce a memorably tough effort to thwart Jazzi Top in the Prix de l'Opera, a pair of victories that saw Pat Smullen to excellent effect. Not bad for a filly who started the season with just one unplaced effort in an all-weather maiden to her name.

"At the start of the season I could have told you I liked her very much and she would win races, and that I'd hope to find some black type with her, but there's no way I could have hoped she would end up where she did," Palmer admits.

"She is just so genuine with a wonderfully high cruising speed and the ability to quicken. Then she has the guts and tenacity to see the race out to the end."

In terms of personal satisfaction, Palmer cannot split Covert Love's Group 1 wins. "Obviously the Irish Oaks was very special – I'll never be able to have my first Group 1 winner again and I'll never again have a first Classic winner. But the atmosphere on Arc day in Paris was also really special and the pressure was higher because we were the favourite, so it was enormously exciting. In Ireland we would have been delighted to be in the first three."

If Covert Love's progress might have been hard to predict, there were other more obvious three-year-old types who contributed to Palmer's tally, among them 2,000 Guineas sixth Home Of The Brave, who won the Free Handicap and a Group 3 in Ireland, and the filly

▸▸ *Continues page 136*

New Providence, short-headed in the Nell Gwyn before adding the Summer Stakes at York to her Group 3 success as a two-year-old. It wasn't all wine and roses, however: much to the trainer's frustration, highly rated Aktabantay – his first Group winner in 2014 – did not trouble the scorers, while five-year-old Short Squeeze narrowly missed out on more than one decent prize.

On the other hand, Palmer's two-year-olds certainly made their mark, which is probably just as well given that they formed the majority of his 66-strong battalion at Kremlin Cottage. Group races were claimed by Prestige Stakes winner Hawksmoor, Galileo Gold (bought by Al Shaqab before his Vintage Stakes victory) and tough gelding Gifted Master, who took a lucrative sales race at Newmarket a week before making all in the Autumn Stakes.

Taken as a whole, such juvenile strength gives their trainer plenty to look forward to in 2016, when Palmer has some lofty targets in mind. "Hawksmoor is still immature and has some growing to do. She'll be a much better filly next year when she'll be aimed towards the French 1,000 Guineas. She might even stay the Diane trip – she wants cut in the ground, so France might be her game for a while.

"We could also look at the French Guineas and the French Derby for Galileo Gold. He's a Group 2 winner and he was third in the Lagardere when the ground was too fast. Being a gelding, Gifted Master can't run in the Guineas but we'll bring him back for the Craven or one of those trials."

For all that Palmer cuts a toffish figure, any suggestion of silver-spoon success is rather undermined by the facts: Covert Love was a €26,000 yearling, while dual Group winner New Providence cost £22,000 – "the same price as a family car," he says. Hawksmoor and Gifted Master cost a bit more, at €80,000 and 75,000gns respectively, but they were at the top end of Palmer's range. "We've been lucky because most of these races have not been won by expensive horses. It's really exciting – and it's exactly what I set out to do, so it's gratifying to have done so. I forget whose autobiography it was that talked about training as buckets of misery and moments of bliss. Thank goodness we had the moments of bliss."

After such a stellar year, one question remains: how precisely do you follow that? "I've always wanted to keep making progress, train more winners, win more prize-money, more Group winners than I did the year before," Palmer says. "That will remain the overriding goal for the rest of my career. My dream is one day to get to the top – but whether I do or not, that goal is always going to be there, to beat my personal best."

On that score, Palmer has already established quite a benchmark.

▸▸ Team effort: (clockwise from top left) Hawksmoor (right) wins the Group 3 Prestige Stakes at Goodwood; Home Of The Brave is led down to post before his victory in the European Free Handicap at Newmarket; Gifted Master (right) lands the Group 3 Autumn Stakes at Newmarket; (below) Hugo Palmer was pleased to have so many "moments of bliss"

'I want to keep making progress, train more winners, win more prize-money. My dream is to get to the top'

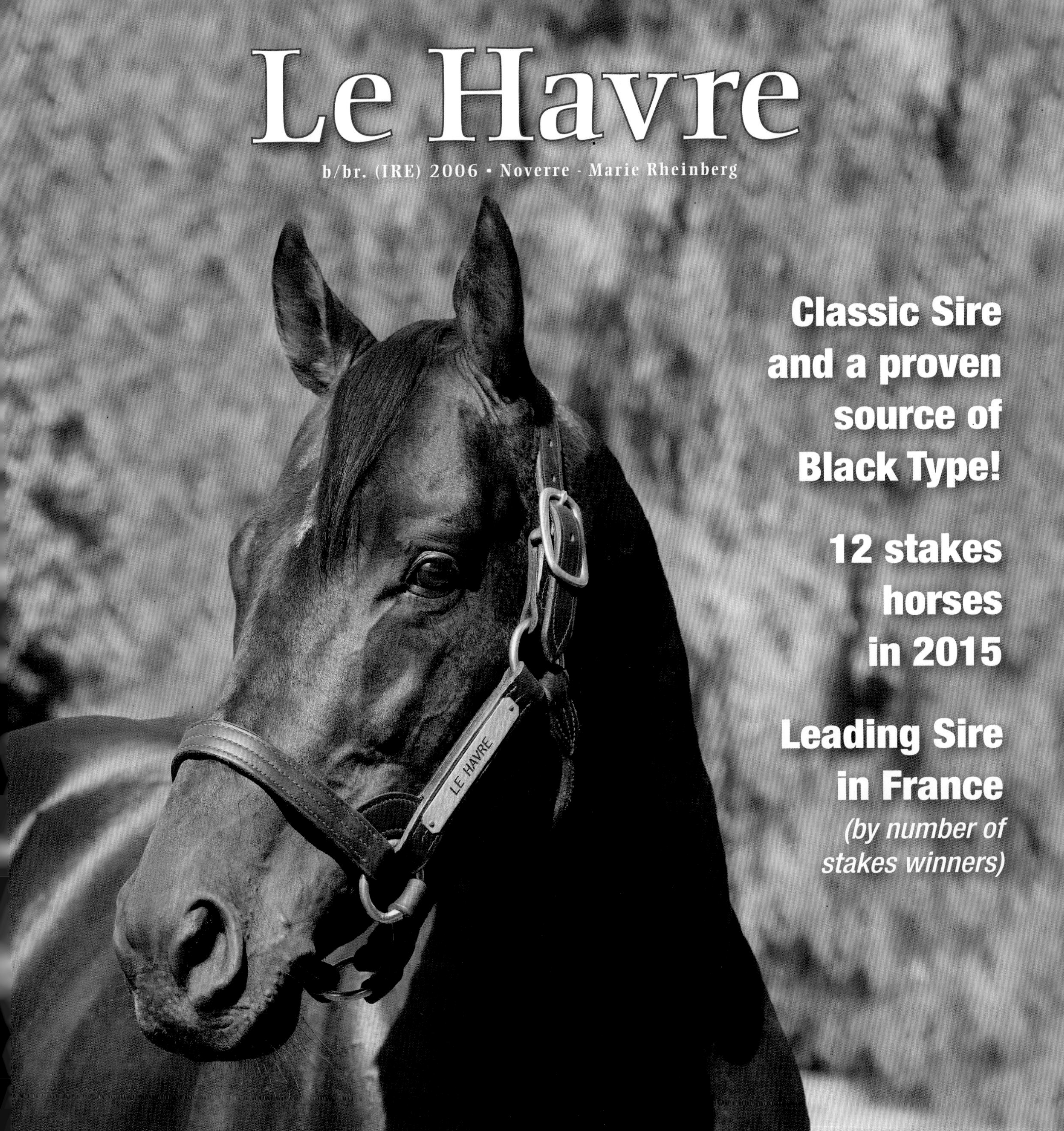

Also standing:

- **RAJSAMAN** : top class miler by champion sire **Linamix**
- **AIR CHIEF MARSHAL** : one of the leading French 2 yo sire in France by **Danehill Dancer**

LA CAUVINIÈRE

Sylvain Vidal +33 (0)6 20 99 10 15 haras@lacauviniere.com • **Mathieu Alex** +33 (0)6 26 59 19 18 malex@lacauviniere.com

www.lacauviniere.com

KILLER QUEEN

David Elsworth's Arabian Queen scored the upset of the summer with her 50-1 success over Golden Horn in the International at York

By Steve Dennis

FOR a graveyard, it was all rather exhilarating. The Juddmonte International had been its usual capricious self, casting down the hot favourite and elevating an outsider, yet there was no fluke about the result. Arabian Queen ruled supreme.

York's biggest race of the season – the best race in the world, on ratings – is unofficially known as the 'graveyard of champions' owing to its propensity for shock results, dating from the first running of the race in 1972 when, under the Benson & Hedges Gold Cup banner, Roberto meted out the only defeat in the awe-inspiring 18-race career of Brigadier Gerard.

The 2015 renewal was not expected to be filed under that category despite being diminished – not for the first time in a British Group 1 this summer – by the late withdrawal of a leading contender on account of unsuitably soft ground. The dual 2,000 Guineas winner Gleneagles, a frequent absentee during a frustrating

campaign, was again benched to leave a race in which any one of a high-class triumvirate would have been a thoroughly credible winner.

Derby and Eclipse winner Golden Horn, scratched at the 11th hour from the King George, was taking his chance this time despite good to soft ground that, at York, is always a little more tiring than elsewhere. Eclipse runner-up The Grey Gatsby, winner of more prize-money than any other horse ever trained in Yorkshire, was there to take advantage should the favourite falter, as was the fast-improving Royal Ascot winner Time Test. Arabian Queen was unconsidered at 50-1, although given her recent third place in the Nassau Stakes her odds seemed a little generous.

The bookmakers were ignoring her, and that mindset was giving her trainer David Elsworth a bad day. The irascible genius was grumpy that his filly had been ignored by all and sundry, including the press and the racecourse management. Elsworth's attitude to journalists is straightforward enough – he doesn't like them much – and although a Racing Post reporter had called him for a quote, it had been a short, unproductive and unquotable conversation.

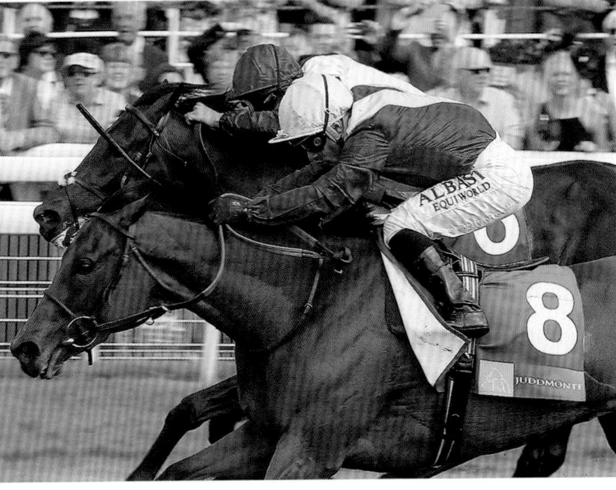

"It's not so much that the press didn't talk to me before the race that irritated me," he said, to a different Post hack at the end of the glorious day. "It was the dismissive manner with which they regarded her chance. I've devoted my whole life to racing and achieved a little bit of success, but the attitude of people is 'What's Elsie doing? He must be off his head'. I don't like that.

"I might be a crotchety old bugger, but I've been in the business for 60 years, so I get embarrassed to see people think a filly I'm running in a race like that is a 100-1 shot."

Arabian Queen, a diminutive filly out of another of Elsworth's success stories in Barshiba, had shown ability at two when winning the Group 2 Duchess of Cambridge Stakes at Newmarket but had appeared short of the top grade in three starts in Group 1 company before that encouraging performance behind Legatissimo at Goodwood. She seemed to be improving, but enough to beat the unbeaten Golden Horn? You can have 50-1. And yet . . .

The race itself was unadorned by any elaborate tactics. Dick Doughtywylie, pacemaker for Golden Horn, went off too fast – as is the way of so many pacemakers – and was ignored, leaving Arabian Queen and Silvestre de Sousa to happily set their own pace in second spot. When the field absorbed the pacemaker a furlong and a half out, the scene was seemingly set for Golden Horn to accelerate clear of his rivals. But first he had to pass Arabian Queen. And he couldn't.

He may have drawn level with Arabian Queen inside the final furlong, but this time the good little 'un was too strong, too game for the good big 'un. Frankie Dettori threw it all at the colt but the filly was his master by a neck. The Grey Gatsby was third and Time Test fourth – and don't imagine for a moment that the 'big three' all ran identically below form. Arabian Queen beat them on merit. Somewhere, elsewhere, Elsworth – who won the Juddmonte 25 years ago with another brilliant filly in In The Groove – was grinning to himself.

The 'crotchety old bugger' shunned the prize ceremony – "I've been a big supporter of the race for a long time, but it was only as an afterthought I was invited to lunch. They didn't think it was worth inviting me to lunch, so I didn't think it was worth me going up to take their prize" – and it was left to owner Jeff Smith, whose stable of fine horses goes back more than 30 years to Chief Singer, to collect the silverware.

Elsworth, though, when he finally emerged from his self-inflicted purdah to meet the terrible press, earned the last word. "She's had sinus operations, which is why she didn't run in the Guineas. She's had problems but got over them. She's the best filly in Europe."

▸▸First lady: (opposite page) Arabian Queen with David Elsworth at Egerton House Stables, Newmarket; (above, clockwise from top) Arabian Queen fends off Golden Horn in the Juddmonte International; takes victory by a neck; and is led back in triumph by groom Laura Gardner

IN THE PICTURE

Frankel stands proud at Ascot as the Queen unveils bronze statue

Frankel has a permanent place at Ascot after the Queen unveiled a life-size bronze of Sir Henry Cecil's great champion on the first day of the 2015 royal meeting. The statue overlooks the parade ring and faces the winner's enclosure Frankel graced five times in his unbeaten 14-race career, including twice at Royal Ascot.

The striking bronze by Mark Coreth is one of four, the others being at the National Horseracing Museum in Newmarket, York racecourse and Banstead Manor Stud. The piece was commissioned by Juddmonte Farms, the breeding operation of Frankel's owner Prince Khalid Abdullah.

Lady Cecil, widow of Frankel's trainer, said: "Ascot played a special part in Frankel's career and it is fitting that such a magnificent statue will stand at the course to celebrate his achievements. Mark Coreth has captured the presence, power and strength of Frankel. I cannot imagine a more fitting testament to his talent."

Coreth, who was selected to produce the commission after a competitive process, said: "It was an honour to be asked to create this sculpture of this extraordinary horse. The creative process was a delight and the sculpture tries to capture the power and vitality of Frankel. Having a sculpture of arguably the finest racehorse ever unveiled at the greatest racing venue in the world was incredibly daunting. It was nevertheless a very proud moment and I hope the sculpture helps people to remember the excitement and exhilaration they experienced when watching Frankel during his racing career."

The statue took eight months to produce. Coreth made a number of visits to Frankel's stables, measuring the now seven-year-old horse and studying his poise and posture. The artist also interviewed those who work closely with Frankel, including his grooms.

After drawing a range of initial sketches, Coreth then produced the sculpture in his studio near Shaftesbury on the Dorset-Wiltshire border. The artist created an aluminium wire skeleton which was then covered in clay and sculpted into shape. From this clay model, a mould was created and Coreth cast sections of the sculpture in bronze before they were joined together.

Instant reactions to the statue on social media after the unveiling were mixed. "The Frankel statue has a noble presence and textured surface. Beautiful," said Laurel Humbert on Twitter and Keith Michael Murray described it as "magnificent", but Ian Mallard was less impressed, saying: "I think I could actually pull a face in a mirror and look more like Frankel than that statue."

Picture: EDWARD WHITAKER (RACINGPOST.COM/PHOTOS)

LEVEL 3
LEVEL 2

TRAILBLAZER

Muhaarar scorched through the season to take champion sprinter honours with four successive Group 1 triumphs

By Julian Muscat

YOU cannot help but notice the irony. In the year the Commonwealth Cup at Royal Ascot was instituted to give three-year-old sprinters a helping hand, one of their number rampaged through the division as though to the manor born. In Muhaarar, Britain had a sprinter of hypnotic talent.

He shredded the theory that sophomore sprinters are impotent against the massed ranks of older horses until the second half of the season. He also belittled the notion that embryonic sprinters who set out on the Guineas trail are too

washed out to contend for the July Cup.

In so doing, Muhaarar reminded us that class is everything. Those caveats about sophomore sprinters might apply in a normal year, yet Muhaarar was anything but normal. He was a thoroughbred comet who blazed to four successive Group 1 triumphs – a rare level of dominance that ranked with the similar feats of Habibti in 1983 and Dayjur in 1990. And guess what? They were three-year-olds too.

Expertly handled through a long campaign by Charlie Hills, Muhaarar started his rise to the sprinting summit in the Commonwealth Cup. While it is impossible to know how pivotal that race proved in aiding the colt's development, its inauguration took Hills off the horns of a dilemma.

That is because Muhaarar's earlier attempt on the Poule d'Essai des Poulains elicited more questions than answers. Drawn widest of all in stall 18 over Longchamp's notoriously trappy mile, jockey Paul Hanagan opted to rein back and forfeit ground throughout a race in which Muhaarar pulled mercilessly for his head.

That combination of unhappy circumstances often sees horses taper away with exhaustion in the closing stages. But that is not what happened at all. Muhaarar made ground from the rear on reaching the straight and kept running to the line, looking for all money like a horse well worth another tilt against the best three-year-old milers.

"After the race Paul [Hanagan] said the horse had definitely stayed the mile," Hills reflected at the end of the campaign. "I had a long chat with [owner Sheikh Hamdan's racing manager] Angus Gold about where to go next, and with Gleneagles and Territories [first and second in the 2,000 Guineas] seemingly heading for the St James's Palace Stakes, we started thinking about the Commonwealth Cup."

The Group 3 Jersey Stakes, in which Muhaarar would have to shoulder a penalty, was also considered for his Royal Ascot assignment, but Sheikh Hamdan saw little sense in running his colt, already a Group 2 winner as a juvenile in the 2014 Gimcrack Stakes, in a Pattern race of lesser status. Hills agreed, viewing the Commonwealth Cup as "an attractive route into the sprinting programme".

Over the years Hills had seen three-year-olds burn themselves out in attempting to stretch their stamina. "Before, if you had a Middle Park winner, you had to try and make them stay a mile at three," he said. "There wasn't much

»» *Continues page 144*

▸▸ Hot property: Charlie Hills with Muhaarar at his Faringdon Place yard; (previous page) Muhaarar ends his career on a high note with a dazzling triumph in the British Champions Sprint

else you could do. Now, I really feel that the sprint programme for three-year-olds is going to stand them in good stead in the future."

The difference in performance levels between overstretched three-year-olds and those campaigned over their optimum trip can be striking. Muhaarar's attempt on the Poule d'Essai des Poulains came in contrast to Adaay's campaign. Also owned by Sheikh Hamdan, the William Haggas-trained Adaay turned straight to sprinting at the start of his sophomore campaign. When he completed his Royal Ascot preparation with a convincing defeat of Limato in the Group 2 Sandy Lane Stakes at Haydock, Hanagan opted to ride him, rather than Muhaarar, in the Commonwealth Cup.

It would not happen again. Muhaarar won with such elan that Hanagan became his constant companion. The combination duly followed up in the July Cup, when Muhaarar overcame a loss of balance over Newmarket's undulations to nail Tropics on the line, and won again at Deauville in the Prix Maurice de Gheest over six and a half furlongs.

That latter victory, gained narrowly by half a length, prompted some to wonder whether Muhaarar was as good as he had looked at Royal Ascot. Yet while Muhaarar rested up, Esoterique, his immediate victim in France, made off with a pair of Group 1 races: the Prix Jacques Le Marois and Sun Chariot Stakes. The form really was copper-bottomed.

There was no particular reason for Muhaarar taking a three-month hiatus from racing after Deauville. "He certainly didn't need it," Hills said. "His weight was fine throughout the season, and so was his condition. In that sense he was a straightforward horse to train. He was always sound, never returned a below-par scope and never needed the vet."

Indeed, the only difficulty Hills encountered came before the colt set foot on a racecourse. "In his early two-year-old days he had a lot of nervous energy. He was always anxious to get on with things, and a little edgy with it. He could suddenly leap forward when his rider lowered his goggles, but he settled down once he started racing. It made a man of him."

Muhaarar's finest racecourse performance was also his swansong. He raced with customary zest through the early stages of the Qipco British Champions Sprint before he asserted with authority to inflict a first defeat on Twilight Son, who had won his five previous starts including the Group 1 Betfred Sprint Cup at Haydock. Hills's star held his form through the entire season before unleashing his best at the last with a decisive two-length victory.

So how good was Muhaarar? That success on Champions Day saw him advance his Rating Post Rating to 127, the highest accorded any sprinter since Dream Ahead in 2011. His mark may be 2lb shy of the best

▸▸ *Continues page 146*

IN THE FAST LANE

Muhaarar's blistering display in the British Champions Sprint was bettered by only one performance in the 2015 European turf season – and that was Golden Horn's tour de force in the Eclipse.

The champion sprinter reached a Racing Post Rating of 127 in his Ascot swansong, making him the best European sprinter since Dream Ahead in 2011. Since 2000 Muhaarar has been bettered by only three other European-trained sprinters – Mozart (2001), Oasis Dream (2003) and Dream Ahead (2011) all had an RPR of 129.

Across all distances in Europe this year, Muhaarar's 127 was on a par with Golden Horn's Derby and Arc displays but below the 132 peak in the Eclipse.

Even before Champions Day, Muhaarar had already recorded the best sprint RPR of the year in Europe – 124 for his Commonwealth Cup win, also at Ascot. Next best was the American sprinter Undrafted with an RPR of 123 for his Diamond Jubilee Stakes success at Royal Ascot.

BEST SPRINT RPRS IN EUROPE IN 2015

Horse	*RPR*
Muhaarar	127
Undrafted (right)	123
Brazen Beau	122
Mecca's Angel	121
Muthmir	121
Tropics	121
Twilight Son	120
Goldream	119
Gordon Lord Byron	119
Mustajeeb	119

YOU CAN FIND OUR PRODUCTS
AT EXCLUSIVE SPECIALIST RETAILERS
AND ONLINE AT **WWW.SWAROVSKIOPTIK.COM**

BY APPOINTMENT TO
HER MAJESTY QUEEN ELIZABETH II
SWAROVSKI OPTIK
SUPPLIER OF BINOCULARS

THE NEW EL
LIMITLESS
PERFECTION

The new EL Family from SWAROVSKI OPTIK is the best ever. Its FieldPro package takes comfort and functionality to a new level. Its perfect optical performance and precision, outstanding ergonomics, and revamped design add the finishing touches to this long-range optical masterpiece. Enjoy moments even more – with SWAROVSKI OPTIK.

SEE THE UNSEEN
WWW.SWAROVSKIOPTIK.COM

SWAROVSKI
OPTIK

posted by his sire, Oasis Dream, in the 2003 Nunthorpe Stakes, but he is Oasis Dream's most talented runner to date.

In that respect Muhaarar makes the perfect replacement for his grandsire Green Desert, who died at Sheikh Hamdan's Shadwell Stud, in Norfolk, this year. That consideration was uppermost in connections' minds when they decided not to send Muhaarar to the Breeders' Cup. "It would have been dreadful had something gone wrong with him in the US," Hills said. "We'd have been mortified."

Hills would have been celebrating a fine year with his sprinters even without Muhaarar to carry the torch. Four-year-old Cable Bay ran consistently throughout the season before he closed his career by winning the Group 2 Challenge Stakes. And in Cotai Glory, Magical Memory and Strath Burn, the trainer has three front-line speed merchants for 2016.

Strath Burn was fancied to ruffle up Muhaarar in the Champions Sprint but returned home lame after finishing in the ruck. "He had a little problem with one of his knees but will be fine for next year," said Hills, 37, who has ensured a smooth transition after taking over from father Barry at Faringdon Place, Lambourn, in August 2011. This was his fourth full season and his best yet, earning him seventh place in the trainers' championship.

Among those lying in wait for the Hills battalions in next year's big sprint races will be Goldream, from the Newmarket stable of Robert Cowell, another noted handler of sprinters. Goldream is best at five furlongs, the distance over which he won a pair of Group 1 races in 2015. The gelded six-year-old, another son of Oasis Dream, plainly has the will to win, having landed the King's Stand Stakes and Prix de l'Abbaye by a short head and a short neck respectively, although his best RPR of 119 in the Abbaye left him 8lb short of Muhaarar's high standard.

With the Henry Candy-trained Twilight Son also due to reappear, it may well require a horse of Muhaarar's calibre to claim the accolade of champion sprinter in 2016.

Angel delight on the Knavesmire

YORK'S Ebor festival is a proud occasion for northern folk, an opportunity to put on a show of top-class racing, fashion and fun, and for sheer joie de vivre nothing beats cheering on a local winner who defeats the big names from down south or overseas.

Undoubtedly the biggest buzz of the 2015 meeting came when Mecca's Angel, a striking grey filly from a relatively unheralded stable, blitzed to a commanding victory in the Coolmore Nunthorpe Stakes. Her success marked a career highlight for David Metcalfe, Michael Dods and Paul Mulrennan, respectively Mecca's Angel's owner, trainer and jockey. Each was gaining his first win in a Group 1 race and, to the packed galleries on the Knavesmire, it was a triumph for one of their own.

Well, almost. Metcalfe is a businessman based in Darlington, near where Dods trains in County Durham. But to quibble about that is to split hairs; Darlington may be across the county border but it is barely 40 miles from York as the crow flies. As for 33-year-old Mulrennan, the London-born jockey has spent the whole of his professional career in Yorkshire.

Mulrennan was in floods of tears as he rode Mecca's Angel into the hallowed winner's enclosure. He later maintained the reception given to Mecca's Angel was more vociferous than that accorded Frankel when the wonder horse landed the Juddmonte International Stakes three years earlier. "The reaction of the crowd was unbelievable," Mulrennan said. "It meant the world. I have no reason why; perhaps it's me and Michael [Dods] being from up north, and it being someone different to the usual suspects."

While the accolade of champion sprinter for 2015 belongs to Muhaarar, Mecca's Angel's Nunthorpe victory stands out as the most inspiring Group 1 triumph. She cost Metcalfe a relatively meagre 16,000gns as a yearling, yet her deeds are such that her yearling full-sister fetched a whopping 825,000gns when she was sold at Tattersalls in October.

Victory was handsome vindication of her connections' determination to run her only when conditions were suitable. Mecca's Angel has always excelled with a bit of give underfoot and conditions were just right at York. She was the only horse who could live with the electric pace of American two-year-old Acapulco – herself a dazzling winner of Royal Ascot's Queen Mary Stakes two months earlier. Acapulco, in receipt of 24lb from Mecca's Angel, entered the final furlong with a seemingly unassailable advantage, yet so emphatically did the Dods filly reel her in that she tallied by two lengths.

The Nunthorpe was Mecca's Angel's second victory from three outings in 2015, which took her career record to eight wins and three second places from 14 starts. She is to race on as a five-year-old in 2016, after which Metcalfe has indicated she will be sold at public auction.

OWNERS – A GOLDEN OPPORTUNITY

ROA membership is the equivalent of just 63p* a day but the benefits are immense

- SIS sponsorship (worth an average of £4,000 against ownership costs alone – annually per horse)
- Free racecourse admission and priority car parking (worth over £200 a year)
- Automatic third-party insurance (worth £290 a year)
- BHA 20% fee discounts (worth £55 on average)
- Thoroughbred Owner & Breeder magazine (worth £55 for 12 issues)

Plus much more

Join 7,250 owners today.
Call 020 7152 0200
or visit **roa.co.uk**

*£230/365 days - £0.63
Terms and conditions may apply to benefits

IN THE PICTURE

Girl power at Shergar Cup as Bell savours champagne moment

Sammy Jo Bell was the star of the show in the Shergar Cup at Ascot in August as she led the Girls team to a landmark success, sparking a champagne celebration with teammate Emma-Jayne Wilson in the winner's enclosure.

Bell (*right*), who enjoyed a breakthrough season in the apprentice ranks, had been called up only three days earlier to replace the injured Cathy Gannon in the Girls team alongside Wilson and captain Hayley Turner, but she won two of the six races, making her the first woman to take the Alistair Haggis Silver Saddle as the event's top rider.

"It's definitely the best day in my career – it's been outstanding," Bell said. "I want to say how gutted I am for Cathy that she couldn't ride, but I'm delighted to get the opportunity. It's been a real whirlwind – it's all happened very quickly. It will take a long, long time to better this day."

Bell, 24, was the first apprentice to take part in the Shergar Cup but she proved more than a match for some of the world's top riders with her wins aboard Mick Appleby's Royal Signaller in the Shergar Cup Stayers and Richard Hannon's Shell Bay in the Shergar Cup Classic. With Wilson winning on Missed Call in the Shergar Cup Challenge, the Girls team amassed 80 points – 13 points clear of the GB & Ireland team – to record their first victory in the event's 15-year history.

Canadian rider Wilson, a Shergar Cup regular, won the award for ride of the day after her short-head triumph on James Fanshawe's Missed Call. She felt the Girls' victory had answered doubts about whether female riders could compete on equal terms with men.

"There are people out there that still ask the question, but I don't see how you could argue it now. Look at the scores. It's 80 to 67. Done and dusted! Apparently we still had something to prove and I hope this shuts up all the doubters."

Three weeks later Turner – for so long the torchbearer for female riders in Britain – announced she would retire at the end of the season. She will become a pundit on At The Races and said she had "other things in the pipeline".

Turner, 32, the most successful female jockey in British racing history, was joint-champion apprentice in 2005, rode a century of winners in 2008 and enjoyed Group 1 successes in Britain aboard Dream Ahead and Margot Did in 2011, followed the next year by a Grade 1 winner in the US.

In picking up the torch from Turner, Bell has a hard act to follow – but she has made a good start.

Picture: CHRISTOPHER LEE/GETTY IMAGES

Dubai Duty Free
SHERGAR CUP

By Nick Pulford

KNOWING when to stop is the most difficult decision in any sporting career; just look at Tony McCoy, who wrestled with the dilemma for five years. The trick is to find that sweet spot between squeezing out every ounce of what can be achieved by not going too early and avoiding damage reputation by not leaving it too late. In racing you can add the ever-present danger of serious injury, or worse, to the thought process.

The unlucky people don't get to choose, and nor do racehorses. Trainers are fond of saying that a horse will tell them when it's time to stop, but what that really means is that a trainer has to be guided by physical signs, instinct and trusted team members to reach that decision on the horse's behalf. The good trainers are the ones who make the right call more often than not.

So it was with Willie Mullins, who finally called time on Hurricane Fly's spellbinding career in August but only after giving him one more season in which he was able to extend his world record of Grade 1 wins and seal his place in the affections of the jump racing public.

When that time came, Mullins could be content he had done right by Hurricane Fly to the very end, and been repaid in kind. "He's a legend," the Irish jumps champion trainer said. "This day was always going to come and it's great that we're doing it on our terms, rather than due to an injury or something like that. He had everything – speed, stamina, incredible bravery and aggression."

Those qualities were reflected in Hurricane Fly's remarkable career statistics. The son of Montjeu won 24 of his 32 races over jumps, including an unprecedented 22 Grade 1 triumphs and set an earnings record for a hurdler. For seven straight seasons and 30 races he competed exclusively in Grade 1 company, mixing brilliance and durability, and he won at least one top-level race in each of those seasons. Mullins said his personal highlight was the 2011 Champion Hurdle on Hurricane Fly's first visit to the Cheltenham Festival, after niggling problems had prevented his appearance in the previous two years, but there were so many to choose from.

In winning the Champion Hurdle for a second time in 2013, Hurricane Fly became only the second horse to regain the title (after Comedy Of Errors, who won in 1973 and 1975) and his long honours list also included a record five Irish Champion Hurdles. He overtook four-time winner Istabraq with his fifth Irish Champion in January, which turned out to be his final success.

On that unforgettable day at Leopardstown, emotion outweighed statistics as throngs of people rushed from the stands, the rails and the bars to the winner's enclosure – running, galloping, jumping barriers and jostling for the best position to grab a photo of the champion when he returned in triumph. One or two bookmakers even left their posts, flying from betting ring to parade ring to be there. After the waves of applause had finally subsided, Ruby Walsh said: "Apart from Cheltenham, I've never heard a horse get a reception like that."

Later in the year, after Hurricane Fly's retirement, Walsh reflected on their partnership. "I was very lucky to ride in my career the horses I consider to be the greatest chaser and greatest hurdler of their generation, Kauto Star and Hurricane Fly," he said. "They had everything: the ability and the longevity. They also had soundness of mind and limb. You can have all the money in the world but you need a bit of luck to come across horses like these and I'm eternally grateful Willie Mullins came across that fellow while I was riding."

In the cold light of day after the emotion of Leopardstown, Walsh was ruled by his head and not his heart in opting to ride Faugheen in the Champion Hurdle at Cheltenham. Paul Townend came in for the ride on Hurricane Fly and they were a gallant third in the Mullins 1-2-3, albeit no match for Faugheen as they finished six and a half lengths behind the winner.

Walsh returned for Hurricane Fly's final two runs of the season, what turned out to be the last of his career, as he moved up in distance. He was second in the World Series Hurdle at Punchestown behind Jezki, his regular rival of the past couple of seasons (the score ended 6-3 to Hurricane Fly), and then sixth in the French Champion Hurdle, won by the David Pipe-trained Un Temps Pour Tout.

In the summer of 2014 Mullins was on the horns of a dilemma with Hurricane Fly, who had been decisively beaten in the Champion

▸▸ *Continues page 152*

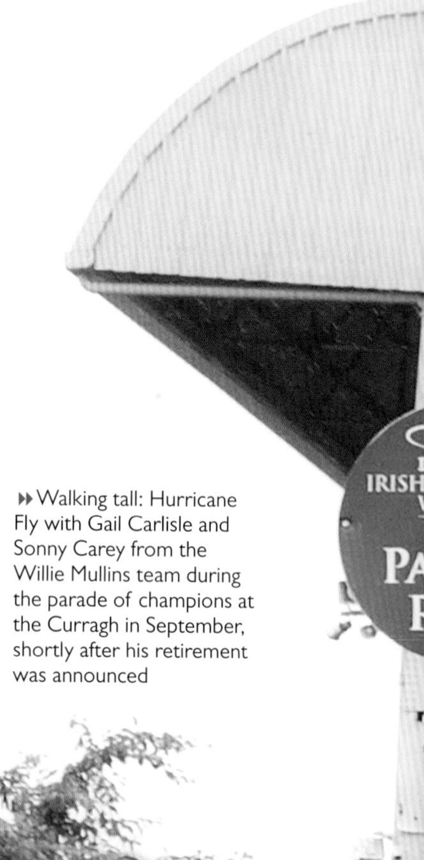

▸▸ Walking tall: Hurricane Fly with Gail Carlisle and Sonny Carey from the Willie Mullins team during the parade of champions at the Curragh in September, shortly after his retirement was announced

FORCE OF NATURE

Hurricane Fly, a multiple Champion Hurdle winner in Britain and Ireland, bowed out at the age of 11 after an emotional final campaign

Hurdles at Cheltenham and Punchestown and, to most eyes, seemed unlikely to be able to live with the emerging younger generation. Mullins, in football parlance, decided to take one game at a time.

That approach led to three consecutive Grade 1 victories at the start of his last season, culminating in that great day at Leopardstown when Hurricane Fly appeared to have Jezki's measure before his rival made a race-ending mistake at the last. To Mullins, here was the ultimate justification for giving Hurricane Fly another season. "When push came to shove he answered the call as he has done so many times in the past," he said amid the tumult in the winner's enclosure. "It's hard to believe he's an 11-year-old and not five or six."

The summer of 2015 brought a different decision, and again Mullins and owners George Creighton and Rose Boyd could be satisfied it was the right one. The final word belongs to Gail Carlisle, Hurricane Fly's faithful companion, who joined the Mullins team seven years ago and soon took on a pivotal role with the horse she described as having a "me, me, me" attitude.

"I started looking after him before the 2010 season and he took priority over everything in my life," said

▸▸Famous fifth: Ruby Walsh salutes the crowd after Hurricane Fly's emotional Irish Champion Hurdle victory in January

SUPER FLY
A LEGEND IN NUMBERS

24 Wins in 32 runs over hurdles

22 Grade 1 wins

2 Champion Hurdle wins (2011 and 2013)

5 Irish Champion Hurdle wins (2011-15)

10 Wins out of 10 at Leopardstown

173 Best RPR, achieved three times

£1,894,422 Career earnings

Mullins' head girl. "My holidays had to wait until Fly went on his holidays, and I came back to work when he came back in. He was a little dude but his attitude helped make him what he was. All the good ones have their own kinks and he definitely had his."

Hurricane Fly was worth the effort, even the countless times he stepped on Carlisle's feet while he was being brushed down, because he gave back so much more with all the glory days. He will never be forgotten by Carlisle, nor by the many others who fell under the spell of what Mullins described simply as "the horse of a lifetime".

'So many great days' for super Sizing

ANOTHER hero of Irish jump racing bowed out in May when Sizing Europe was retired at the age of 13 after a glittering career that stretched for ten seasons.

Trained by Henry de Bromhead and owned by Ann and Alan Potts, Sizing Europe numbered the 2011 Queen Mother Champion Chase at Cheltenham among his eight Grade 1 victories.

"He'll be very hard to replace and we had so many great days with him that it's simply impossible to pick just one of them as a highlight," De Bromhead said. "We have plenty of nice horses capable of winning good races, but I don't know if any will ever fill his boots. He has been the horse of a lifetime for all involved."

Sizing Europe's peak performance was his five-length Champion Chase victory over Big Zeb, which earned a career-high RPR of 176. He ran in the next four editions, finishing runner-up twice, fourth and then seventh to Dodging Bullets in the 2015 race, which turned out to be his last racecourse appearance.

The first of Sizing Europe's Grade 1 triumphs came over hurdles in the 2008 Irish Champion Hurdle and he was an unlucky loser of the Champion Hurdle at Cheltenham the same year, but he truly blossomed when he went chasing.

His novice season brought two Grade 1 wins, including the Arkle Chase at Cheltenham, and as a senior chaser he followed his Queen Mother Champion Chase triumph with victories in the 2011 Tingle Creek, the 2012 Dial-A-Bet Chase and two Punchestown Champion Chases in 2012 and 2014.

The last of those wins was charged with emotion after Sizing Europe staved off retirement with a remarkable performance at the age of 12, raising the roof at Punchestown and prompting connections to carry on for another season.

He won the Grade 2 Gowran Champion Chase to another rapturous reception on his reappearance in the 2014-15 season, but time eventually caught up with him. "We gave it a good bit of thought and we're happy that he's retiring in one piece," De Bromhead said.

In all Sizing Europe won 22 of his 45 races, placing on a further 13 occasions and earning more than £1.3m in prize-money. In retirement he has been retrained for racehorse to riding horse shows by Rosemary Connors, the talented equestrian rider who played a key role in his racing career by partnering him in his flat work for De Bromhead.

Vetrol·Medical
Premium Quality Veterinary Products

AKKER®

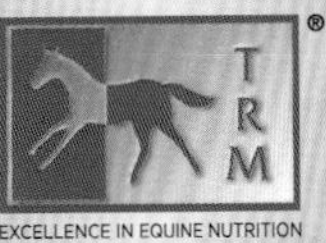

STERI-7

Tel 01730 815800 | www.farmstable.com

OUT OF THE DARKNESS

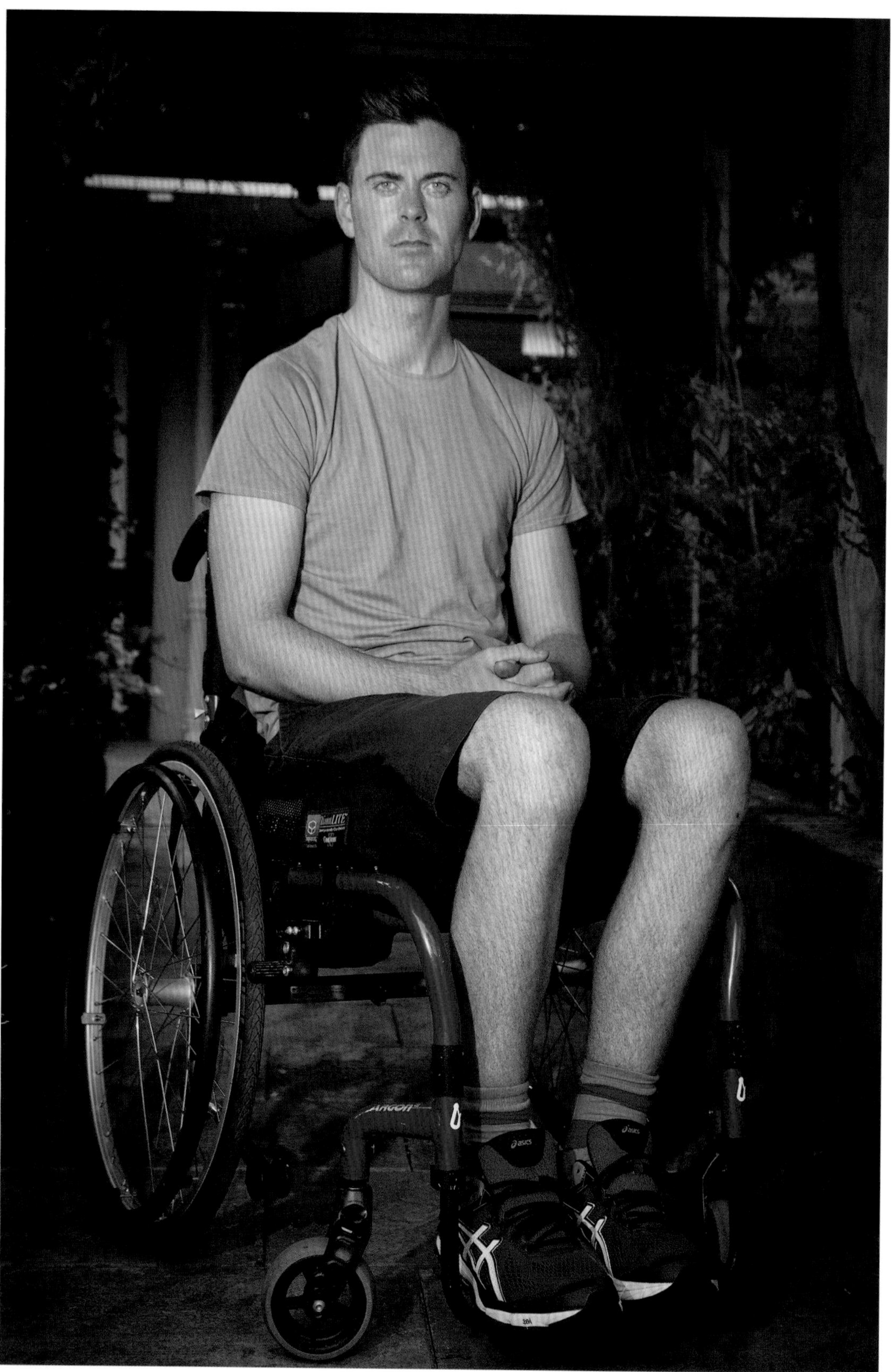

Robbie McNamara was gripped by negativity after being paralysed in a fall at Wexford in April but now he is looking forward to following his long-held dream of being a trainer

By Jonathan Mullin

IT WASN'T a first-to-last white-knuckle ride or all-hands-to-the-pump arm-wrestle up the home straight, but in many ways Robbie McNamara produced the greatest performance from a jockey this year. Nobody will forget the gut-wrenching moment the news came through of McNamara's fall at Wexford on April 10 and, soon, the sombre realisation that his injuries would finish his career as a jockey.

A pall hung over Irish racing in the following days. But the manner in which McNamara fought his way back from a perilous situation, his innate, articulate bravery, made it easier for everybody else. For all his qualities as a jockey – and they were many – he has been even more impressive as a person in facing the challenge of his life.

Once the most stylish amateur in the saddle, McNamara had ridden two winners at the 2014 Cheltenham Festival – one a masterful front-running ride on Spring Heeled to win the Kim

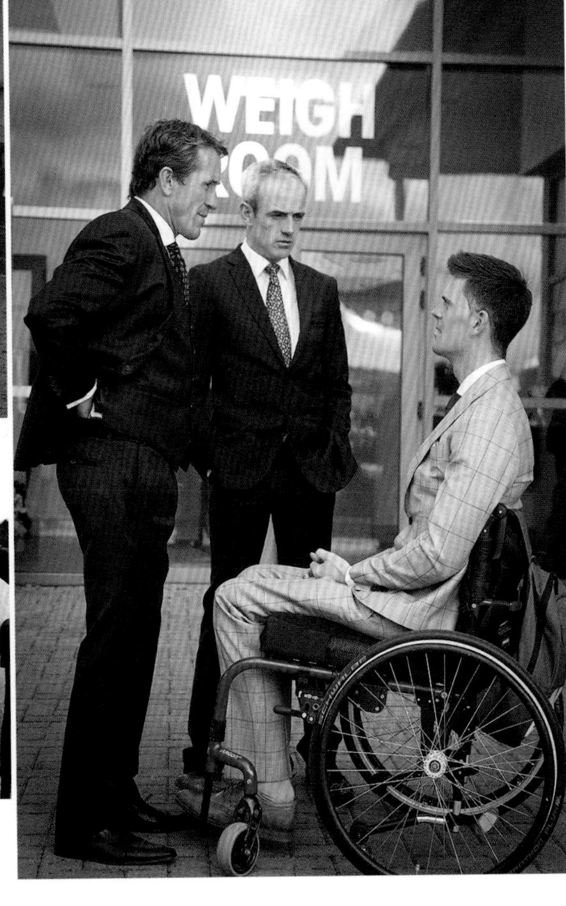

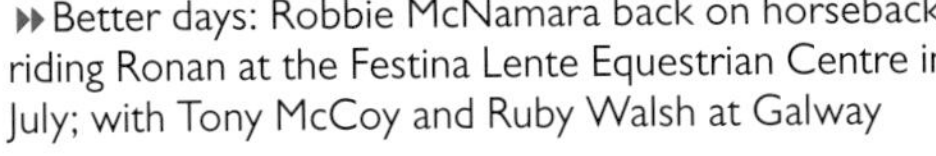
▸▸ Better days: Robbie McNamara back on horseback riding Ronan at the Festina Lente Equestrian Centre in July; with Tony McCoy and Ruby Walsh at Galway

Muir, the other a patient, perfectly timed success on Silver Concorde to beat the best of the weighing room in the Champion Bumper.

They were his first festival winners but shellacking the professionals was nothing new for McNamara, far from it. In a newspaper column last year, Bryan Cooper estimated that, but for McNamara's 6ft 3in stature, he would be "definitely in the top five or six jockeys in the country". And so the most stylish of amateurs went professional last season.

Four months after the decision was made to turn pro, that sickening spill from Bursledon in an ordinary handicap hurdle on a Friday afternoon ended a career in the big time before it even began. "I remember everything about the fall and the hours after," McNamara, 27, recalls, "but then nothing at all until two days after when I came round in the Mater Hospital after the operation, and on the Saturday night I remember my parents were there by my bed, my brother Andrew was there, and they were all crying. I said to them, 'if you want to cry, f*** off and do it somewhere else, because I'm not crying'."

Broken ribs, a collapsed lung, internal bleeding and fractured vertebrae were the war wounds from the fall but, very quickly, it was clear the psychological damage would prove an equal peak to conquer.

Eight weeks after life-saving surgery in Dublin's Mater Hospital, McNamara left for the National Rehabilitation Centre in Dun Laoghaire and from there, in September, he departed to begin his new life. A life that, within a year or so, will involve training horses.

"The thing in the Mater that frightened the living shit out of me was that I thought it was all over, for a week and a half I thought I was gone. Dead. And it frightened me so much to feel that negativity, that I couldn't find any positives. My personality was gone," says McNamara, who has always spoken with chilling honesty about his darkest days this summer.

"There was none of the calmness that I'd always have. I was shaking. My head was between my knees. It scared me that this would change my personality, that my way of floating along and dealing with things was gone. All my life that's the way I was. Sure, I'd get pissed off and annoyed but an hour later I'd be grand.

"In the Mater I couldn't shake it off. Dark thoughts all day and all night, and I think the medication was a lot to do with it. My head was gone, I couldn't think for myself and I was so frightened. Like, I knew my fate, I knew I was paralysed. But I knew I could still do everything on my own. At the start that was a big help but it did wear off. The first thing they tell you in Dun Laoghaire is not to worry about the other patients, don't be thinking 'oh, this poor lad is worse than me' and so on. As soon as you get into your room on your own they don't matter. It's what wrong with yourself.

"I was writing on Twitter at the start and I was feeling good, but people probably noticed there was nothing from me for a month," he says, with a two-word explanation of just where he was holed up for that time: "rock bottom".

"They say that spinal shock lasts six weeks and I was well aware that no feeling was going to come back but I still had that glimmer of hope. When that six-week mark hit, that's when my fate really set in. That was going to be tough on its own, but that was also the same time I came off the medication. The two hitting together? Christ . . . " he says, teeth gritted, the memory still scraping a nerve.

"Everyone knew I was struggling but didn't know how bad I was. Mark Enright and Mikey Fogarty [fellow jockeys] were a big help, they were the two I confided in. They got me back on an upward curve."

At the top of that upward curve, says McNamara, was what he calls his "epiphany", a Thursday in July when he climbed from the mire and realised that life was manageable, that his way of floating through adversity was possible.

"That Thursday I chatted to a very good social worker, told her that I couldn't possibly go any lower. She said that you can gauge when you come out of rock bottom and that you can take solace that you went as low as you possibly could and you got out of it. In saying that, if something like that happened again, I'd be gone, I wouldn't be able for it. But it is there for me that I know I got that low and came through. I swear to God I haven't had a bad day since. I'm probably better than before I got the fall."

Since the summer he has kept himself busy with media work and was back among colleagues and old friends at Galway and Listowel. He plans next year to begin the new phase of his career in racing.

"If you'd asked anyone five years ago they'd have told you training was always what I wanted to do. From day one I wanted to be a trainer, so I've always kept my eyes open and tried to learn how different trainers do things."

That knowledge, together with the determination McNamara has shown in abundance since that fateful day in April, means only a fool would bet against him.

IN THE PICTURE

Chelmsford makes fresh start – but it's not exactly smooth

Chelmsford City became the newest racecourse in Britain – and the fifth all-weather track among the 59 in total – when it held its first meeting on January 11. 'New', of course, being something of a misnomer as the track rose from the ashes of Great Leighs racecourse.

Great Leighs – which was Britain's first new racecourse for 81 years when it opened in April 2008 – lasted only nine months before the company behind the project went into administration and the doors were closed. After several abortive attempts to relaunch the track, a consortium headed by Betfred boss Fred Done took over in December 2013 and invested £15m to get the track up and running again. Finally, 2,188 days after Great Leighs closed, the racecourse was reborn as Chelmsford City.

The distinction of being the first horse to win at the relaunched Essex track went to Tryster, trained by Charlie Appleby and ridden by Adam Kirby. The picture shows the stalls opening for that landmark first race with Tryster in Godolphin blue (third left).

Chelmsford City was granted 58 race meetings in 2015 by the BHA, although there were problems along the way. Crowd numbers were limited at the first three meetings, with the general public having to wait until the 'proper' opening on February 1, when the attendance was 1,900.

That meeting brought the first rumblings of discontent with the racing surface, which was reported to be riding slow with a lot of kickback. The racecourse management launched a review of the Polytrack surface, which dated back to the Great Leighs days, and remedial work – principally a full rewaxing of the track to bind it together better – was undertaken at a "significant six-figure" cost.

There was also embarrassment when the official weighing scales failed to work properly on a number of occasions at the early fixtures.

Despite those issues, the reinvention of the racecourse was received warmly by racing professionals, particularly in view of its proximity to Newmarket, and the owners have emphasised their commitment to boosting prize-money levels on the all-weather, offering a minimum of £2.2m in the first year.

There was a statement of intent when the inaugural race was worth £20,000 and that attracted the Group-class Tryster, who turned out to be a notable first winner at Chelmsford. His victory was the first step in a five-race unbeaten sequence on the all-weather that culminated with the Winter Derby and the All-Weather Middle Distance Championships and earned the lucrative sum of £215,000.

Picture: EDWARD WHITAKER (RACINGPOST.COM/PHOTOS)

Stobart
Stobart
Stobart
racingplus
Stobart

PIONEER SPIRIT

Clive Brittain, whose optimism broke boundaries with a string of audacious big-race triumphs, retired this year against a sad background

By Peter Thomas

THE landscape of Newmarket is a constant one. It makes sporadic, minor concessions to progress, bending uncomplainingly in the wind of change before regaining the shape that has evolved out of necessity over 400 years.

Occasionally, however, the town's human vista alters unimaginably almost overnight, losing features that had seemed as immovable as the Heath itself. On the final day of the Flat season, Clive Brittain retired and nothing in racing's headquarters will ever be quite the same again.

At the age of 81, Brittain may not have been in his pomp for a little while, but it's only a couple of years since he danced his way back into our collective consciousness when star filly Rizeena restored him to the status of Group 1-winning trainer at Royal Ascot and the Curragh.

They were wins that reminded us of a

colourful thread in the sport's fabric stretching all the way back to the day in 1949 when a scrawny five-stone pony racer from Wiltshire turned up on the doorstep of the legendary Noel Murless at Beckhampton stables with his heart set on becoming a jockey.

That goal soon faded into the distance, but Brittain followed his guv'nor to Warren Place in Newmarket three years later and never left. His ambition was to be a very good stable lad, and not much beyond that, but when Murless retired, the man who began life training Welsh mountain ponies to pull milk carts had built enough of a reputation to start up on his own.

Armed with the proceeds of a punt on his old yard's 1971 Oaks winner Altesse Royale, he got off to a flying start at his new premises in Pegasus Stables before he was head-hunted by wealthy owner Captain Marcos Lemos to train from Carlburg, on the Bury Road – and a Newmarket institution was created.

By Brittain's side for the next glorious four decades was his wife of 58 years, Maureen, another former member of the Murless team, who became the social and administrative hub of the Carlburg operation through glory years that began in earnest with the 1978 St Leger win of Julio Mariner and hit top gear when Lemos's nervous but brilliant filly Pebbles landed the 1,000 Guineas in 1984.

Clive and Maureen became the town's most enduring and popular couple as his remorselessly optimistic outlook paid dividends on the track. His pioneering spirit had its detractors, but it produced a Japan Cup win with Jupiter Island in 1986 and a Kentucky Derby second with Bold Arrangement the same year.

With his 'can do' confidence and his 'why not?' attitude, Brittain broadened horizons like nobody before him and very few since, reaching his highest pinnacle when landing the 1985 Breeders' Cup Turf with Pebbles, employing a streak of animal cunning by bribing a friendly gateman to let him in the 'tradesman's entrance' and spare her the rigours of a pre-race parade that "would have blown her brain".

All the while, Maureen charmed the great and the good, dispensing champagne and goodwill that ensured a steady flow of owners into a yard whose working day always began at 5am and never finished until Clive went to bed.

Tragically, the sun that always seemed to shine on Carlburg was dimmed when Maureen's health began to decline last year and she was admitted to hospital suffering from dementia. It was a cruel blow that hastened the retirement of a man who had previously smiled his way through knees that were wrecked in a car crash, an artificial hip that was never quite the same as the real one and skin cancer that he fought off manfully yet not without hardship.

The physical discomfort he could cope with, but the loss of his beloved wife to a condition that brings suffering without release left him without the will to carry on. The success of the yard had turned Brittain from stable lad to owner of one of Newmarket's prime pieces of real estate, but the game was no longer the same when it had to be played alone.

In a moving Racing Post interview shortly before his retirement, he said: "I'm a wealthy man, but to have Maureen back as she was, I'd give this lot up and start all over again. I don't give the past too much thought, but her illness has taken the wind out of my sails and I find myself thinking back to the immaculate way she did everything. She'd run the house and the business side, we'd have breakfast parties and dinner parties and she had the knack of making everybody feel special.

"Her not being here anymore was the catalyst for me retiring – we were a team and when you've only got half a team, you're not the same. She was the brains of the outfit and being without her is so hard to deal with."

Since time immemorial, Brittain has been seen heading for the Heath in the half-light, getting up early to beat the crowds, employing his instinctive genius every day of the week to land further British Classics with Mystiko (1991 2,000 Guineas), User Friendly (1992 Oaks and St Leger) and Sayyedati (1993 1,000 Guineas).

For Brittain, however, the time was right to move on. Somehow what was once his world no longer held its worth when measured alongside the things that really matter.

WORLD CLASS

Full name Clive Edward Brittain

Born Calne, Wiltshire, December 15, 1933

First winner Vedvyas, Doncaster, April 1, 1972 (33-1)

First Group 1 winner Julio Mariner (1978 St Leger at 28-1)

British Classic winners Julio Mariner (1978 St Leger), Pebbles (1984 1,000 Guineas), Mystiko (1991 2,000 Guineas), User Friendly (1992 Oaks, St Leger), Sayyedati (1993 1,000 Guineas)

Breeders' Cup winner Pebbles (1985 Turf)

Japan Cup winner Jupiter Island (1986)

Richest win £775,862, Pebbles (1985 Breeders' Cup Turf)

Most wins in a British season 63 in 1992

Highest position in trainers' table 3rd in 1992

Glory days: (from top) Clive Brittain's brilliant filly Pebbles and jockey Philip Robinson with owner Captain Marcos Lemos after the 1984 1,000 Guineas; the trainer's trademark jig greets Rizeena's 2013 Moyglare Stud Stakes success; Brittain at home surrounded by big-race mementoes

IN THE PICTURE

Quest For More takes final Northumberland Plate held on turf

Quest For More became the last winner of a Northumberland Plate on turf in June when he took the final edition of the historic race before Newcastle's Flat track was ripped up to be replaced by an all-weather surface.

The Roger Charlton-trained five-year-old (yellow and black, nearest rail) won by a length and a quarter to signal the end of an era for the race colloquially known as the Pitmen's Derby, as it used to be a holiday occasion for mineworkers. First run in 1833, the Plate has been held at Newcastle's Gosforth Park track since 1882.

The race will continue to be the centrepiece of Newcastle's Flat racing calendar but in 2016 it will be run on Tapeta for the first time with prize-money boosted to £150,000 and a £75,000 consolation race. Jump racing will still be held on turf during the winter months.

The switch to all-weather by Arena Racing Company, which runs Newcastle, was controversial and divided opinion among racing professionals. After riding Quest For More to victory, jockey George Baker said: "It's extremely sad. I've been up here only a handful of times but it's far and away one of the best tracks in the north and it's a crying shame it's being changed."

That view was shared by many trainers. The act of destroying the widely admired turf course was criticised by Ed Vaughan (who called it "an act of vandalism"), Luca Cumani ("a disaster"), Mark Johnston ("sad") and David Barron ("ridiculous"), while Ralph Beckett said: "It is difficult to think of a more depressing announcement for the sport of horseracing."

Others, though, said Britain's first all-weather track north of the Trent was a welcome development. "It will definitely take off, regardless of how many people moan about it," said Brian Ellison, a proud Tynesider, who was born on Northumberland Plate day 63 years ago.

Fellow Malton trainer Richard Fahey was firmly behind the switch. "I was about the only person in favour when I first heard about the plans. We desperately need an all-weather course in the north and, if it has to be at Newcastle, so be it. Just looking at the configuration of the course and the plans, it promises to be the best all-weather track in Britain."

The final turf meeting was held on September 4 before the £11m redevelopment, which includes the installation of a mile floodlit straight. Having previously staged 17 Flat meetings on turf, Newcastle was granted 37 all-weather fixtures in the 2016 allocation – 21 afternoons, 11 twilight meetings and five evenings.

Picture: JOHN GROSSICK (RACINGPOST.COM/PHOTOS)

Newcastle Racecourse
JOHN SMITH'S
CITIPOST

BACK FROM THE DEAD

Jump jockey Brian Toomey made a miraculous return to race-riding this summer – two years after a horror fall that almost claimed his life

By Steve Dennis

ONE morning, just before winter officially passed on the baton to spring, a young jockey climbed aboard a horse and went up to the gallops to ride work. Nothing unusual about that, but all is not always as it seems.

This was a young jockey, yes, but more compellingly an ex-jockey. Even more compellingly, he was an ex-person, having once been dead for six seconds before returning hastily to the land of the living. Many people in such circumstances would have settled for the quiet life, for any sort of life, but not this one. Racing nearly killed Brian Toomey, but it was the only thing he lived for, so he went back to his old life anew.

Throughout his resurrection, recovery, recuperation, rehabilitation, reinvigoration, Toomey's sole intent was to be a jockey again, to race-ride as he had before. Fairytale stuff, of course, except that this fairytale came true. As February turned into March, Toomey began to write the final chapter. Are you sitting comfortably? Toomey was, on the back of Kings Grey, on the Middleham gallops. Then we'll begin.

"When he first started schooling I think I was more nervous than he was, but he just took it all in his stride," said trainer Phil Kirby, under whose matey supervision the 26-year-old began the final leg of his incredible journey. Kirby's words hinted at the disconcerting fearlessness, the unrelenting focus, with which the

young Irishman approached the task at hand.

In Toomey's mind, there was only very occasionally the slightest doubt that he would resume his career as a jockey if the authorities would allow it. His breeziness and general sangfroid about the fall that almost ended it all and about his intentions to return as swiftly as possible to the same theatre of risk have been a central theme of the story.

A few months after that fall, from Solway Dandy at Perth on July 4, 2013, after 18 days in an induced coma, after his family had been advised to say their goodbyes and asked about organ donation, just before a titanium plate was bolted across one-third of his skull to protect the battered brain beneath, Toomey dismissed recent events with the blithe bravado of youth, with its ineffable invincibility. "When I got to hospital, my brain was swelling up so much they had to remove part of my skull, because they said it would kill me otherwise. And now I'm just getting better from that. I want to be a jockey again. I'm not interested in anything else. I'll get there."

And so he did, and so he has. It took time, of course, more time than Toomey would have wished, and along the way even this undemonstrative man experienced the odd long, dark, sleepless night of the soul that goes with this sort of territory. In an interview with the Racing Post, he spoke candidly of his internal turmoil.

"Even my friends and family didn't know how bad things were, I

▸▸ Miracle man: (far left) Brian Toomey rides out on Kings Grey at Phil Kirby's yard in Middleham, North Yorkshire; (above, clockwise from left) weighing out to ride Kings Grey at Southwell in July; interviews with the media; Toomey (centre) with brother Sean, sister Aine and parents Marian and Johnny; in the parade ring; with fellow jockeys Sean Curran (centre) and Will Kennedy

didn't want to let on how much it had affected me. I've had sleepless nights, my balance was bad, and for a long time my memory was very bad. I was worried it would never get any better, that I'd never come out of it.

"When I began thinking that way my determination took over, I tried even harder, wouldn't give in to the prospect of not making a full recovery. I wanted my recovery to be as good as I could possibly make it – but it took a long time to get it that way.

"As soft as it sounds, the first time I went up the gallops was nothing special to me, because I'd been dreaming about it for long enough beforehand, so when I eventually started doing it again it was just like picking up where I'd left off."

Toomey tried to pick up where he'd left off as soon as possible, as soon as the BHA sanctioned him to begin riding out again a calendar year after that black day at Perth. This February, he reapplied for his licence and waited impatiently, conscious that his future was in the balance.

"For the purposes of Brian's application we treated him in the

▸▸ *Continues page 164*

same manner we would any other rider, the bar was set at the same level we expect of all professional jockeys," said Jerry Hill, the BHA's chief medical adviser. "No allowances were made for his injuries and the length of his absence from the sport, which makes all the more remarkable the scale of his recovery."

The long months of grinding rehabilitation at Oaksey House in Lambourn, the revival of his riding technique at Jack Berry House in Malton, the anxiety over whether his future would be the one he chose or the one he was lumbered with were all over, all worthwhile in the light of the official piece of paper that said, in true fairytale style, 'Mr Toomey, you shall ride again'.

"My parents are very proud of me – they never sat me down and said 'are you sure this is the right thing?' because they knew it was my goal, they knew it was the one thing that would really help my recovery. They're chuffed that I've done what I wanted to do," said Toomey, as his re-entry into race-riding approached.

"I'm so happy about coming back. It'll mean I've achieved the impossible, I've achieved my goal. I know there will be people who will say I'm mad to want to come back, but it's been my dream since I was a boy to be a jockey and it's a job and a life I love."

The vehicle for his return was the horse he'd been riding out for four months, honing a fresh edge on the skills blunted by inactivity but not by loss of bottle. "I've never worried, not even a little bit in the back of my mind, about having a fall," he said. That horse was the Kirby-trained 11-year-old Kings Grey, a successful chaser who nevertheless remained a novice over hurdles, and who was found an ostensibly simple opportunity in a five-runner selling hurdle at Southwell on July 12.

The media interest was colossal. After all, people who have died don't often return to the day job, large as life, or at least as large as a willow-thin jockey can be. Toomey left the racing pages, went via the back pages to the front page, a medical miracle, Lazarus Man. The day itself was one not for wild celebration but for quiet, introspective jubilation – after all, Toomey was just doing his job.

Unfortunately, Kings Grey was not up to the job despite his 1-3 odds, leading early but dropping away quickly and being pulled up before the second last. After what had gone before it might have been considered an ignominious performance but the day was not about the winning, simply about the taking part.

"It wasn't a fairytale ending, but just being alive is a fairytale ending, never mind being back on a horse," said Toomey, his feet back on the ground, a jockey again. "I've come back after being practically dead. I want to get my career back. That's the dream."

His family, fully cognisant with what might have been the ultimate nightmare, are content to allow him to pursue his dream. "It was nerve-wracking for us, but to see him come back safe is a great relief. We are always going to worry but we'll have to put it to one side," said Toomey's sister Aine.

Toomey himself has ambition to make an impact on the track rather than in the pages of The Lancet. He wants his name to appear on the honour roll of the Grand National and the Cheltenham Gold Cup, but beneath his natural ebullience he is well aware that the very appearance of his name in the racecard is the definitive success story. Hope is what fuelled him through his darkest days and hope is what Toomey's story can offer to us all.

"Hopefully my story can inspire people not just in racing but in the wider world, because what happened to me happens to people every day, and for me to do what I'm doing will show them that there's hope even in the worst of circumstances."

▸▸ For the love of it: Brian Toomey is back on the racecard and back in the saddle for his ride on Kings Grey at Southwell. Unfortunately the 1-3 shot could not make it a perfect comeback, being pulled up before the second last

'Just being alive is a fairytale ending, never mind being back on a horse. I've come back after being practically dead'

When working with horses, you cannot compromise on safety or strength. Made using advanced PVC technology all Duralock fencing is safe, strong and requires no maintenance.

Call +44 (0)1608 678238 or visit www.duralock.com

quality defined, safety assured

IN THE PICTURE

Delight to despair as Owen loses beloved Brown Panther

Michael Owen endured "the saddest day of my life" in September when Brown Panther, the high-class stayer he bred and part-owned, broke a hind leg as he attempted to clinch a second successive win in the Irish St Leger and had to be put down. Only three months earlier the former England striker had posed for this intimate portrait with his pride and joy at his Manor House Stables, near Chester, and in a Racing Post interview he said: "I can't bear thinking of life without him. It's that bad."

The seven-year-old was sitting in second place at halfway in the Irish St Leger when he quickly dropped out and was pulled up by Richard Kingscote having sustained the catastrophic injury.

In an emotional posting on social media site Sportlobster, Owen said: "It's the saddest day of my life. The toughest, most honest, most brilliant horse I will ever set eyes on passed away today doing the thing he loved most. A shattered hind leg that was irreparable according to the first-class team at the Curragh ended his life.

"I was with him when he was born, shared an experience for seven years that will never be repeated and gave him his last kiss goodbye. What an honour to own and breed him. I love you Panther, life will not be the same without you."

Owen, who bred Brown Panther out of his first racehorse Treble Heights and owned him jointly with Betfair founder Andrew Black, travelled the world to watch his star compete in the Breeders' Cup, Melbourne Cup and Dubai, where he scored his last big victory in March with a clear-cut success in the Group 2 Dubai Gold Cup.

That took his earnings past £1m and added to a roll of honour featuring Royal Ascot triumph in the 2011 King George V Handicap, the 2013 Goodwood Cup and, most spectacularly of all, his runaway victory by six and a half lengths in the 2014 Irish St Leger.

In that Racing Post interview in June, Owen reflected: "If you asked the man in the street if he could name a racehorse, I bet Brown Panther would be one of those he might give you. He is becoming a people's horse, a real favourite. That's brilliant."

Brown Panther's popularity was evident in the outpouring of grief after his death. "It really is overwhelming the genuine affection in which Brown Panther was held," said trainer Tom Dascombe, "and it is touching to know that complete strangers and many people within our industry share our despair."

Picture: EDWARD WHITAKER (RACINGPOST.COM/PHOTOS)

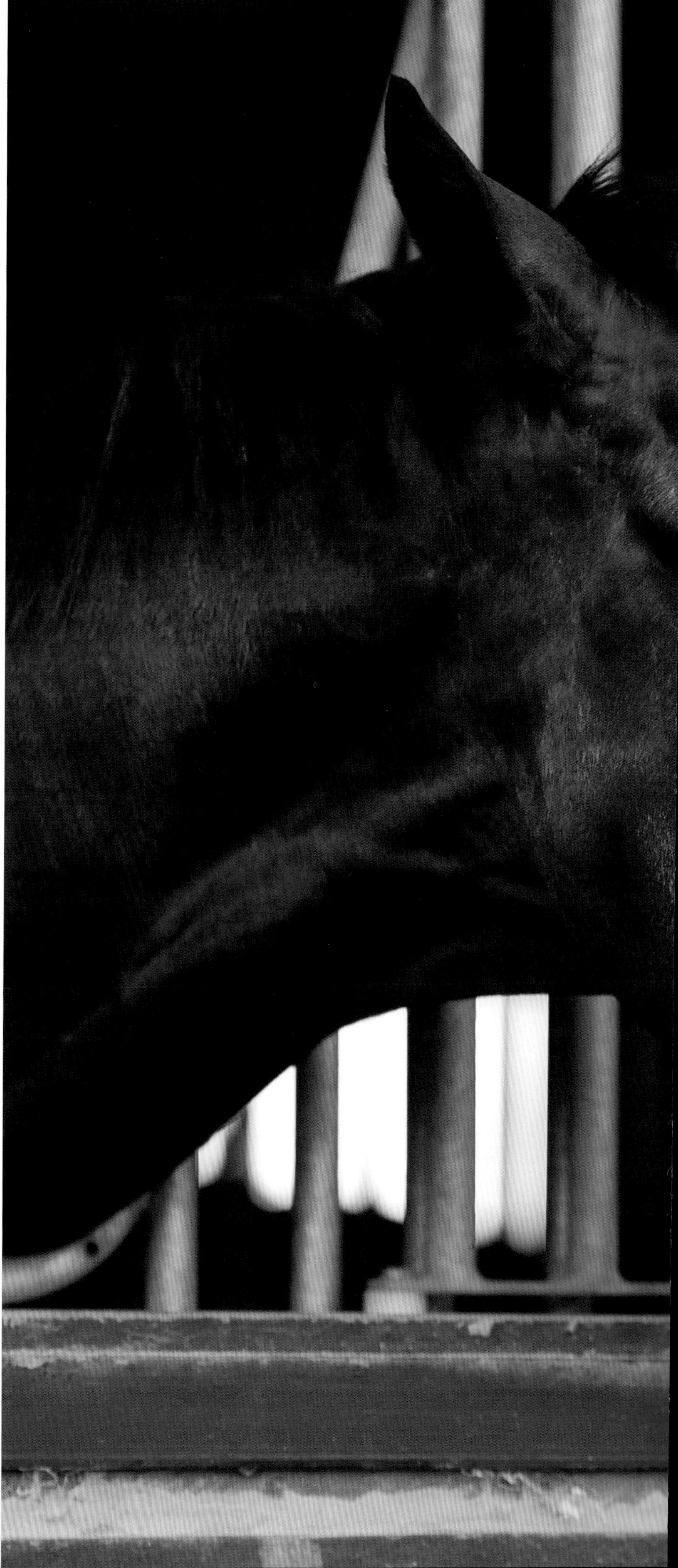

CROWNING GLORY

American Pharoah became the 12th Triple Crown winner in US racing history, ending a drought that had stretched back to the 1970s and etching his name alongside greats such as Secretariat

By Nicholas Godfrey

"AND here it is, the 37-year wait is over," bellowed race-caller Larry Collmus, his voice drowned out by an outpouring of emotion, adulation and plain relief from the boisterous Belmont Park stands. "American Pharoah is finally the one. American Pharoah has won the Triple Crown!"

For the 90,000 in attendance on a gloriously sunny afternoon in New York on June 6, this was the ultimate 'I was there' sporting moment. For everyone involved in US racing – for anyone interested in horseracing anywhere on the planet – the waiting was finally over. Amid euphoric scenes, American Pharoah had earned a place among the greats with a truly dominant performance to

win the 147th Belmont Stakes, thereby becoming the 12th horse to complete the US Triple Crown. The drought was over: at last, the US racing community could drink deep from its holy grail.

In the 36 runnings since Affirmed became the third horse in six years to achieve the feat in 1978, 13 horses had arrived at the Belmont Stakes attempting to complete the sweep. In one of the most notorious losing streaks in sporting history, all 13 had failed (admittedly, one of them, I'll Have Another, did not start in the Belmont after an eve-of-race setback).

The 14th did start, however, and he was not destined to fail. Representing the most recognisable face in US racing, trainer 'Uncle Bob' Baffert, American Pharoah crushed his rivals with a wire-to-wire victory, making all to take the $1.5m event by five and a half lengths to earn an immediate place in the equine pantheon alongside the legendary likes of Citation and Secretariat. The 25 years that separated Citation (1948) and Secretariat (1973) was the previous longest gap between Triple Crown winners before the drought was finally ended by American Pharoah.

Baffert, 62, knew enough about the so-called Belmont curse, having encountered Triple Crown failure three times before with Silver Charm (1997), Real Quiet (beaten a nose at Belmont in 1998) and War Emblem (2002).

"Thirty-seven years we've waited for this but, you know what, this little horse deserves it," he said. "The way he's been all winter and this spring has been incredible. I knew he was training well but you've got to have the horse. Down the backside I knew if he was a great horse, he was gonna do it. And he's a great horse."

****

GREAT expectations had always surrounded American Pharoah. "Bob never hypes a horse for me, but he kept telling me, 'This is the one, this is the one. I've been waiting my whole life for a horse like this,'" owner-breeder Ahmed Zayat told US reporters in the days before the Belmont. "This is a dream come true," added the Cairo-born Egyptian-American businessman, who bred American Pharoah from his 2009 Kentucky Derby runner-up Pioneerof The Nile.

New Jersey-based Zayat, who originally made his money from selling non-alcoholic beer to Muslims in his native country, entered the US racing world after selling the business for a reported $280m in 2002. American Pharoah was the second foal of Zayat's mare Littleprincessemma, named after the owner's daughter; the colt was officially sold for $300,000 as a yearling but in reality was bought back via a bloodstock agent after failing to make the $1m asking price.

It was fortunate for Zayat that nobody was properly interested. He sent the young horse to his main trainer, the west-coast legend Baffert. "Day one we felt that he

▸▸ *Continues page 170*

had brilliance in him – his demeanour, his aura, his conformation, the way he moved," Zayat said.

Baffert said he liked American Pharoah from the off but there was to be a rude awakening on his two-year-old debut in August 2014 in a Polytrack maiden at Del Mar, the summer home of California's racing elite. Ten months before his run into racing folklore at Belmont, the bay colt – once listed as a ridgling – with a faint white star on his forehead, an unusually short tail and a curious spelling was sent off heavy favourite. After losing composure beforehand, he seriously screwed up, finishing only fifth of nine. According to the Daily Racing Form, "Baffert had touted American Pharoah as his best two-year-old. Someone sitting in Baffert's box remarked after the race that if that was his best two-year-old, he was in trouble."

Baffert's faith was unabashed: the horse continued to work brilliantly and he was chucked into the Grade 1 pool less than a month later at the same venue for the Del Mar Futurity – albeit with a few changes designed to calm anxieties. "We took the blinkers off, put cotton in his ears and schooled him a lot," the trainer recalled. "He trained well, we decided he was ready and we threw him in there at the last minute."

He also engaged a new rider in War Emblem's jockey Victor Espinoza, enjoying an Indian summer in a career approaching the veteran stages thanks to his association with California Chrome, who had forfeited the 2014 Triple Crown at the Belmont. "He [American Pharoah] is a little bit of a headcase," Baffert told Espinoza. "You got along with War Emblem. Maybe you will get along with this guy."

Not favourite for the only time in his career, American Pharoah made all to score by nearly five lengths. "He's always shown he's different," Baffert said. "He behaved himself and showed what he could do. He did what we thought he'd do the first time." He did it the next time as well with a carbon copy on his dirt debut in the Grade 1 FrontRunner Stakes at Santa Anita, where American Pharoah was sent to the front and stayed there without any semblance of danger.

An injury described as a "deep, deep foot bruise" to his near-fore – a suspected suspensory problem never showed up on x-ray, according to Zayat – deprived him of the chance to stamp his authority in the Breeders' Cup Juvenile; in his absence, the race was won by Texas Red, miles behind American Pharoah on his previous outing. He could not beat American Pharoah in Eclipse Award voting either and the Baffert colt was named North America's champion two-year-old.

****

THOUGHTS turned immediately towards the Triple Crown. American Pharoah took the Arkansas route to Churchill Downs, barely breaking sweat for a pair of daylight victories at Oaklawn Park in the spring. Although the opposition was not exactly top drawer on either occasion – he was sent off at 2-5 and 1-10 – both victories held significance. Sloppy track conditions when he made all to win the Rebel Stakes in March suggested that whatever might beat him in the future, it would not be the weather. Stepped back up to Grade 1 company next time out for his final Kentucky prep in the $1m Arkansas Derby, American Pharoah demonstrated his versatility by sitting just off the pace instead of being sent straight to the lead.

Evidently this was no one-dimensional front-runner, an attribute that was to serve him well at Churchill Downs three weeks later on the first Saturday in May. Then, as might be imagined, he would be made to work a little harder in the race that really mattered.

American Pharoah arrived at Churchill Downs for the storied $2m contest burdened with the mantle of

▸▸ Three steps to heaven: (left to right) American Pharoah wins the Kentucky Derby at Churchill Downs on May 2; a fortnight later, he adds the Preakness Stakes on a sloppy track at Pimlico; his five-week quest for the Triple Crown – and US racing's 37-year wait for another winner – ends gloriously as jockey Victor Espinoza salutes victory in the Belmont Stakes

being this year's 'horse most likely'; just listen to D Wayne Lukas, who saddled outsider Mr. Z. "I think we're going to see something really special, though I don't want to put Bob on the spot here," the 79-year-old said. "If you stop and look at a couple of noses and nods, he's come the closest to the Triple Crown as anyone in 20 years. I think it could be his year."

By common consent, the 141st edition of the Kentucky Derby featured the most talented field for some time but perhaps the biggest threat came from within American Pharoah's own barn in the Baffert-trained Dortmund, who was unbeaten in six. "I'm sitting on these two outstanding individuals, so I feel like I've got the No. 1 and the No. 2 in the draft," Baffert said. "I think the California horses are pretty tough this year."

Baffert was right on the money, though for a while it seemed as if the burden of expectation was hanging heavy on American Pharoah. In front of a record crowd of 170,513, the favourite (at just under 3-1) raced wide at both turns before being produced at the head of the stretch and then needing serious coercion in an ugly, whip-flailing drive from Espinoza to put away a gallant runner-up in Firing Line, trained in California by former Newmarket man Simon Callaghan. In the end, he was vanquished by only a length, with Dortmund a couple more back in third. "I feel like the luckiest Mexican on earth," Espinoza said. "He has been a special horse since the first time I rode him. He has a lot of talent and is an unbelievable horse. Turning for home I started riding a little bit harder. At the eighth pole I just couldn't put that other horse away, but he got it done."

Everyone involved in US racing

▸▸ *Continues page 172*

BLASTS FROM THE PAST

Horse and owner had intriguing back stories

A curious tail An unusual characteristic of American Pharoah is his short tail. Various theories have emerged, including the suggestion that it was chewed off by fellow Zayat Stables homebred Mr. Z when the pair were stationed in Florida as young horses. Bob Baffert has offered a different story. "I think he was in the pasture one day and there was a mountain lion chasing him," he suggested. "That was the closest he could get."

A curious tale Owner-breeder Ahmed Zayat's biography was well rehearsed in the US press. Five years previously Zayat went through bankruptcy in the wake of a lawsuit by Fifth Third Bank, which claimed Zayat had defaulted on $34m in loans, while a federal lawsuit dating back to 2003 alleging he welched on $1.65m in offshore-casino bets re-emerged in the wake of the Preakness.

"It's a fraud," Zayat told the Associated Press, adding that he was being blackmailed and had asked for the suit to be thrown out. "It's a scam from A to Z. It's total fiction. It's a total lie." The lawsuit was thrown out.

▸▸ Hero worship: American Pharoah is the centre of attention at Belmont Park after sealing his Triple Crown success

covets the Kentucky Derby but perhaps Zayat had more reason than most after no fewer than three second places in a five-year spell via Pioneerof The Nile (2008), Nehro (2011) and Bodemeister (2012), the horse named after Baffert's young son Bode. An emotional victory was almost too much for the Zayat family to bear. "No more seconds," said Ahmed Zayat, crying tears of joy; his son Justin, an integral part of the operation, had a more visceral response: he threw up.

A record crowd of 131,680 also turned up a fortnight later at Pimlico in Baltimore for the Preakness Stakes. Unfortunately the weather did not turn up, as the race was run minutes after a torrential downpour that turned the track into a sea of mud; not that it mattered to American Pharoah, who overcame a potentially unfavourable inside draw to slosh away from his rivals. As quiet here as he had been animated at Churchill Downs, Espinoza kept it simple by putting American Pharoah straight on the lead and avoiding all the kickback. While an opening split of 22.90s was one of the fastest in Preakness history, the final time of 1m58.46s was the slowest since 1956, testament to how easy it had been for the winner.

With his main opponents – such as Dortmund and Firing Line – getting stuck in the mud, he had little to beat but did so with a dominant seven-length triumph over 29-1 longshot Tale Of Verve. "He's just an incredible horse," Baffert said. "What he does is amazing. The weather really scared me but great horses do great things and I think he showed that today."

****

AND so to New York, where after nearly four decades of hurt for US racing, American Pharoah was set to become the latest horse to meet his date with destiny. "The sport without a star is not a sport," said Zayat as American Pharoah spread the feelgood factor across the beleaguered US racing community.

"I really feel a lot of positive energy because of this horse," Baffert said. "I know a lot of people are hoping – they put their hat on something big like this. A horse like what he's done, there's a certain aura about him. And he has caught everybody's attention. I'm so glad that they gave him to me to train. I think Bode could train this horse."

However, there is a reason why the Belmont is nicknamed the 'Test of the Champion', and that is because the 1m4f event is a severe challenge, one that had been failed by every Triple Crown aspirant since Affirmed completed the historic sequence in 1978. The list of the vanquished at Belmont featured iconic names: Spectacular Bid, Sunday Silence, Smarty Jones, California Chrome. Each of them won the Kentucky Derby and

▸▸ *Continues page 174*

'A horse like what he's done, there's a certain aura about him. And he has caught everybody's attention. I'm so glad that they gave him to me to train'

Need More
Horse power?

Call now to find out how Dodson & Horrell
can fuel your future success.

Contact our Thoroughbred Team now for more advice and support
0845 345 2627 | www.dodsonandhorrell.com

Preakness Stakes, only to fall at the final hurdle.

"I never thought I'd go through this again," Baffert said. "I'm reminded every year of Real Quiet and Silver Charm. He's a different horse than they were. You really don't know until the whole series is over how good the horses are. I'm just hoping I brought the right horse here, but we won't know until halfway into the race."

In the event, American Pharoah never really looked like joining the ranks of the Belmont beaten. Kicked to the front after breaking a stride slowly at the gate, he was allowed a surprisingly easy lead and duly ambled around the wide oval of the racetrack known as the 'Big Sandy'. Any stamina worries never came into play as American Pharoah led into the stretch with second favourite Frosted giving vain chase, unable to get closer than a couple of lengths away. After they straightened up, American Pharoah drew clear for an authoritative five-and-a-half-length success as the stands resounded with deafening cheers.

"I didn't know how I was going to feel; now I know and I'm very emotional," Baffert said. "I'm just thinking about my parents – I wish they'd been alive to see this but they were with me today. I was thinking about them the whole race. I feel like I have a very special horse and he's the one that won it, not me."

Espinoza, who turned 43 the week before the race, recalled his two previous attempts at a Triple Crown on War Emblem and California Chrome. "That trophy has given me a lot of stress but to finally get it . . . the third time is the charm," he said. "I came here with a ton of confidence, more than the last two times. I said, 'I hope American Pharoah feels like me.' And he did."

Reviewing the race, Espinoza added: "He broke a step slow but in two jumps I was in the lead where I wanted to be. He's just an amazing horse to ride – the way he hit the ground, you couldn't even feel how fast he was moving. You feel like you're going in slow motion."

The time of 2m26.65s was the sixth-fastest in Belmont history and the best since Baffert's only previous winner, Point Given, in 2001. "This is for the sport," shouted Zayat as he hoisted the trophy aloft. "New Yorkers, all racing fans, this is for you. I feel so honoured, humbled, privileged."

And richer, having sold the breeding rights in American Pharoah, whom he described as a "freak of nature", to Coolmore's US arm Ashford before the race in a deal said to be worth $20m – plus extras if he won the Belmont.

Zayat retained the racing rights and vowed that American Pharoah would continue to race for the remainder of his three-year-old campaign. Frankly, though, it would not really have mattered had he never run again. An enduring place in racing history was already assured.

▸▸ Winning combination: jockey Victor Espinoza and trainer Bob Baffert (red tie) celebrate with the Triple Crown trophy

LEGENDS

THE 12 US TRIPLE CROWN WINNERS

1919 **Sir Barton**
1930 **Gallant Fox**
1935 **Omaha**
1937 **War Admiral**
1941 **Whirlaway**
1943 **Count Fleet**
1946 **Assault**
1948 **Citation**
1973 **Secretariat**
1977 **Seattle Slew**
1978 **Affirmed**
2015 **American Pharoah**

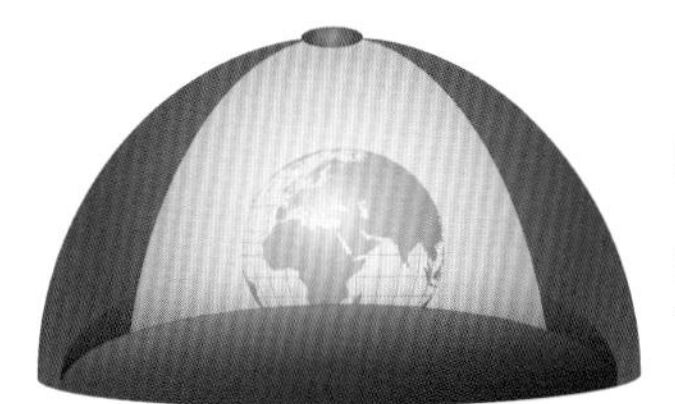

Abu Dhabi The Capital

المؤتمر العالمي لخيول السباق العربية

WORLD ARABIAN HORSE RACING CONFERENCE

ITALY 2016 إيطاليا

MAY 25-29, 2016

Rome, Italy

Sustained By

Coordinated By

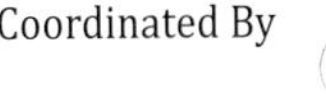

in Cooperation with

Official Partner

Official Carrier

Sponsored By

THE BIGGER PICTURE

Six-time racing photographer of the year Edward Whitaker points his camera at the water to capture a runner jumping the fence in front of the stands during the Harwell Trophy won by the David Pipe-trained Smiles For Miles at Newbury in January

EDWARD WHITAKER (RACINGPOST.COM/PHOTOS)

NOVICE CHASER

Olympic gold medallist Victoria Pendleton took up horse riding this year with the ambitious target of being ready to compete in the 2016 Foxhunter at Cheltenham

By Peter Thomas

TO SOME it was a publicity stunt, to others an affront to hard-working amateur riders everywhere, but it was far closer to the mark to describe Victoria Pendleton's bid to become a no-holds-barred jump jockey in less than a year as exceedingly brave and borderline barmy.

There cannot be many multiple Olympic gold medallists and world champions who, having retired at the top of their game with a sideboard full of silverware, would risk their gilt-edged sporting reputation by marching into a dangerous alien arena and asking to go toe to toe with hardened campaigners; but then Pendleton is not only a track cycling legend but also a sportswoman with an all-consuming work ethic and a need for a quest.

So when she was approached by Betfair to take up the challenge of turning herself into a rider fit to compete in the 2016 Foxhunter Chase at the Cheltenham Festival, she leapt at the chance; after all, she had once been advised she was too small, weak and psychologically feeble to be a professional cyclist, so achieving the impossible was nothing she couldn't handle.

"I was past my cycling best-before date," she says, "and the idea of having something to work for and train for and a purpose to get up in the morning for was something I'd really missed.

"At the start of my career, I was told I didn't have the right mentality to be a champion, and for me it was the biggest driving force – if you say I can't do it, I'm going to put my head down and do it.

"So for me it was never about the competing or proving that you're the best in the world at something – although that's nice – it was more about the progress, pushing yourself each and every day to get stronger, better, faster, quicker to react."

With that in mind, Pendleton

▸▸Pedal power to horse power: (clockwise from far left) Victoria Pendleton gets a feel for the female changing room at Cheltenham; weighing out for her ride on Royal Etiquette at Beverley in September; in the race on Royal Etiquette; riding Mighty Mambo in a charity event at Newbury in July; and after unsaddling

began her quest by rubbing shoulders with the McCoys and Walshes at the Cheltenham Festival, knowing she had little more than 12 months in which to complete her transformation from complete novice to a level that would enable her to compete at the 'Olympics' of jump racing.

She had "shovelled poop" before as work experience, but that was the closest she had come to the racing experience and now she was diving in at the deep end, albeit with the expert help of trainers Alan and Lawney Hill, jumping guru Yogi Breisner and event rider Chris King.

Even with their assistance, however, there were no foregone conclusions about her mission and plenty of obstacles, literally, to overcome, but within 19 weeks of first sitting on a horse she rode in her first race, the George Frewer Celebration Sweepstake charity event over a mile and five furlongs at Newbury, and finished a creditable eighth of 11 on Mighty Mambo.

It was a far cry from what will face her at Cheltenham, but she did what she hoped to do, avoided humiliation and emerged with her enthusiasm intact, ready to face her first race under rules on August 31, in which she was second by a head on Royal Etiquette at Ripon. A 13th-placed finish on the same horse at Beverley the following month may have looked like a backward step, but Pendleton remains on course for her main objective, even if she is painfully aware of the risks and uncertainties involved.

She moved on from the Flat to partnering Sedgemoor Express and According To Sarah, the pair of Alan Hill-trained point-to-pointers assigned to carry her through the next part of her quest. Despite her promising start on the racecourse, the size of the challenge is all too clear.

"To my friends, I'm Captain Sensible," smiles the unstoppably enthusiastic 35-year-old. "You can get hurt cycling, but not that hurt, and this is probably the most dangerous sport there is, so if I don't develop in the way I'm hoping I will, I'm not going to go crazy.

"I saw some horses being schooled right next to me at the outset, so I knew the extent of it before I said I'd give it a try. The fences are high, there's no doubt about it, but it looks incredible. The idea of being in motion at that speed with a creature, together in a partnership, is incredible."

Britain's most successful female Olympian has jumped the queue, that's for sure, but when she lines up to face the daunting Cheltenham fences in March there will be no hiding place and no amount of privilege will protect her from the rigours and perils of the Foxhunter.

Criticism has come her way from those who see the whole thing as a manufactured PR exercise, but a broader public seems to have latched on to her efforts, generating valuable publicity for the sport. There's no doubting Pendleton's commitment, her humility in the face of the task and the goodwill that has come her way from all corners of the racing world.

"The challenge I've taken on is absolutely ridiculous on many levels," she admits, "but I'm blown away by how generous, helpful and encouraging people have been – and how many people have offered to sell me a horse!

"It's a really, really tough sport to be in and I understand some people may not like me, but I'd just like to say I feel so grateful and thankful for this opportunity. I know it probably means nothing to them, but I really am."

If Pendleton ends up good enough to line up with the top amateurs at Cheltenham in March, you can be sure she'll have got there through painstaking preparation and Olympian courage, with trepidation not far from the surface but a lot of love for racing in her heart. The festival must seem awfully close at hand already for the champion facing her toughest task of all.

ARABIAN LIGHTS

The prestigious Sheikh Mansoor Festival gave fresh impetus to the rising profile of Arabian racing – and provided memorable moments for one British trainer in particular

MICHAEL DODS is not the only British trainer who had a breakthrough Group 1 success this year. The other is much less well known even now and, while Mecca's Angel blazed to Nunthorpe glory at high speed for Dods, her landmark winner came at a more sedate pace – although in no less dramatic fashion.

The trainer is Beverley Deutrom and her speciality is Arabian racing, the branch of the sport that goes back to the very origins of the thoroughbred and has its own distinctive flavour. The different rhythm of Arabian racing and the characteristics of the horses – smaller, slower and with shorter necks and dished faces – are becoming more familiar to racegoers at major thoroughbred meetings and it was on Lingfield's Derby and Oaks Trials card in May that Deutrom landed her first Group 1 in Britain.

The Sheikh Zayed Bin Sultan Al Nahyan Cup was the British leg of a global series that has raised Arabian racing to new heights and culminates in a valuable finals day in Abu Dhabi in November. In the world of Arabian racing this was no ordinary race, and it produced an extraordinary finish.

Many races in this sphere are won from the front, with most horses below the top class lacking a change of pace, and Deutrom feared the worst for Lahoob – one of her two representatives in the ten-runner contest over a mile – when the grey was slowly away.

"When I saw him jump out and he was at the back, I thought 'oh no, that's it'," admits the trainer, who is based in East Sussex during the summer months and in Dubai over the winter. "But Harry Bentley gave him a brilliant ride. He was patient, whereas a lot of jockeys would have hassled the horse and then he'd have probably said 'no, thanks'. Harry just sat and waited, and amazingly the horse picked up. Arabs don't tend to pick up like thoroughbreds, so I was quite surprised to see him come flying down the outside."

Lahoob's strong finish gave him victory by a neck from the favourite, Al Hibaab, with the French-trained Ghazwa another neck back in third, and none of the seven thoroughbred races later in the day could produce a finish like that.

▸▸World in motion (clockwise from far left): Karar wins the Sheikha Fatima Bint Mubarak Apprentice World Championship race at Sandown in July; Lahoob in the Lingfield winner's enclosure after taking the British leg of the Sheikh Zayed Bin Sultan Al Nahyan Cup; apprentices and officials line up at the Sandown prize-giving; delegates at the sixth World Arabian Horse Racing Conference, held in Warsaw in May; Beverley Deutrom, who trains Karar and Lahoob

Pictures: **MORHAF AL ASSAF & DEBBIE BURT**

"It was amazing, and very exciting to win a Group 1. I won a Group 1 in Oman with Maghazi in 2011, but I'm not sure the rest of the world count that," says Deutrom, 51, who went close to a double at Lingfield when Maghazi was runner-up in the HH Sheikha Fatima Bint Mubarak Ladies World Championship, the other Arabian race on the card.

Like the Sheikh Zayed Bin Sultan Al Nahyan Cup, the HH Sheikha Fatima Bint Mubarak Ladies World Championship is part of the Sheikh Mansoor Global Arabian Festival, which is billed as a 'one world, six continents' competition. The other two race series in the festival, the Wathba Stud Farm Cup and the HH Sheikha Fatima Bint Mubarak Apprentice World Championship, also had British legs, in another boost to the growing profile of this form of racing.

Deutrom was successful again in the apprentice race at Sandown in July with another grey, Karar, who had been eighth to stablemate Lahoob at Lingfield. There was a kind of revenge involved, too, as the runner-up was Man Of Dreams, who had beaten Maghazi into second place at Lingfield.

A major aim of the Sheikh Mansoor Festival is to provide opportunities for apprentices and female riders and Irish apprentice Ian Queally, who showed his talent with a 20 per cent strike-rate on the Flat in Ireland in 2015, won a place in the grand final in Abu Dhabi with victory on Karar. "This is my first time on board an Arabian horse," he said. "The instructions were to ride easily, but the horse was slow and one-paced at the start and I had to push quite hard to keep him in contention, but he picked up nicely at halfway and travelled well after that."

Deutrom was also on the winners' list with a handicap victory at the long-established Dubai International Arabian Races at Newbury in July, which had a further boost this year with Dubai Duty Free sponsoring one of the three Group 1 races on the card.

Major honours that day went to trainer Julian Smart, who took two of the Group 1 races with Djainka Des Forges and Gazwan. Both were ridden by Bentley, once again showing his versatility in a year that also saw him record a half-century in the British thoroughbred Flat season for the first time.

Lahoob was fourth to Gazwan but by then he had added to a memorable season for Deutrom. "A couple in the Lingfield race subsequently won Group 1s, which franked the form, and Lahoob went to Holland in June and won a Group 3 in the Sheikh Zayed Cup," she says.

The Dutch race was the eighth of the 13 races in the Sheikh Zayed Bin Sultan Al Nahyan Cup prior to the finals in Abu Dhabi – which feature the Sheikh Zayed Bin Sultan Al Nahyan Jewel Crown, the world's richest Arabian race with a purse of €1.2m (£880,000) – and Deutrom is grateful for the opportunities provided by the Sheikh Mansoor Festival under the direction of Lara Sawaya, executive director of the festival.

"It's on a different level now and for me it's much better," says the trainer, who remembers racing for £100 prizes when she first started in Arabian racing in the early 1990s, whereas Lahoob's Lingfield win was worth £34,000. "I love the big days, with the big crowds, and I love the competition, there's no point winning an easy race. I like to have a challenge.

"Quality-wise this is the best year I've had and for consistency too, my strike-rate's about 26 per cent. It helps to have the right horses. We had a good team this year and everything seemed to go right. In the past we've had viruses and this year we had a fairly clean run, which was great."

Deutrom was nominated in the trainer category of this year's Sheikha Fatima Bint Mubarak Darley Awards, the glittering event held in Hollywood each April that honours the top performers in the sport, and is set to be in the reckoning again after such a successful season.

At heart, though, even such a competitive person is driven first and foremost by her love of the horses. "I bought an Arab at an auction, rode it, trained it, won my first race and got totally hooked. That was in 1991," she says. "Arabians think a bit more than thoroughbreds, so they can be a bit trickier. I'm lucky enough to have a small number and I can treat them as individuals, which makes a huge difference. They're lovely, great characters."

THE BIGGER PICTURE

Dramatic action on the frozen lake of St Moritz, Switzerland, during the 'White Turf' meeting held on three consecutive Sundays in February. This picture shows Arabian horses from the HH Sheikha Fatima Bint Mubarak Ladies World Championship, a 14-race global series culminating with a finals day in Abu Dhabi in November

SWISS-IMAGE.CH / ANDY METTLER

Our selection of the horses and people – some established, some up-and-coming – who are likely to be making headlines in 2016

LUMIERE

Mark Johnston was both confident and nervous before Lumiere ran in the Group 1 Cheveley Park Stakes at Newmarket in September. The reason, the trainer explained, was that he considered the filly "the best horse I've had for a long, long time".

He is so convinced of her ability and her suitability for a Classic mile that three weeks before the Cheveley Park "I told someone I'm sure she'll win the Guineas". It was just he wasn't quite so confident she would win the Cheveley Park, as Lumiere had gone in her coat and lacked experience after only two outings.

Johnston needn't have worried. The grey filly defeated market rivals Illuminate and Besharah with a game success from the front; if this was what she was like when not in peak condition, it was even more promising.

The trio had been closely tied on form throughout the season (Illuminate beat Besharah, who then beat Lumiere) but Johnston's filly had the last word as she lived up to the high hopes that had followed her from the start. Adrian Nicholls and Russ Kennemore both sang her praises after riding her in workouts early in the summer, with the latter telling Johnston it was "the fastest I'd ever been up the gallop and I'd been scared because I couldn't pull her up at the end".

Will she develop into something more than a juvenile speedster? Johnston, who includes the marvellous filly Attraction (1,000 Guineas) among his Classic winners and had Lumiere's sire Shamardal as a juvenile before his French 2,000 Guineas victory for Godolphin, has no doubt.

AIR FORCE BLUE

Save the date: April 30, 2016. That is the day Air Force Blue is expected to make his next appearance, in the Qipco 2,000 Guineas at Newmarket, and it will be one of the unmissable events of the year. Is it too early to mention the F-word? Well, apologies for any offence caused, but here goes.

The Aidan O'Brien-trained colt will approach the mile Classic in much the same position as Frankel five years earlier: a brilliant Dewhurst winner, highly rated by connections and handicappers alike, but with the task of going from star two year-old to superstar three-year-old.

Frankel had a prep run for the Guineas, which is not usually O'Brien's way, but the Rowley Mile was the all-important first proving ground. In winning by six lengths at Newmarket, he left no doubt that he was bound for greatness and many will expect to see a similarly dominant performance from Air Force Blue.

O'Brien's colt will be still two days short of his actual third birthday on Guineas day and, having made such a vibrant mark as a two-year-old without the precociousness often conferred by an early foaling date, he is clearly expected to make further massive strides as he grows from the equine equivalent of boy to man.

"It felt like there was plenty more to come," jockey Ryan Moore said after the Dewhurst. "He's a big horse and is still filling that frame. There should be more to come over the winter, with a bit of luck."

Might those last five words cool some of the hype surrounding Air Force Blue and remind us of the essential fragility of horses and our dreams? Probably not.

RICHARD HUGHES

In his first full season Richard Hughes will carry with him a fund of public goodwill after his daring exploits in the saddle as well as a high level of expectation that he will follow in the footsteps of his late father Dessie by turning from top jockey to top trainer.

Hughes, 42, dipped his toe in the water with a handful of runners before the end of the 2015 Flat season but the big test will come only after a winter's preparation at the historic Danebury yard in Hampshire that he described as a "hidden jewel" when he first visited. As Hughes said himself: "I honestly feel my first full year will be the most important year in my training career."

If that vital campaign goes right, Hughes will have laid the foundations for a second career as successful as his first. Champion jockeys do not always make great trainers – in recent times Lester Piggott and Pat Eddery were no more than moderately successful – but a key difference with Hughes is that he deliberately retired at a young enough age to give himself every chance of building that second career.

Hughes is under no illusions about the size of the task he has taken on. But it is one he was born to, has planned for, and will attack with relish.

VAUTOUR

"I stuck my neck out and said 'this horse is going chasing', and I'm glad it's worked out [because] I can just see Willie Mullins giving me a hard time if it hadn't." Ruby Walsh's firm conviction about Vautour after his victory in the 2014 Supreme Novices' Hurdle was proved right with a breathtaking victory in the JLT Novices' Chase on his return to Cheltenham and the festival's top rider was left in no doubt what should come next. "He's definitely a Gold Cup horse," Walsh said after that 15-length demolition, which stamped Vautour as one of the most exciting chasers around.

Merely jumping the feared Cheltenham fences was not enough for Vautour ("he was like a gazelle," Walsh said) and Mullins admitted his heart was in his mouth as he watched. For the rest of us, as Mullins acknowledged, there was a 'wow, wow, wow' effect as Vautour sailed over the obstacles and drew right away from a pair of Grade 1 winners.

Walsh believes Vautour could win over any distance, hinting (though not explicity saying) that here is another chaser with the versatility of Kauto Star, who won two Tingle Creek Chases at two miles as well as two Gold Cups and five King Georges.

In that respect it was interesting that Mullins was aiming for the two-mile Champion Chase at the Punchestown festival until Vautour failed to sparkle in his prep gallop.

Mentioning Vautour in the same breath as Kauto Star may be premature, but there is no doubting his potential as a top-class chaser. "He's the real deal – I may be wrong but you have to dream," Walsh said. As he well knows, it promises to be some ride.

PEACE AND CO

Even the best four-year-old hurdlers can have difficulty adjusting to the senior ranks but, if any are going to take high rank this season, the likelihood is that they will come from the Nicky Henderson stable.

Henderson dominated the juvenile hurdle division last season, landing a 1-2-3 in the Triumph Hurdle when Peace And Co led home Top Notch and Hargam, with ten lengths back to Devilment in fourth place. Although Hargam subsequently flopped when odds-on at Aintree, the first two were put away after Cheltenham and clearly Henderson believes they are capable of further progress.

That certainly applies to Peace And Co, whose Cheltenham victory came on only his fourth outing (three for Henderson after a debut win in France). Henderson admitted he was "gobsmacked" when Peace And Co won by 19 lengths on his British debut at Doncaster, which already put him close to Triumph-winning standard. Although there was a dip next time in his Cheltenham prep (it was a case of educating him, the trainer said), he improved to an above-average RPR of 155 at the festival (only Our Conor and Zaynar have given better Triumph-winning performances since Racing Post Ratings started).

Seven of the last nine Triumph winners have become high-class performers in the senior ranks and Barry Geraghty, who rode Peace And Co at Cheltenham, has no doubt the best is yet to come. "Physically he's immature, and a horse with a future," he said. "He has the size and scope for a fence, but he also has the pace for a hurdler." Exciting times lie ahead.

DOUVAN

Even in a stable of superstars, Douvan was quick to put himself in the spotlight with a series of stunning performances. Now, having established himself as a headline act, greater fame and fortune surely awaits.

Recruited from France in the summer of 2014, Douvan could not have been more impressive in his first season with Willie Mullins. He won all four starts over hurdles, peaking with an RPR of 160 in winning the Supreme Novices' Hurdle at Cheltenham and virtually matching that standard with another Grade 1 victory at Punchestown to round off his perfect first campaign.

Each triumph was accompanied by rave reviews and the usually restrained Mullins bubbled with excitement even before Douvan destroyed the opposition at the two big end-of-season festivals. At Cheltenham he scored by four and a half lengths from his stablemate Shaneshill, who won a Grade 2 by 13 lengths on his next outing, and at Punchestown he beat Sizing John (third at Cheltenham) by seven and a half lengths.

The tricky part for Mullins came in the summer when he had to decide whether to follow his natural inclination to send Douvan novice chasing or aim for the Champion Hurdle. With Douvan 11-4 favourite for the Arkle Chase and 10-1 second favourite behind stablemate Faugheen in the Champion Hurdle, it did not seem Mullins could go wrong but there was a lot to weigh up, not least where Douvan fitted into the overall scheme of his all-conquering stable.

It was exactly the same dilemma Mullins had faced 12 months earlier with Faugheen ("Douvan looks every inch a chaser, though I said the same about Faugheen," he said at Cheltenham) and he called that one right. Time will tell if Mullins has chosen the right script but all the signs are that Douvan will be centre stage again.

JOHN FERGUSON

The dominant trainer of the summer over jumps was John Ferguson, with close to double the number of winners of his nearest rival, and he already had a personal-best on the board before the 2015-16 season entered the core winter period. This was a notable change of pace even for a trainer who always makes hay while the sun shines – this summer he had 50 winners by the end of September, up from 26 the year before.

With three consecutive half-centuries on the board, Ferguson, 55, now faces the challenge of pushing on towards the three-figure mark and increasing his impact in the winter season. That

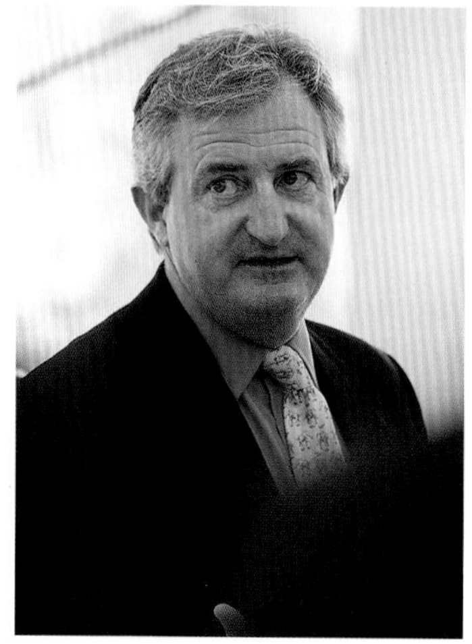

has not been easy in the past with his team of Flat-breds, who are much better suited by good ground, but he has won two Grade 1s over hurdles and a Grade 2 over fences, and gradually more store horses have been brought into the fold.

This summer also brought another significant addition to the set-up at Bloomfields, just outside Newmarket, when Aidan Coleman was signed as retained jockey. The 27-year-old former champion conditional is seen as one of the riders 'most likely to' in the post-McCoy era and their link-up was an immediate success.

The real proving ground as a 'winter trainer' are the big festivals, where Ferguson's story has been one of near-misses and misfortune. With that strong summer behind him, Ferguson will be hoping this is the season when his luck finally turns.

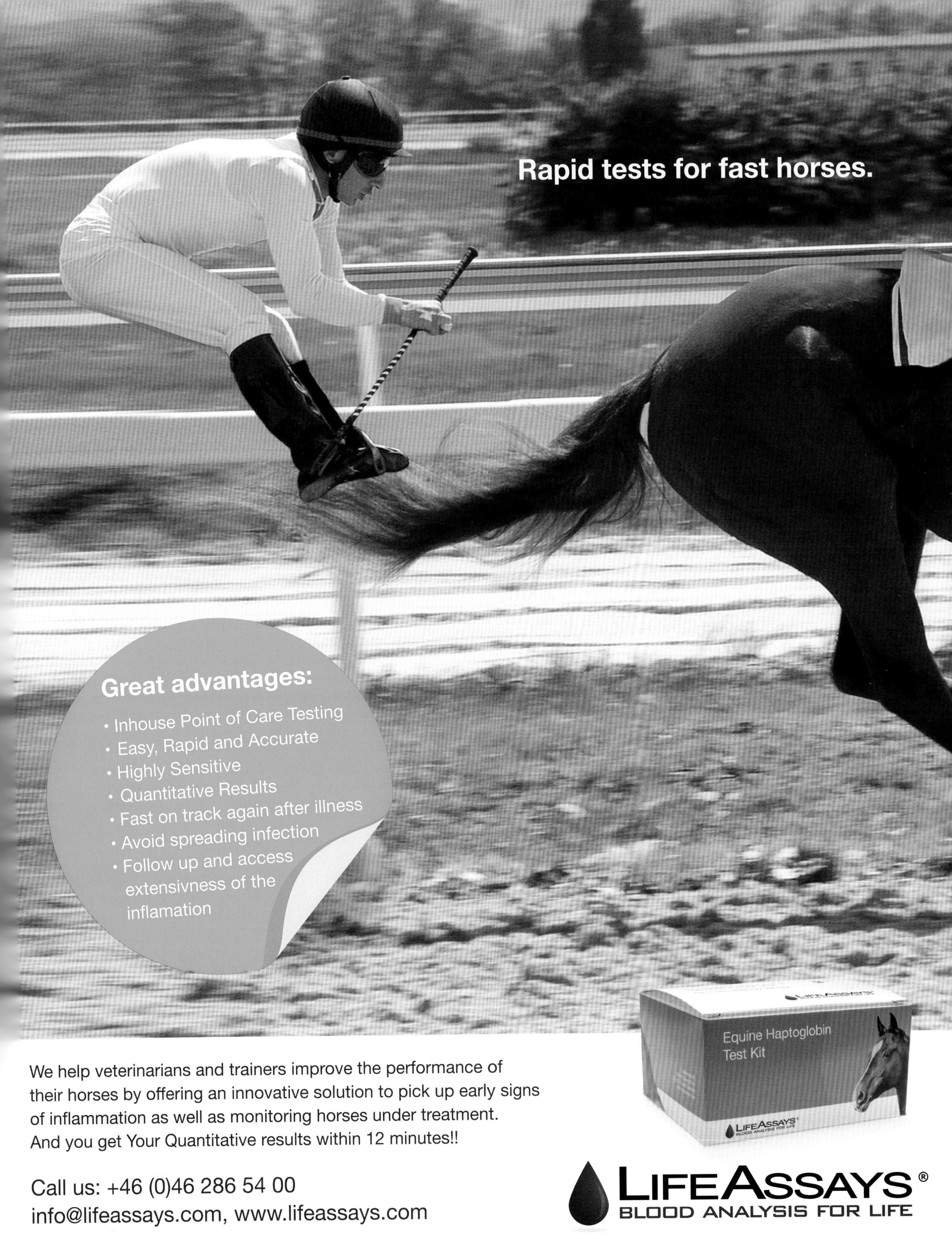

Rapid tests for fast horses.
Great advantages:
• Inhouse Point of Care Testing
• Easy, Rapid and Accurate
• Highly Sensitive
• Quantitative Results
• Fast on track again after illness
• Avoid spreading infection
• Follow up and access extensivness of the inflamation
Equine Haptoglobin Test Kit
We help veterinarians and trainers improve the performance of their horses by offering an innovative solution to pick up early signs of inflammation as well as monitoring horses under treatment. And you get Your Quantitative results within 12 minutes!!
Call us: +46 (0)46 286 54 00
info@lifeassays.com, www.lifeassays.com
LIFEASSAYS®
BLOOD ANALYSIS FOR LIFE

SHALAA

When Frankie Dettori describes a horse as "the best two-year-old I've sat on in my life" the words are worth heeding, but just in case we weren't taking him seriously this year's Derby and Arc-winning rider added: "I'm not exaggerating."

Dettori had just leapt off Shalaa (right) after their decisive victory in the Prix Morny at Deauville in August, the fourth leg of a five-race unbeaten sequence for the John Gosden-trained juvenile that culminated with a second Group 1 success when making all in the Middle Park Stakes.

Gosden joined in the plaudits after the Middle Park, reporting that rival jockey Ryan Moore had said he had never gone so fast over four furlongs of the Rowley Mile. The trainer compared Shalaa favourably to his 2002 Middle Park winner Oasis Dream, who went on to be champion sprinter at three. "He's of that mould," Gosden said. "He's very, very fast – the fastest two-year-old I've trained. He reminds us all of Oasis Dream."

Gosden was forced to send Oasis Dream straight into all-aged company as a three-year-old (finishing third to Choisir in the King's Stand) but now has the option of the Group 1 Commonwealth Cup for three-year-olds at Royal Ascot. The first edition of that race was won by Muhaarar, who then stepped into all-aged company to win the July Cup, Prix Maurice de Gheest and British Champions Sprint, and Shalaa looks set to follow a similar route. As early as July, Gosden said the Commonwealth Cup was "a huge target".

Shalaa's potential is obvious. His RPR of 119 in the Middle Park was 2lb behind Oasis Dream's mark in the same race but 6lb better than Muhaarar when he was third in the 2014 Middle Park. Gosden's exciting colt will start 2016 as a leader of the sprint pack and is going to take a lot of catching.

LIMATO

Riding Limato is "like driving a Ferrari" according to Andrea Atzeni and, despite a less than smooth journey on his final outing as a three-year-old, trainer Henry Candy has high hopes he will hit top gear as a miler in 2016.

Atzeni's excited comment came after Limato's breathtaking victory in the Group 2 Park Stakes over seven furlongs at Doncaster in September. That was the Group 1 Commonwealth Cup runner-up's first outing beyond sprint distances and, with a career-best RPR of 123, appeared to confirm Candy's view that his best days lay ahead over a mile.

For his last run of 2015, Limato stayed at seven furlongs for the Group 1 Prix de la Foret and was a fast-finishing second to French 2,000 Guineas winner Make Believe, having had to come round the whole field in the straight.

Candy was far from downcast, feeling it was one race too many for the gelding. With Group 1-winning sprinter Twilight Son also in his team, the veteran trainer looks set for another exciting year.

SIMON CRISFORD

Racing managers, like teachers, may be seen by some as "those who can't" but Simon Crisford has confounded that negative view since leaving his long-time role with Godolphin and starting a new life as a trainer. Not only is Crisford, 53, doing the job he dreamed about in his younger days, he is doing it rather well.

Victory in the Group 3 Solario Stakes with the promising juvenile First Selection was a standout moment but there was more to Crisford's first year than just one horse. Among British trainers with 50-plus runners, nobody could match Crisford's 28 per cent strike-rate and he showed his skill with handicappers such as Peril, Gang Warfare and Phyllis Maud (all three-time winners).

Of course, support from his old contacts in Dubai meant Crisford was no ordinary first-season trainer and his 43-box Newmarket yard was full from the outset.

With such backing, his already evident skills and a first proper winter of planning, Crisford looks likely to do even better in 2016.

MOON RACER

Little-known Irish trainer Michael Ronayne hit the jackpot when he bought Moon Racer as an unraced four-year-old for €5,000, won a valuable bumper with him and then sold him for £225,000 to join David Pipe's stable.

Even that huge sum might prove money well spent judging by Moon Racer's impressive victory in the Champion Bumper and the high hopes held for him. Pipe toyed with sending Moon Racer over hurdles following a 12-length bumper win at Cheltenham on his British debut but decided instead to put him away for five months until the festival, where he won decisively despite a slow start.

"The form of this bumper is working out better and better each year and he's got an engine," Pipe said. "There's no reason why he can't come back here next year as a novice hurdler."

Pipe's right about the race – four of the previous six winners went on to Grade 1 success over jumps (two of them at the festival) – and this season will test whether he's right about Moon Racer too.

Wingate
signs & graphics

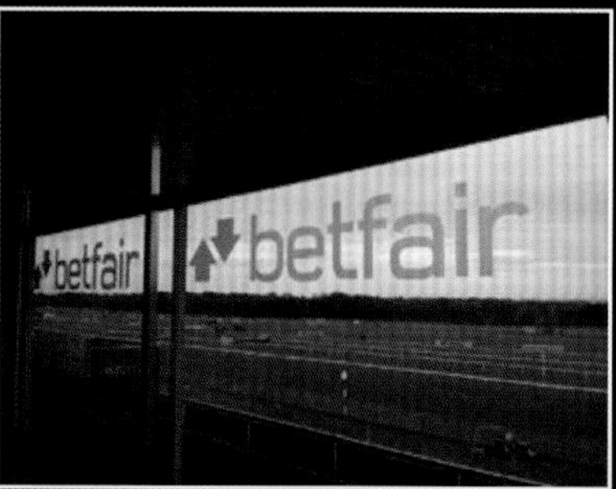

Your message on the inside track of racing

As a family run business we understand the importance of brand and how it translates on and off the UK's racecourses.

Maximising your brand exposure: creatively, professionally and ensuring value for money.

- Signs and banners
- Event activation
- Promotions
- Vehicle wrapping
- Bespoke branding campaigns
- Services for sponsors, venues and business requirements
- Supporting your own racing requirements: branded colours, rugs and clothing

Contact us for advice and to discuss your requirements.

Wingate Signs are proud of their association with The Jockey Club and its sponsors.

Wingate Signs & Graphics Ltd
Phoenix Buildings
Heywood Road, Prestwich
Manchester M25 1FN
Tel: 0161 772 0129 • Mob: 07736 243 256

www.wingatesigns.co.uk

BALLYDOYLE

Khalid Abdullah waited for exactly the right horse before bestowing the honour of naming him after the late, great Bobby Frankel, his American trainer, and (understatement alert) that turned out well.

Similarly the name Ballydoyle would not have been given lightly to a representative of Ireland's most famous training establishment but the filly chosen for the privilege still faces a difficult task to establish herself as the best in Aidan O'Brien's team, never mind of her generation.

Ballydoyle (pictured, blue and orange) was born with the right pedigree, as a sister to Irish 1,000 Guineas winner Misty For Me, and ended her juvenile season as a Group 1 winner in the Prix Marcel Boussac at Longchamp in October (a race won by Misty For Me five years earlier). Her winning time was nearly two seconds quicker than that recorded half an hour later by Ultra in the colts' version, the Prix Jean-Luc Lagardere.

That all sounds good but, having assumed favouritism for both the 1,000 Guineas and Oaks after that victory, she was knocked off her perch five days later by stablemate Minding, who gave an even more impressive display in the Fillies' Mile at Newmarket.

The previous month, when Minding had beaten Ballydoyle by three-quarters of a length in the Moyglare Stud Stakes, the difference was said to have been made by the easy ground. At Newmarket, however, Minding simply looked different class (119 on RPR compared with Ballydoyle's 113).

Fast summer ground might bring out the best in Ballydoyle – "she's a beautiful mover," O'Brien said – and her pedigree suggests both the 1,000 Guineas and Oaks may be within her scope. Yet if she is to truly live up to her name with Classic success, she first has to become the best Ballydoyle has got.

ED GREATREX

On February 27, on only his third ride, Ed Greatrex landed his first win aboard the Andrew Balding-trained Perfect Mission at Kempton and never looked back. Eight months later, when the Flat title season finished on Champions Day, the 17-year-old apprentice was among the winners with victory on Godolphin's Musaddas in the Balmoral Handicap – his 35th of the year.

That left another 60 before he loses his claim and, with several of his more experienced rivals soon to join the senior ranks, he looks set for a strong title bid in 2016.

Greatrex, of course, has had advantages in life. Dad is Lambourn trainer Warren Greatrex and mum Lois – Warren's first wife – manages Kingwood Stud in the village, while the young rider is enjoying a first-rate education at Balding's Kingsclere academy.

Yet there is obvious talent and he has shown his skill on big days and several tricky tracks – both aspects combined at Epsom on Oaks day with 16-1 winner Elbereth, his biggest success before Musaddas.

DAN SKELTON

Click on Dan Skelton's website and the first thing you'll notice is the numbers that whirr round, fruit machine-style, before coming to rest on his latest totals of 2015-16 winners and prize-money, his overall number of domestic winners and his total of Graded winners.

Already the numbers are impressive and they are likely to be even more so by the end of his third season as a trainer. Paul Nicholls' former assistant had 27 winners in his debut campaign, 2013-14, and almost trebled that figure to 73 last season, which put him joint-eighth among British trainers by that measure.

The next step for Skelton, 30, is to add more quality to his Warwickshire yard and improve on last season's 12th place by prize-money earned. He had five Graded winners in his first two seasons, including the valuable Ladbroke with Willow's Saviour in 2013, but a first Grade 1 and a live Cheltenham Festival contender will be on the wish list for the ambitious trainer.

KEITH DALGLEISH

Being based outside the traditional training areas may seem like a disadvantage but Michael Dods and Mick Appleby are two of those who have defied any perception of second-class citizenry from their yards in County Durham and Nottinghamshire, and Keith Dalgleish – now established as Scotland's leading trainer – is another.

Dalgleish, 32, was 16th by number of winners in the British Flat trainers' list after Champions Day and, with 69 on the board by that stage, 2015 was another personal-best campaign. In fact, he has increased his total every season since racking up 39 winners in his first year at Belstane Stables, Carlurke, Lanarkshire, in 2011.

What he has lacked so far is a headline-making big winner, although it may not be far away. Tommy Docc was a half-length runner-up in this year's Queen's Vase at Royal Ascot and, in promising Flat filly Maleficent Queen and smart bumper winner Meet The Legend, he has bright prospects under both codes.

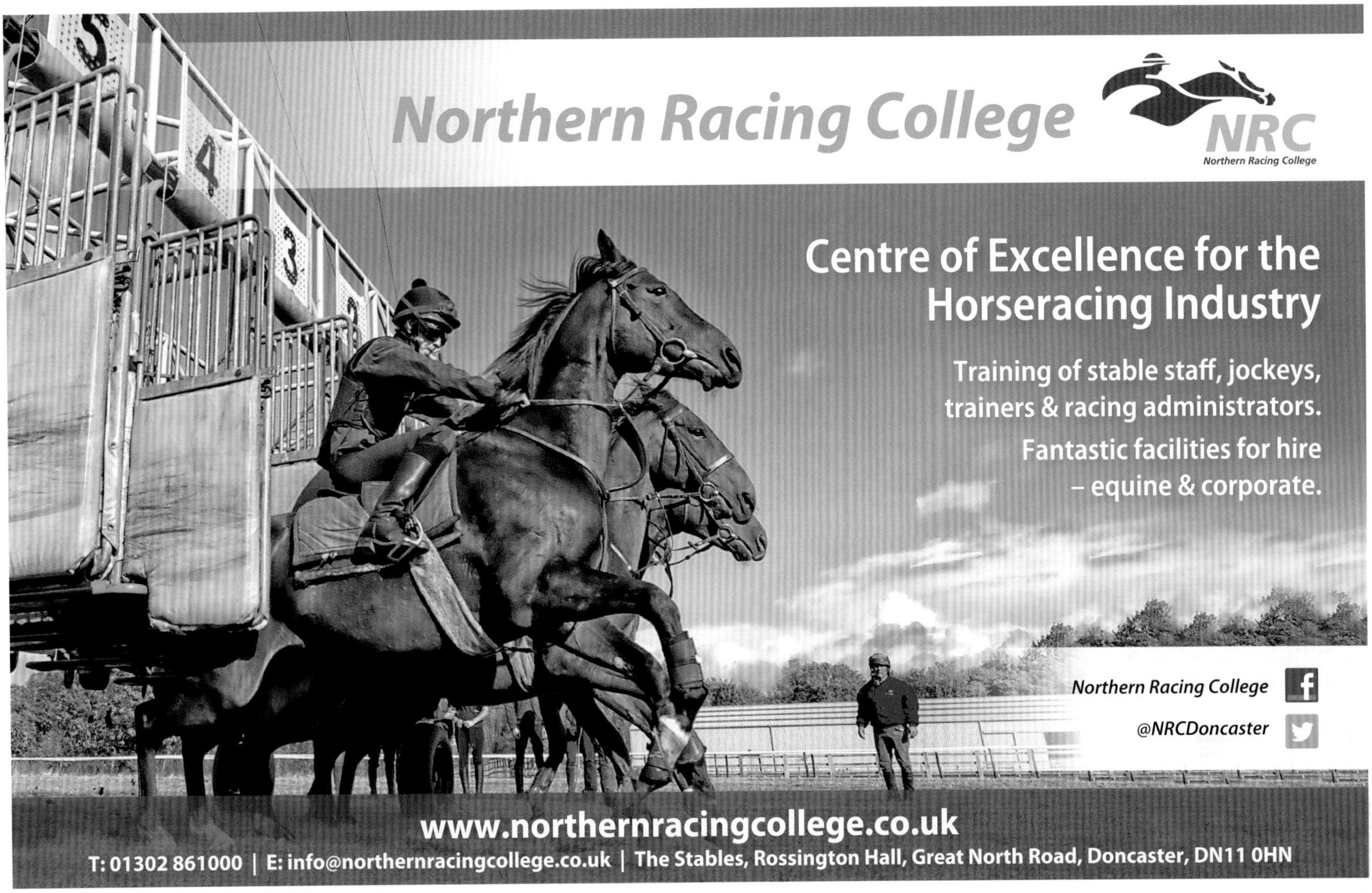

Northern Racing College

NRC
Northern Racing College

Centre of Excellence for the Horseracing Industry

Training of stable staff, jockeys, trainers & racing administrators.

Fantastic facilities for hire – equine & corporate.

Northern Racing College

@NRCDoncaster

www.northernracingcollege.co.uk

T: 01302 861000 | E: info@northernracingcollege.co.uk | The Stables, Rossington Hall, Great North Road, Doncaster, DN11 0HN

IF RACING ABROAD SOUNDS FOREIGN TO YOU, YOU HAVEN'T TRIED CHATEAU RACING

Great hosts...nothing too much trouble. Racing was excellent.
Mr & Mrs J.G., Cheshire

Our 1st visit, but not our last. We loved every minute
Mr & Mrs R.B., Staffordshire

Super week's holiday... our 3rd visit!
Mr & Mrs D.H., Chichester

THE FRENCH HORSE RACING EXPERIENCE IS SECOND TO NONE!

Over 50 racecourses, breathtaking settings, passionate crowds and a warm welcome await!

RACING AS IT SHOULD BE!

Some familiar names;

Philip Hobbs, Willie Mullins, Richard Johnson

and some familiar horses;

Silviniaco Conti, Balthazar King, Douvan

have been spotted by our guests during our **8 seasons** as market leaders in provincial French racing holidays.

CHATEAU RACING

PRICES START FROM 300 EUROS/225 POUNDS PER COUPLE*

This includes **airport, racecourse and restaurant transfers, racecourse entry,** and a **double room with breakfast** at La Sapinière, our country chateau set in 6 acres of gardens.

CALL +44 (0) 1428 685 874 (UK) OR +33 (0) 228 040 984 (FRANCE)

Email: info@chateauracing.com

*Price quoted is for a 3 night stay in a standard double room with 2 days of racing.
Airport transfers available from Nantes, Rennes & Angers only.

www.chateauracing.com

MARTELLO TOWER

The Mullins name was etched across the honours board at the 2015 Cheltenham Festival but, as well as Willie's eight, one of the winners belonged to Mags Mullins, who landed the Albert Bartlett Novices' Hurdle with Martello Tower (right, yellow colours).

Mags is the sister-in-law of the champion trainer, who had to settle for a half-length second in the Albert Bartlett with Milsean (as well as fourth with Arbre De Vie). In a race dominated by the Mullins clan, Mags's son Danny rode Milsean for his uncle, having partnered Martello Tower in exercise that morning.

Danny had ridden Martello Tower to his biggest previous win, in a Grade 3 at Limerick last December, but was not on board at Cheltenham as he had been replaced as owner Barry Connell's retained rider by Adrian Heskin.

If it all sounds complicated, Martello Tower is simple enough. "He's just so tough and always keeps going – you never get to the end of him," said his trainer, whose debut festival winner came with only her second runner.

Albert Bartlett winners have a decent record of progressing, either as high-class staying hurdlers or chasers, and Martello Tower's stamina and class (his RPR of 154 was around the same mark as At Fishers Cross and Bobs Worth among previous winners) give him every chance of further success.

DAVID MULLINS

The family name has marked out David Mullins from the start but so has his talent in the saddle. The son of Cheltenham Festival-winning trainer Tom Mullins, and nephew of Willie, has made a flying start as a conditional jockey and is already a trusted member of the Gigginstown set-up.

Within a few months of his first professional success over jumps in December 2014, the 19-year-old had been runner-up in the Irish Grand National on Rule The World, won at Aintree on Grand National day in a conditionals' handicap hurdle and landed the Galway Blazers Handicap Chase on Rogue Angel at the Galway festival.

Those successes appear to be only the start for this highly promising young rider.

ZUBAYR

They say you should never go back but both Paul Nicholls and Willie Mullins were keen to revive former glories when the British and Irish champion trainers had a fierce bidding war at the French sales over juvenile hurdling prospect Zubayr, described as the "absolute standout" of those on offer.

The Nicholls team won the battle at €380,000 for the dual middle-distance Flat winner, who is bred on the same lines as the Mullins-trained four-time Grade 1 winner Nichols Canyon and comes from the Aga Khan operation that produced Nicholls' 2011 Triumph Hurdle winner Zarkandar.

Price and pedigree bring great expectations and no doubt the 2016 Triumph will be the number-one aim for Nicholls' "gorgeous individual".

OWEN BURROWS

Few trainers get such a good head start as Owen Burrows, who has taken over as private trainer to Sheikh Hamdan Al Maktoum at Kingwood House Stables, Lambourn, following the second retirement of Barry Hills. Among the string are Massaat, second favourite for the 2,000 Guineas (albeit a considerable distance behind hot favourite Air Force Blue, to whom he was runner-up in the Dewhurst), and Royal Lodge third Muntazah.

Burrows, 40, assistant to Sir Michael Stoute for 13 years, had 600 rides as a conditional jockey based with Martin Pipe. He also rode for Josh Gifford and David Nicholson before moving to Newmarket. He already knows the Kingwood horses well, having worked alongside Hills during the 2015 campaign in preparation for taking over in his own right. Hills, who retired in 2011 but took out a licence again to supervise the Kingwood string after the death of his son John in June 2014, will still be on hand in an advisory role.

The stable has had around 20 winners in the past couple of seasons and that is the benchmark for Burrows. "Owen was the only person we interviewed," Hills said. "He's level-headed and has a good background in racing. It's a wonderful opportunity for him."

JACK KENNEDY

There was no stopping Irish teen sensation Jack Kennedy – not until a fractured toe in September interrupted his impressive debut year. At that stage, only four months after his first ride, the 16-year-old with the illustrious name had reached 20 winners (14 over jumps, six on the Flat) and been hailed as a star in the making.

The former pony racing champion, from Dingle, County Kerry, is based with Gordon Elliott and the jumps is where his future lies. But the highlight of his blazing summer was his valuable Flat handicap victory at the Galway festival on the Willie Mullins-trained Clondaw Warrior and he went close to an even bigger success for Mullins in the Ebor when he was second on Wicklow Brave.

He may look back on the injury as a blessing of sorts, keeping his claim intact for longer and giving him more time to learn his trade and make a title bid. He will never be as famous as the other Jack Kennedy but in racing circles he looks certain to make a name for himself.

Moorcroft

Racehorse Welfare Centre

This centre in the south of England was set up to ensure that retired racehorses whatever age, can be re-trained to find another career in life. Much care and attention is given to each individual horse and when fully retrained new homes are found. The centre retains ownership for life and visits these horses every year to ensure that all is well.

This charity depends on generous donations from horse lovers. Many horses need a time for rehabilitation due to injury etc and start to enjoy an easier life after their racing careers. Visits by appointment are welcomed. Please ring Mary Henley-Smith, Manager on 07929 666408 for more information or to arrange a visit.

Tel: 07929 666408
Email: moorcroftracehorse@gmail.com

www.mrwc.org.uk

VALUE RACING CLUB

Winning Together!

Value Racing Club provides affordable racehorse ownership for an all-inclusive price with no hidden costs or extras

WHAT WE OFFER & BENEFITS:

- An opportunity to become involved in racehorse ownership
- A one off cost covers the season with nothing else to pay
- Weekly updates via email or phone from your Racing Manager
- Stable visits arranged to watch your horse work on the gallops
- Free owners & trainers badges each time your horse runs
- Each syndicate keeps 100% of any prize money won
- Horses train with Dr Richard Newland, Jamie Snowdon & Chris Wall
- 77% overall strike rate of our horses finishing in the first three

Big race wins in 2015 include the £70,000 Imperial Cup & the £30,000 Betfred Summer Hurdle

Web: www.valueracingclub.co.uk
email: contact@valueracingclub.co.uk
Twitter: @valueracingclub

Call James for more information: 07939 800769

Fully bespoke horse walker matting

Installation of matting

Bonded installation

Nationwide delivery

HORSEMAT

SPECIALIST IN EQUESTRIAN MATTING

Horsemat has been supplying high quality products into the equestrian market for over 10 years. From bespoke horse-walker matting to complete stable solutions. We hold vast stocks and varieties of heavy duty, solid rubber mats as well as EVA foam and porous crumb matting. Also we supply products that help establish strong paddock grass to make those hard winters at the stables a little easier to manage.

For honest, professional advice please contact the Horsemat team

Tel: **01787 886929**

www.horsematshop.co.uk

sales@horsemat.co.uk

BELMONT PARK
DRAFT KINGS
DRAFT KINGS
DRAFT KINGS

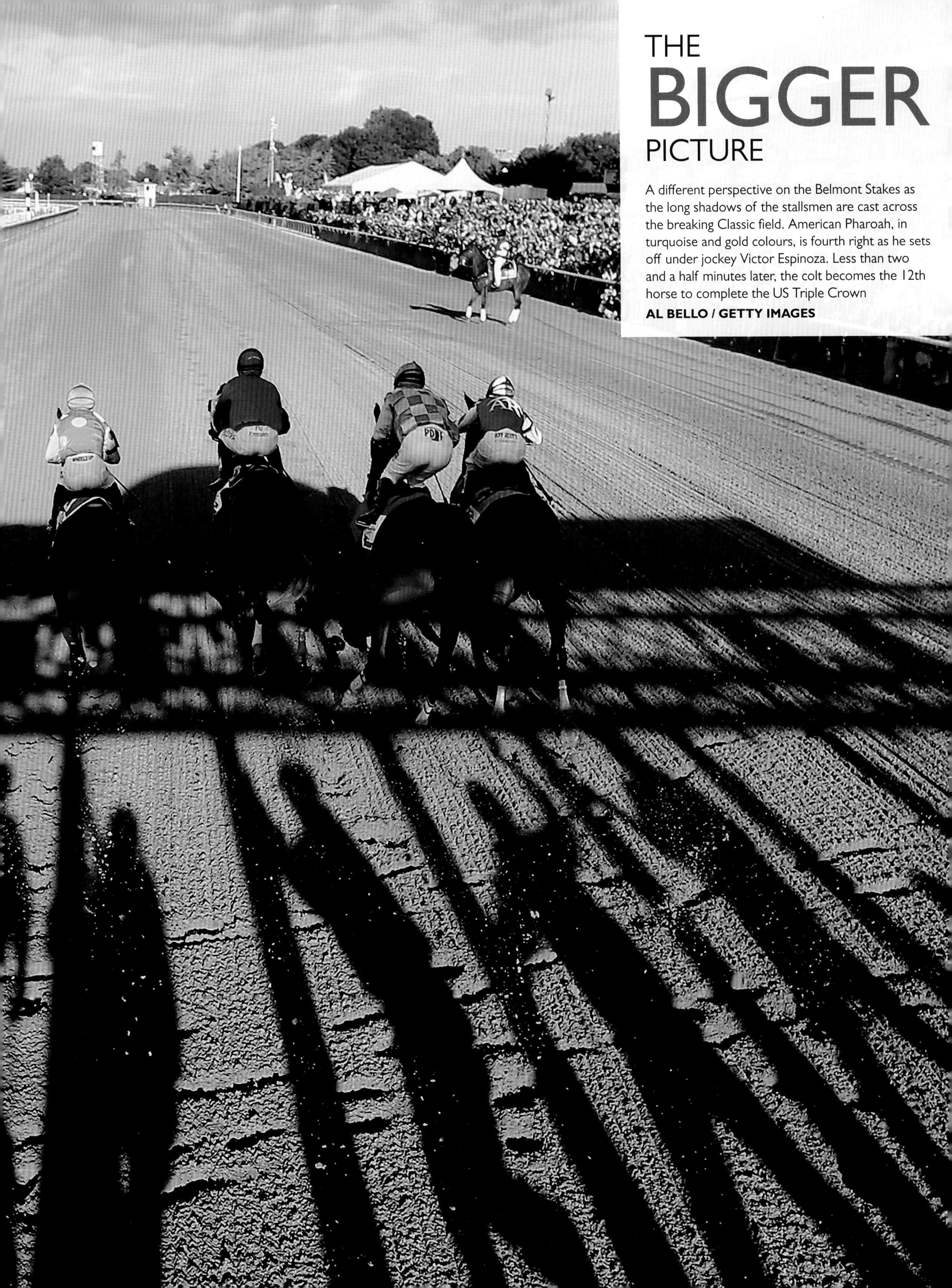

THE BIGGER PICTURE

A different perspective on the Belmont Stakes as the long shadows of the stallsmen are cast across the breaking Classic field. American Pharoah, in turquoise and gold colours, is fourth right as he sets off under jockey Victor Espinoza. Less than two and a half minutes later, the colt becomes the 12th horse to complete the US Triple Crown

AL BELLO / GETTY IMAGES

final furlong

stories of the year – from the serious to the quirky

Young stars tipped for the top

Conditional titles expected to be just the start for Bowen and Burke

SONS of prominent jumps trainers took the 2014-2015 conditional jockeys' titles in Britain and Ireland – and both are tipped to scale greater heights as their careers progress.

Sean Bowen came out on top in Britain after a tight race with Nico de Boinville, the Cheltenham Gold Cup-winning rider of Coneygree. Less than 12 months after turning professional, the son of Welsh trainer Peter Bowen won by 51 winners to 44, having started the final week only two ahead. He crowned his title-winning season with victory on Just A Par in the bet365 Gold Cup on the final day at Sandown.

Jonathan Burke had a much easier ride to the Irish title, amassing 42 winners to win by 15 from defending champion Kevin Sexton. The 19-year-old son of County Cork trainer Liam Burke also enjoyed big-race success with Grade 1 victory on Sizing John at Leopardstown in December – and another outside Ireland with Sizing Granite in the Maghull Novices' Chase at Aintree. Both were in the colours of major owners Alan and Ann Potts, for whom Burke became retained rider in September 2014.

Burke, who finished fifth in the overall Irish riders' standings in 2014-15, said: "Getting the job was a big highlight of the season and the two Grade 1 wins were great. Becoming champion conditional jockey was something I had in the back of my head when I turned professional."

The summer brought another big victory in the Potts colours for Burke when Shanahan's Turn, trained like his other big-race winners by Henry de Bromhead, landed the Galway Plate – a race won by his father in 2007 with Sir Frederick.

▸▸ Bred for the job: Sean Bowen (left) and Jonathan Burke are both sons of trainers and have been quick to make their mark

"An ounce of breeding is worth a ton of feeding," senior jockey Davy Russell said after the Plate, paying tribute to Burke. "There are some really good young lads here right now. You've got Johnny and Paul Townend and Bryan Cooper and they're all top-notch. They'll be shoving all of us old lads out of the way soon."

Great things are also expected of Bowen, who at the age of 17 became the youngest to take the British conditionals' title, joining a roll of honour that includes Tony McCoy, Richard Johnson and Sam Twiston-Davies.

Paul Nicholls, who has Twiston-Davies as his No.1 jockey and Bowen as stable conditional, said: "I've had lots of young riding talent through my hands and at this stage Sean is as good as any of them. He's a natural. Horses run for him, which is a priceless gift. I can see him going right to the top."

Biddick and O'Connor reach new standards

POINT-TO-POINT records tumbled in Britain and Ireland as riders Will Biddick and Derek O'Connor scaled new heights in their championship-winning seasons.

Biddick, 28, took his fourth consecutive British title with a record total of 68 winners, beating the mark of 56 set by Oliver Greenall in 2008 and equalled by Oliver's brother Tom in 2009.

Somerset-based Biddick's previous best was 42 winners in his first title-winning season (2011-12) but he now has the powerful backing of the Barber family, which is closely linked with champion jumps trainer Paul Nicholls.

Jack Barber, 23, in his second season training the point-to-point string after the retirement of his grandfather Richard, took his first title with 51 winners – all but four ridden by Biddick.

"Jack's horses were a massive part of me retaining the title," Biddick said. "To get the record is very satisfying. This has been a phenomenal season."

O'Connor has been the dominant rider in Irish points for more than a decade and he claimed his 11th title with 90 winners, 21 clear of defending champion Jamie Codd.

Just as notably the 32-year-old became the first to ride 1,000 pointing winners when he was successful on Death Duty at Cragmore, County Limerick, in February. "I'm absolutely thrilled to have reached the milestone, it's one of those occasions I'll never forget," he said.

To put O'Connor's achievement into perspective, the British record in point-to-points held by Richard Burton is 414 winners.

●Festival heroine Quevega a proud mum

QUEVEGA, the record six-time winner at the Cheltenham Festival in the Mares' Hurdle, delivered her first foal in May, a filly by Beat Hollow. Quevega's part-owner Ger O'Brien said: "It's a different type of excitement to when Quevega was winning at the festival, but if this one's half as good as her mother she'll be some mare."

●Memorable year of firsts over jumps for Blackmore

RACHAEL BLACKMORE made Irish racing history at Down Royal in March when she became the first female to ride as a professional over jumps and later had the joy of her first winner in the paid ranks.

Blackmore, 25, from Killenaule, County Tipperary, was fifth on her professional debut aboard the Shark Hanlon-trained Redwood Boy in a handicap hurdle. In September she had her first winner with a determined short head victory on the Hanlon-trained Most Honourable in a 2m½f handicap hurdle at Clonmel.

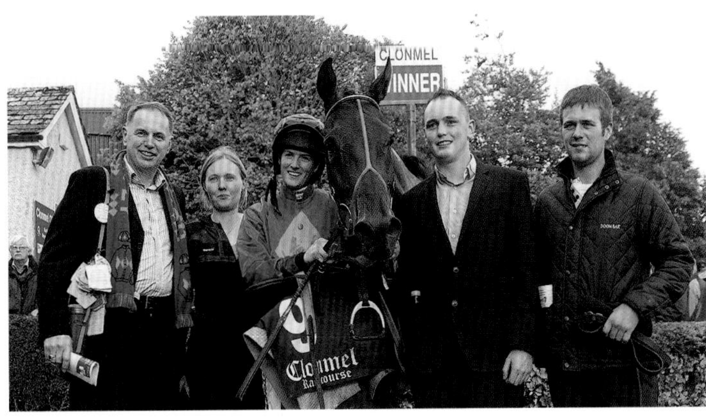

"I can't believe it has happened," she said after her landmark winner (pictured). "This horse was also Andrew's [McNamara] last winner, so he's a special horse for everyone in the yard.

"I ride out mainly for Shark, who thought it would be a good idea for me to turn [professional], so I decided to give it a go."

The Annual Awards

Our pick of the best of 2015

Horse of the Year (Flat)
Golden Horn

In colours that were a reminder of glory days past, he had an old-fashioned campaign that took him from spring to autumn without ducking any challenge – the cambers of Epsom, older rivals, varying distances, rain-affected ground, rough races, the great Treve on her home turf. He appeared in every month of the European turf season and the races were always compelling – even in shock defeat – as he blossomed first into a Classic star and then into the top European performer of the year.

Horse of the Year (jumps)
Coneygree

There was what he did: the first novice to win the Cheltenham Gold Cup in more than 40 years and the best novice chaser since Racing Post Ratings started. There was how he did it: blazing a trail from the front under his first-time Gold Cup jockey, only three and a half months after first jumping a fence in public. And there was who he did it for: his small stable bound by strong ties to his late breeder Lord Oaksey. A rare triumph.

Ride of the year (Flat)
Frankie Dettori on Golden Horn

French jockeys have often had difficulty with Epsom and numerous British-based riders have failed to conquer Longchamp, but Dettori showed he was a master of both with his Derby and Arc triumphs on Golden Horn. The Arc ride in particular was a masterpiece: tacking across gradually from his graveyard draw, settling in a forward position and then capitalising to full effect with a powerful drive up the straight.

Ride of the year (jumps)
Nico de Boinville on Coneygree

For a rider barely a year into his professional career with no previous Cheltenham Gold Cup experience, it took rare nerve to set out to dictate the pace in the festival showpiece in front of Ruby Walsh, Tony McCoy et al. Even more, it took rare skill to judge that pace to perfection and keep his cool while turning up the heat on his pursuers. A Gold Cup veteran from the top rank would have been proud of that ride; for De Boinville, it was a hell of a debut.

Race of the year (Flat)
St Leger

The race that had it all. The St Leger is often derided as the lame duck of the Classic season, but this year four high-quality horses came to the furlong pole together before two duelled to a thrillingly close finish. Then came a stewards' inquiry that turned Doncaster into a pressure cooker, followed by a surprise verdict and visible displays of the effects of triumph and disaster on the human combatants.

Race of the year (jumps)
Champion Hurdle

The first day of the Cheltenham Festival is the most eagerly awaited and the Champion Hurdle was responsible for much of the anticipation. A small field densely packed with brilliance and rivalries – old champ v young buck, Britain v Ireland – faced off with the air that something important was going to happen. It was – the magnificent Faugheen retained his unbeaten record with a compelling all-the-way victory that lived up to every inch of newsprint lavished upon the race in the preliminaries.

Comeback of the year
Litigant

Heartwarming human stories aplenty – like resurrection men Frankie Dettori (metaphorically) and Brian Toomey (literally) – but the vote goes to an incredibly fragile horse who was nursed along by Lambourn trainer Joe Tuite and came back to win the Ebor after 491 days off the track. "That was a tremendous training performance with the winner," said Willie Mullins, second with Wicklow Brave, and there could be no higher compliment.

Unluckiest horse
Secret Gesture

Any overseas raid carries an acceptance of playing by different rules, but Ralph Beckett was rightly vexed when his mare was demoted to third in the Beverly D at Arlington. She was a clear winner but had caused minor interference to third-placed Stephanie's Kitten. The appeal fell on deaf ears, even with Steve Cauthen as a witness. Sometimes the law is an ass.

Disappointment of the year
John F Kennedy

The winter favourite for the Derby was still clear market leader at 9-2 on the morning of his seasonal debut, with eight weeks to go until Epsom. Then he ran and it all went wrong. He was third of three on that comeback, then seventh of seven behind Golden Horn in the Dante and he did not even turn up at Epsom.

THE AP McCOY SPECIAL ACHIEVEMENTS AWARDS

Horse of the Year *Uxizandre* The one who fulfilled the cherished wish for a last Cheltenham Festival winner

Ride of the year *If In Doubt* A fortnight before announcing his retirement came this gem in the Skybet Chase at Doncaster, with McCoy refusing to give up on the hairy jumper. "Fantastic," said trainer Philip Hobbs's wife Sarah

Bombshell of the year *"I'm gonna tell you something else Rishi . . . "* The 11-week countdown to retirement was about to begin

'I was there' moment of the year *The bittersweet final farewell at Sandown* Uplifting and memorable

Services to racing *The one and only AP McCoy*

The Robin Williams Memorial 'Carpe Diem' Award
Richard Johnson

As if inspired by Williams' exhortation in Dead Poets Society to "seize the day", the perennial runner-up to AP McCoy was among the winners at his first meeting of the 2015-16 jumps season after the retirement of his nemesis.

The WC Fields Knowing When You're Beat Award
Paul Nicholls and Silviniaco Conti

"If at first you don't succeed, try, try again. Then quit. There's no point being a damn fool about it," quipped the great comedian. Perhaps Nicholls has had similar thoughts after his dual King George winner failed for a third time in the Cheltenham Gold Cup.

The Macavity Award for not being there
Gleneagles

Like TS Eliot's 'mystery cat', the dual Guineas winner brought bafflement and despair by not being seen at Goodwood, Deauville, York and Leopardstown.

The Roses 'Thank You Very Much' Award from the bookmakers
Annie Power

Layers avoided what they said would have been a £40m-£50m payout on the first day of the Cheltenham Festival when the mare's final-hurdle fall scuppered the last leg of the Willie Mullins 'good things' four-timer.

The 'Thank Goodness It's Not Steps' Award for services to music
Kylie Minogue

The Aussie pop princess took post-racing entertainment up a notch with her sellout concerts at Newmarket and Haydock in June.

The Shoeless Joe Jackson Award
Seb Sanders

Like the baseball great who once played in his socks, Sanders weighed out without his boots at Goodwood in September, breaking no rules save the one involving common sense.

The Victor Kiam 'I Liked It So Much . . . ' Award
The Duchess of Cornwall

The race named in honour of Charles and Camilla when they visited Sligo in May was won by Mollyanna and the Duchess was so impressed she bought the six-year-old mare in partnership a few weeks later and transferred her to Jamie Snowden's stable in Lambourn.

The Shattered Glass Ceiling Award
Katie Walsh and Sandra Hughes

Thunder And Roses' triumph in the Irish Grand National was a landmark win for the female jockey-trainer combination.

The Tyrannosaurus Rex Award for failing to keep up with the process of evolution
Michael Tebbutt

The jockey coach caused uproar with his comment that "girls can't ride" in a BBC interview with Katie Walsh about women in sport.

The Jeremy Corbyn Award for overturning the established order
Arabian Queen

Barely worth a mention before the start of the race, the David Elsworth-trained 50-1 shot shocked hot favourite Golden Horn with a neck victory in the Juddmonte International.

The Simple Minds 'Don't You Forget About Me' Award
Silvestre de Sousa

Discarded by Godolphin, the Brazilian went back to being a freelance and became champion jockey for the first time.

The Jurgen Klinsmann Award for theatrics
Irad Ortiz

The top US jockey made a meal out of alleged interference from Secret Gesture in the Beverly D Stakes, leading to a controversial disqualification for the British-trained mare.

The Bob Beamon Award for spring-heeled leaping
Coneygree

The novice chaser jumped his Cheltenham Gold Cup rivals into the ground with an exhilarating display on only his fourth start over fences.

The 'It's Not Me, It's You' Falling-Out Award
Adam Kirby v Frankie Dettori

Arguments raged after Postponed and Eagle Top became embroiled in a custody battle over a strip of ground in the Hardwicke Stakes, pitting Kirby on one side against Dettori and John Gosden on the other, with Luca Cumani caught somewhere in between.

The Gerry Rafferty 'If You Get It Wrong You'll Get It Right Next Time' Award
Freddy Head

Having made his first attempt in Group company with Solow over nearly two miles at Longchamp, the French trainer dropped him back to a mile and campaigned him to a series of top-level successes.

The 'It's Not Goodbye, It's See You Soon' Award for short-lived retirement Jamie Spencer

The former champion jockey returned to the saddle almost as soon as he'd given up

RACING POST

racingpost.com/mobile

JONATHAN PEASE
Interview with the Arc-winning soon-to-retire trainer, pages 6-7

ALASTAIR DOWN AT LONGCHAMP
Classic book extract, page 10

€1.7m FRANKEL FILLY

Four arrested after Coleman is attacked in weighing room

Leading jockey smacked in the face says witness to astonishing Southwell fracas

REAL MADRID, MAN UTD & MAN CITY ALL TO WIN 7/2

CORAL

Coleman in alarming incident at Southwell

ONE of the biggest shocks of 2015 on a British racecourse came not on the track but inside the jockeys' room at Southwell, where leading jump rider Aidan Coleman was allegedly punched after two men gained access through a back door.

The incident followed the last race of the day at Southwell's meeting on September 29. One of the men was restrained inside the weighing room while the other was held on the ground outside by judge Nick Bostock and trainers David Thompson and Charlie Pogson until police arrived. Two men and one woman were arrested on suspicion of assault and criminal damage and another woman was arrested for obstructing police.

Coleman, who escaped with minor injuries, including two chipped teeth, schooled six horses at Charlie Longsdon's yard in Oxfordshire the following morning before riding in the afternoon at Chepstow.

"Us jump jockeys are a tough bunch," he said.

The incident prompted a BHA investigation and a security review by Southwell and other tracks amid concerns about levels of alcohol consumption on racecourses.

Paul Struthers, chief executive of the Professional Jockeys Association, said: "One of the big attractions of horseracing is how close the public are able to get to the jockeys and how accessible they are, and we would not want this to change. Thankfully these incidents are very rare indeed but they highlight the importance of a responsible approach to alcohol sales and the need for appropriate security arrangements."

●Whip? Check. Helmet? Check. Goggles? Check. Boots? . . .

Seb Sanders caused controversy at Goodwood in September when he rode without boots in what the BHA said was a first in modern British racing history.

Sanders, with his breeches covering the lower part of his legs, rode the Roger Teal-trained Langley Vale to finish fourth in a six-furlong handicap. When he went to weigh out without boots, the rule book was consulted and it was determined he was within his rights to do so.

BHA spokesman Robin Mounsey said: "No rules have been broken. Jockeys are required to wear certain safety equipment, including body protectors and helmets, but this doesn't extend to footwear."

Sanders' actions divided opinion among racing professionals and attracted criticism from punters on social media but the 43-year-old defended his decision.

"I got held up getting to Goodwood and didn't have time for a sweat so I left the boots off to make the weight," he said. "That's all it was and I think a mountain's been made out of a molehill."

●One direction? Not at Wexford

WEXFORD took a different turn in April when it became the first racecourse operating in Ireland or Britain to switch direction.

Having raced clockwise since its opening in 1951, Wexford changed to the left-handed direction long used on its point-to-point course situated on the inside of the main track.

Many who have ridden on the point-to-point track said it would be a better way to go on the racecourse proper and, after a series of gallops trials, the first left-handed jumps meeting was held on April 21.

The switch was well received, with trainer Liz Doyle, who had a double at the historic meeting, saying: "It rides much smoother. They jump much safer and finish much safer. It's been a huge success."

Wexford was the first major track to switch direction since Belmont Park, in New York, in 1921.

●Jockeys battle for whip hand in finish

PARX racetrack in Pennsylvania saw an unusual mid-race mugging in September when one jockey stole the whip of a rival.

Angel Castillo lost his whip when his mount Interchange got in a tangle with favourite Distant Thoughts, ridden by Pierre Hernandez Ortega.

In response, Castillo leaned over and took the whip straight out of Hernandez Ortega's hand, driving forward to finish a strong second while Distant Thoughts weakened to second last.

The Pennsylvania stewards let the result stand and did not even call an inquiry, taking the view that "they did not think the horse did anything wrong," according to an official.

Elizabeth Armstrong - Equine Artist

Original Contemporary Art & Commissions on Request

www.elizabetharmstrong.co.uk

For the Finest in Fencing
CHOOSE NORCROFT

Over four decades of expertise in fencing the world's leading Stud Farms & Training Centres, supplying Pressure Creosoted Post & Rail Fencing, Stud Entrance & Paddock Gates - **NORCROFT** provide the complete service from concept to completion.

NORCROFT are UK, Ireland and European distributors for KEEPSAFE & SQUARE DEAL - The Original and Only Proven Wire Systems from Keystone Red Brand Products.

NORCROFT
Paddock Fencing

CONTACT RICHARD S JERMY
NORCROFT EQUESTRIAN DEVELOPMENTS
1 Norton Road, Loddon, Norwich, Norfolk NR14 6JN
Tel: 01508 520 743 ◆ Fax: 01508 528 879
Email: enquiries@norcroft.com
www.norcroft.com

Farce as non-runner becomes a runner

FIASCO of the year? It would be hard to beat the farcical chain of events in the Speculative Bid affair at Ascot on King George day when the well-backed favourite in the high-profile International Handicap was declared both a non-runner and a runner after leaving the stalls without his rider.

With the riders already weighed in, the stewards first announced an inquiry, then decided Speculative Bid (pictured) was a non-runner and finally, 90 minutes later, that he had been a runner after all. Amid the confusion after the weighed-in signal, bookmakers started to pay out on bets on the 7-1 winner without the 20p-in-the-pound deduction they were entitled to make if the 4-1 favourite was a non-runner, then had to refund bets on Speculative Bid as a non-runner only to be told that, officially, he had taken part in the race.

The betting industry refunded more than £500,000 in stakes and bookmakers described the debacle as "a total shambles" and "first-rate bungling".

The BHA was forced to apologise more than once for what chief executive Nick Rust called "a regrettable episode". After an internal investigation, disciplinary action was taken against one official but the BHA refused to name that person or the punishment imposed.

As for Speculative Bid, he appeared to do his best to repay the bookmakers with narrow defeats on his next two starts when a well-backed favourite (at 7-4 and 5-1) at Newmarket and York's Ebor meeting.

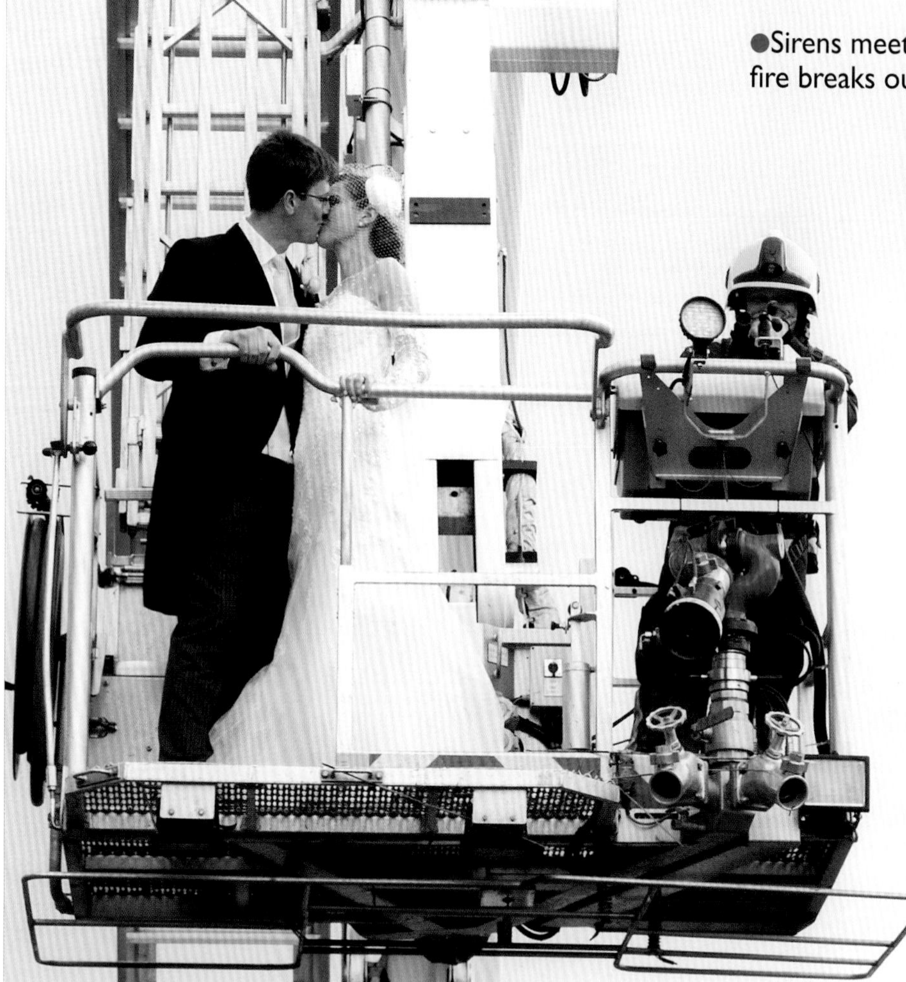

●Sirens meet wedding bells as fire breaks out on Fry's big day

Champion Hurdle-winning trainer Harry Fry and his bride Ciara O'Connor had a wedding-day drama in June after a major fire broke out in the County Limerick village of Adare shortly before the ceremony was due to start.

The village was closed to traffic as eight fire crews fought the blaze in a group of cottages close to the church but the wedding was able to proceed after a 30-minute delay.

Later, as the couple were leaving for the reception, one of the fire crews offered to hoist them up in the platform cage, giving them an unusual photo of their big day.

●Front-runner encounters unusual obstacle – especially for a Flat race

IT WAS one of those 'I'm sorry, I'll read that again' moments. The Racing Post's in-running comment on front-runner Tight Lipped in a Kempton amateur riders' Flat handicap in January read: 'Led, hurdled swan after 5f, headed halfway, soon pushed along, weakened 3f out.' Yes, that's right, he really did hurdle a swan early in the mile-and-a-half race.

Ross Birkett, who was on board Tight Lipped, said: "As we swung into the back straight I looked up and saw the swan three horse-widths off the rail a furlong ahead, with a further four swans not far away on the inside of the track.

"I figured as soon as the swan saw us he would start to jog off, but he carried on walking slowly, as though nothing was happening. Luckily my horse had been hurdling and when he saw the swan he shortened his stride and pinged it. In the head-on shot you can see the swan just tucks in his neck and the horse clears him by a foot."

The swan, part of a protected group that lives on the racecourse, was unharmed, but this was not the first or last incident involving the birds.

The following month Leighton Aspell's mount Mr Cardle narrowly avoided a collision during a novice handicap hurdle, and last year amateur rider Harry Beswick was brought down when his horse hit a swan on the reservoir bend.

There was talk of moving the swans, and Kempton clerk of the course Barney Clifford obtained a licence to do so, but the option was not taken up. At the start of autumn, 32 swans were living near the infield lake and Clifford said the situation would be kept under review.

Short but not sweet as 1-20 shot is beaten

TRIPLE DIP became the shortest-priced loser on the Flat in Britain since 1948 when she was beaten at 1-20 in a fillies' maiden at Lingfield in March.

Mark Johnston's filly was backed in from 1-12 in the morning but was beaten a length and a quarter by 16-1 second favourite Mercy Me in the four-runner race.

Mercy Me's trainer John Ryan said: "I didn't think we'd turn over a 1-20 chance but I did have a few quid on Mercy Me on the Tote for the lads. I thought she might be a good second but told the lads they could buy the beers if it came off."

The record for the shortest-priced loser in British racing history is held by Royal Forest, a 1-25 shot who was second at Ascot in September 1948.

Triple Dip succeeded Alamo City (6-100, Brighton 1966) as Britain's shortest-priced loser since Royal Forest and joined four St Leger winners – Saucebox (1855), Caller Ou (1861), Kilwarlin (1887) and Prince Palatine (1911) – in being beaten at an SP of 1-20.

Another 1-20 chance, the great steeplechaser Jerry M, became the shortest-priced loser over jumps at Newbury in 1909. Three years later he won the Grand National.

●Hollywood golden story comes to sorry end

MORE than 75 years of California racing history was reduced to rubble in a matter of seconds in May when the grandstand at Hollywood Park was blown up to pave the way for a major commercial redevelopment.

The racetrack, founded in 1938 by members of the Hollywood film industry including Walt Disney and Bing Crosby, closed in December 2013 after years of uncertainty surrounding its future. The track's signature race was the Hollywood Gold Cup – won in its first year by Seabiscuit and later by Triple Crown winners Citation and Affirmed – and in 1984 it hosted the inaugural Breeders' Cup, which revisited in 1987 and 1997. In its heyday the track (pictured below in better times) drew crowds of 80,000 but the average dwindled to 3,000 in latter years.

Plans for the 260-acre site include an 80,000-seater sports stadium, theatre, hotel, office, shops and 3,000 homes.

●#banned as Lemaire is caught tweeting

TWEETING cost Christophe Lemaire dear in March when he was banned for 30 days by the Japanese authorities for using social media during the strict 'lockdown' imposed on jockeys prior to race meetings.

The French rider had been preparing for his first meeting since becoming one of the first foreign jockeys – along with Italian Mirco Demuro – to be granted a permanent riding licence in Japan. The ban ruled him out of his first month in Japan as well as the Dubai World Cup meeting.

A Japan Racing Association representative said: "He was suspended because he used Twitter. It is prohibited for riders to contact people outside during their quarantine at a JRA facility. There is no appeal."

In gaining his licence, Lemaire had passed an initial written test in English on the rules of Japanese racing before undergoing an oral test in Japanese. Ironically, when his application was successful he announced the new chapter of his career via Twitter, saying: "Glad to become a JRA jockey. Thanks to all the support. A new life begins!"

●Butler finds novel hiding place from raceday nerves

When My Silver Cloud jumped the last fence in front in a 2m4f handicap chase at Fontwell in April, on his way to giving Paddy Butler his only success of the last jumps season, the trainer did not have a clue. He was in the toilet with his fingers in his ears.

Butler, 66, has been training for 40 years and is one of those stalwarts who keeps going with a small string and only a handful of winners, but he has never got over his raceday nerves.

"I get like this when I think they've got a chance," he said after My Silver Cloud, sent off 6-4 favourite, had won by a length and a half. "I watched him at Plumpton [five days earlier] when he got caught after the last, but I couldn't watch this time. I was in the toilet with my ears covered so that I couldn't hear the commentary. It's been a long time since I've done that."

The trainer, based in East Chiltington, East Sussex, added: "I didn't used to be able to watch them. I got better but today was too much pressure. I've been at it for 40 years and you'd think I would have learned."

Megalala a golden oldie for Bridger

AGE continues to be no barrier to the remarkable Megalala, who won not one but two Flat races in 2015 at the grand age of 14. That made him only the third horse of that age bracket to achieve the feat this century – the others were sprinters The Tatling, who also did it twice, and Redoubtable.

Megalala is different in that he is a middle-distance front-runner and often has to expend much more effort to beat his younger rivals. His second victory of the year, over a mile and a half at Brighton in October, came by a short head after a ding-dong battle with Hermosa Vaquera, nine years his junior.

His first win as a 14-year-old, over a mile and a quarter at Lingfield in June, was also hard earned after he was denied his usual place at the front when he stumbled at the start. He came with a late run to score by half a length, beating 12 rivals all less than half his age.

"He's a cracking old horse and he does it the hard way," said Hampshire-based trainer John Bridger, 73, who is a veteran himself with 44 years as a licence-holder. "We bought him for jumping but he was a bit of a tearaway. He's pretty straightforward now if you just let him run."

The Brighton success was Megalala's 19th win and came on the 128th start of a career that started in bumpers in the spring of 2005. Bridger (pictured with Megalala) sees no reason to stop, saying: "Life wouldn't be the same without him and we'll carry on as long as he's fit and well."

●Garner earns spurs with daredevil ride

TOM GARNER produced an amazing ride in Bratislava, the capital of Slovakia, when winning the Velka Starohajska Chase aboard Mr Pamperito (pictured right, blue colours) in September despite having no irons for most of the 2m6½f race.

"I'm a bit sore and have a high-pitched voice, but it was interesting," said Garner, 24, a conditional jockey with Oliver Sherwood. "The saddle slipped underneath the horse and I had the choice to pull up or try to continue. We went on turning in and he popped the last. We had two hassling me, but he kept on battling and we won by a neck."

●Is it a bird? Is it a plane? No, it's . . .

JOHN CROWNE stood proud as the only bookmaker at Newmarket's late-August meeting to dress up as a superhero in return for free entry. None of his colleagues took up the racecourse's offer but it didn't bother Crowne (above), who spent the afternoon in a Superman outfit. "I don't know why I'm the only one to dress up," he said. "I suppose I'm the only one daft enough."

●Call of nature proves expensive

SPENDING a penny came at a price for William Treacy when the County Tipperary trainer was fined £1,000 by the BHA in September over a failed drugs test.

The banned substance tramadol was discovered after Fethard Player's second in a handicap hurdle on Grand National day at Aintree in April – and there was a strange explanation.

Interviewed by BHA investigators, Treacy, 67, revealed he is on a medication for arthritic pain called Zydol, which contains tramadol. He said he takes it every morning and then visits Fethard Player to give him an apple – and, due to the effects of the drug, occasionally answers the call of nature in his box.

The trainer said: "They are funny tablets, you have to go to the toilet about 20 minutes after taking them, and either that, or the traces of Zydol on my hands, is probably what happened. I didn't realise spending a penny could cost so much."

CONVERSATION PIECES

Horse Racing Art Specialists

Frankel - Champion Stakes, Ascot by Peter Smith

Golden Horn by Terence Gilbert

Please contact us for a FREE Brochure

Telephone: +44 0115 9286512

Email: conversation.pieces@ntlworld.com

WWW.ASCOTGALLERY.COM

HELPING YOU GET AHEAD OF THE REST

TRM®

EXCELLENCE IN EQUINE NUTRITION

Farm & Stable

DISTRIBUTED IN THE UK BY
Farm & Stable Supplies LLP.

Call for same day dispatch: **01730 815 800**
Order online from: **www.farmstable.com**

Manufactured in Ireland by:
TRM, Industrial Estate, Newbridge, Co. Kildare, Ireland.
T: + 353 (0) 45 434 258

/TRMNutrition @TRMNutrition trm-ireland.com

A-Z of 2015

The year digested into 26 bite-size chunks

A is for American Pharoah. The Bob Baffert-trained colt sprinkled some badly needed stardust on US racing by becoming the first Triple Crown winner since 1978.

B is for Berry. Tireless fundraiser Jack Berry saw his vision of a jockeys' rehabilitation centre in the north of England come to fruition with the opening of a £3.1m facility named in his honour.

C is for Charles and Camilla. Prince Charles and the Duchess of Cornwall enjoyed an evening at Sligo races in May as part of a four-day official visit to the island of Ireland, which marked another step in Anglo-Irish reconciliation after the Troubles.

D is for De Sousa. Back as a freelance after parting company with Godolphin, Silvestre de Sousa took advantage of Richard Hughes's retirement and Ryan Moore's injury to claim his first British Flat jockeys' championship.

E is for eight. Willie Mullins set a host of records in the 2014-15 season but none was more astonishing than his eight winners in the 27 Cheltenham Festival races, including a fab four in the Grade 1 races on the opening day.

F is for Frankie. The only jockey recognisable from his first name alone (even though it's really Lanfranco) enjoyed a glorious 2015 capped by his Derby and Arc victories.

G is for Golden Horn. Beneath every great jockey are great horses and Golden Horn was the vital other half in a glittering partnership with Frankie Dettori.

H is for Hayley. In September the racing world was shocked when Hayley Turner, Britain's foremost female jockey, announced she would retire at the end of the Flat season at the relatively young age of 32.

I is for inspirational. Afghan war veteran Guy Disney, who lost his right leg from below the knee on active duty in 2009, made racing history in February when he became the first jockey with a prosthetic leg to ride in Britain. He later competed on Grand Military day at Sandown and at Cheltenham's hunter chase meeting in April.

J is for jockeys' title. For the first time the British Flat jockeys' championship was decided on wins in the 'core' premier Flat racing period, starting on Guineas weekend in May and finishing on British Champions Day in October.

K is for Kauto Star. The greatest steeplechaser since Arkle was put down in

June after sustaining injuries as the result of a fall in his paddock at Laura Collett's eventing yard in Lambourn, where he spent his final years following his retirement from racing in 2012. He was 15.

L is for legacy. John Oaksey left his family, and the world of jump racing, the great gift of his homebred Coneygree on his death in 2012 and he was in many thoughts after the exciting novice chaser beat the seniors in a pulsating Cheltenham Gold Cup.

M is for McCoy. The record-breaking jump jockey bowed out in style at the age of 40, lifting the trophy for his 20th consecutive jump jockeys' title on an emotional final day at Sandown in April.

N is for Newcastle. The centuries-old Flat turf track was removed after the final meeting in September to be replaced by an artificial Tapeta surface as part of an £11m redevelopment.

O is for O'Sullevan. Racing lost its Voice in July when peerless broadcaster Sir Peter O'Sullevan, who commentated on 50 Grand Nationals for the BBC, died at the age of 97.

P is for punters. The most neglected of racing's 'stakeholders' were finally given a formal voice with the formation by the BHA of the Horseracing Bettors Forum, an eight-member panel whose purpose is to make "constructive suggestions about how the sport can develop and change, for the benefit of the betting public".

Q is for Qipco. The Qatar investment group extended its backing of the British Champions Series, British Champions Day, Newmarket's Guineas festival and Ascot in a record sponsorship for British racing. The deal is believed to be worth in excess of £50m and will run until at least 2024.

R is for racing right. Hopes for a new funding mechanism to replace the levy system were boosted when Chancellor George Osborne made a firm commitment to introduce a racing right – under which bookmakers would pay for the right to bet on British horseracing.

S is for situation vacant. There will be a new name on the British jump jockeys' championship trophy next April, with the now-retired AP McCoy having frozen out all of his contemporaries for the past two decades.

T is for Thornton. Another high-profile jockey to retire in 2015 was Robert Thornton, who was unable to return to the saddle after fracturing vertebrae in a fall at Chepstow in April 2014.

U is for Un Temps Pour Tout. One Champion Hurdle that eluded the grasp of Willie Mullins was the French version, which was won by the David Pipe-trained Un Temps Pour Tout from Mullins' Thousand Stars.

V is for value. Or lack of it after a 165 per cent overround on the Grand National sparked controversy and official talks on how to avoid a repeat.

W is for Wetherby. In a reversal of a trend that has seen Warwick become jumps-only and Newcastle switch from turf to all-weather, the Yorkshire jumps venue staged its first Flat meeting in April. Two more will be held in 2016, although the racecourse stressed jump racing remains "the heart of Wetherby".

X is for X-rated. Australian jockey Blake Shinn gave a whole new meaning to being "well exposed" when his breeches slid down after the elastic snapped during a race at Canterbury racecourse, Sydney, in April. Shinn managed to finish third, while winning jockey Tommy Berry had a novel reason for being pleased to finish in front. "It meant I was the only one that didn't have to stare at Blake's arse the whole way up the straight," he said.

Y is for Yarmouth. The Norfolk seaside venue, bedevilled by grass growth problems after remedial work to the track, suffered a major blow when its three-day Eastern Festival in September had to be abandoned at halfway after heavy rain and several horse slip-ups, and its final two fixtures of the year had be transferred elsewhere.

Z is for zero tolerance. The BHA took the lead in the racing world by introducing stricter rules on anabolic steroids, forbidding their use at any point of a horse's life.

FLASHBACK

1965 Starting stalls are used for the first time in Britain

⏩And they're off! The start of the Chesterfield Stakes at Newmarket on July 8, 1965, the first race in Britain to use starting stalls. Winner Track Spare gets off to a flyer from stall one

By Steve Dennis

FIFTY years ago, at Newmarket, a minor two-year-old event became the first race started from stalls in Britain. Half an hour earlier, the July Cup had been won by Merry Madcap, starting as usual from the traditional 'gate'. And so the stage was set for a brief break with tradition and, in winning the five-furlong Chesterfield Stakes, Track Spare – ridden by Lester Piggott – wrote himself an indelible entry in racing's record books.

By 1965 Britain had fallen behind the other main racing jurisdictions in its adherence to an antiquated system for starting Flat races. Stalls had been used for many years in the US, in Australia, in France, in India, but British racing still retained the old starting gate with its inherently chaotic nature. Eventually the Jockey Club examined ways to modernise the system and, after a series of trials, introduced them to the racecourse.

A large crowd gathered at the five-furlong start to watch the horses being loaded for that first race from starting stalls. Just one minute after the advertised post-time, starter Alec Marsh pressed the button to send the dozen runners on their way.

Track Spare was swiftly away from stall one and – befitting a horse who would go on to win the Middle Park Stakes and St James's Palace Stakes – was too fast for his rivals, crossing the line three lengths clear of the field. Runner-up was Tokyo Girl, drawn six, and third was Great Nephew from stall 12, offering no evidence of any draw bias.

Following the Chesterfield Stakes, there were just four more races – all for two-year-olds – scheduled to be started from stalls that year. Progress was remarkably slow given the venture's evident success and it was a long time before starting stalls spread throughout racing's estate.

"Stalls were used only at certain meetings," says Brian Wilson, a former stalls handler whose son Mark is part of the current RaceTech operation responsible for starting stalls and for the teams of handlers. "When I started in 1972 only around half the racecourses were covered and it wasn't until the early 1980s that every Flat race at every track was started from stalls. Eventually we had five teams of stalls handlers covering the country but it was a very slow process."

Now, of course, it's impossible to imagine Flat races being started in any way other than from stalls – on the rare occasions a flag has to be used instead, it's clear that mechanisation is vital, that it's as much about how you start as how you finish. Track Spare and his 11 fellow pioneers changed British racing, got the modern era off to the best possible start.